Sustainable Development of Small Island Economies

Sustainable Development of Small Island Economies

Hiroshi Kakazu

Westview Press

BOULDER • SAN FRANCISCO • OXFORD

Copyright © 1994 by Westview Press, Inc.

Published in 1994 in the United States of America by Westview Press, Inc., 5500 Central Avenue, Boulder, Colorado 80301-2877, and in the United Kingdom by Westview Press, 36 Lonsdale Road, Summertown, Oxford OX2 7EW

Library of Congress Cataloging-in-Publication Data
Kakazu, Hiroshi, 1942–
    Sustainable development of small island economies / Hiroshi Kakazu.
        p.   cm.
    Includes bibliographical references and index.
    ISBN 0-8133-8854-6 — ISBN 0-8133-8855-4 (pbk.)
    1. Sustainable development—Case studies.   2. Islands—Economic conditions—Case studies.   I. Title.
HC79.E5K335   1994
338.9'00914'2—dc20   94-7732
                                                                                         CIP

Printed and bound in the United States of America

The paper used in this publication meets the requirements of the American National Standard for Permanence of Paper for Printed Library Materials Z39.48-1984.

10   9   8   7   6   5   4   3   2   1

Contents

Tables and Figures

vii

Figures

Preface

This volume contains eight chapters focusing on the economic issues of small Pacific islands. These small island economies have been facing similar economic problems such as scale diseconomy in all dimensions of economic activities, overdependency on external trade and assistance, high costs of transportation and other infrastructures, and high vulnerability to natural disasters. All island economies, however, have experienced painful trial-and-error efforts to achieve self-reliant development, particularly since they obtained political independence from their sovereign nations. Other than a few success stories, most of the island economies have failed to achieve self-reliance. I have compared and analyzed various island economies to find sustainable development paths for different types of island economies.

The theoretical models employed are not highly sophisticated, but they are mostly original and more relevant to small island economies than to large-scale economies such as those of the United States and Japan.

My first journey into the study of small island economies began when I was a graduate student at the University of Nebraska in the late 1960s. My first major publication on the island economy was *A System of Input-Output Accounts for Okinawa,* which was submitted as a Ph.D. dissertation to the University of Nebraska in 1971. Even though I have published and edited a number of papers and books on the economy of the Ryukyus since then, that manuscript is still regarded as one of the best accounts on the economy of the Ryukyu Islands.

My second encounter with the subject was at the East-West Center in Honolulu during 1984–1985 when I was a Fulbright Senior Research Fellow. The Pacific Islands Development Program (PIDP) of the center and the University of Hawaii provided me with invaluable intellectual resources and documents on small Pacific islands. The paper on the South Pacific islands, which I wrote at the East-West Center and published as a UN working paper in 1986, has been heavily cited by researchers on island economies. Several of these papers on the South Pacific have subsequently been published, and some important ones are included in this book.

My third opportunity to study the island economy was at the Asian Development Bank, where I worked as a research economist during 1988–1990. My particular task was to find the best sustainable development path for eight South Pacific island economies and the Maldive Islands, all of which were affiliated with the bank. The bank was a very effective base from which to launch field research studies on these islands as well as a rich source of information.

The phrase "island economy" has been gaining its own identity through recent world conferences on island matters. In 1992, I and others organized the International Small Island Studies Association (ISISA) in the Bahamas, and in the same year the International Scientific Council for Island Development under the United Nations Educational, Scientific and Cultural Organization (UNESCO) published an international journal on island affairs named *INSULA*. These positive initiatives are a clear indication that island matters are important not only to islanders but also to mainstream scientists.

This book contains my original as well as published papers on island economies, which have been revised and updated where necessary (see the appendix for original sources and acknowledgments). I am deeply indebted to Professor Hiroshi Yamauchi—my long-standing friend—who coauthored Chapters 3, 5 (with Professor Nobuya Miwa), and 6 and who also provided continued support and encouragement throughout the preparation of this volume. My debt also extends to Professor Te'o I.J. Fairbairn, coauthor of Chapter 2, whose epoch-making book *Island Economies: Studies from the South Pacific* (1985) has greatly contributed to shaping the ideas in this book. I have also benefited from discussions and comments over the years with many friends and conference participants. I am especially appreciative of the help given me by Professors Harry T. Oshima, Shuji Hayashi, Koji Taira, Chung-Hsun Yu, Kwangsuck Lee, Kiyoko Nitz, and the late Professor Shinko Yamashiro.

Thanks are also extended to Judy Yamauchi and my student at the International University of Japan (IUJ), Julie R. Mann, who provided editorial assistance. I would also like to express my deepest appreciation to the Research Institute for Asian Development (RIAD) of IUJ for its financial support of this book. The project also received a prestigious Grant-in-Aid for Publication of Scientific Research Result of the Ministry of Education, Science and Culture. Without the kind and willing support of all these people and organizations, the completion of this book would not have been possible. Needless to say, none of the individuals or institutions named are responsible for any shortcomings in this work.

It is my hope that the book will provide some basis for island researchers, planners, and decisionmakers to contemplate giving more serious attention to the immensely difficult task of achieving self-reliance in the development of island economies.

Hiroshi Kakazu

1

A Genealogy of the Self-Reliant Development of Small Island Economies

The economic development problems of small island economies were discussed as early as the 1940s when the South Pacific Commission (SPC) was formed.[1] The first systematic examination of the problems of small island economies occurred at the Lisbon Conference of the International Economic Association, "Economic Consequences of the Size of Nations," in 1957.[2] The conference discussions, however, centered around the minimum size of firms that would be able to obtain the benefits from economies of scale on production.

The 1962–1964 seminar of the Institute of Commonwealth Studies was perhaps the first serious endeavor to examine the various issues of small island territories.[3] According to R. T. Shand, the seminar was the first in-depth study on the Pacific Ocean islands.[4] Following this seminar, a number of important individual studies on small island economies were published. These include studies by William Demas,[5] Peter Lloyd,[6] E. K. Fisk,[7] R. F. Watters,[8] A. S. Stanley,[9] B. Lockwood,[10] David Vital,[11] H. C. Brookfield and D. Hart,[12] Brookfield,[13] I. J. Fairbairn,[14] B. R. Finney,[15] V. A. Lewis,[16] and S. Schiavo-Campo.[17] In addition, the controversial yet interesting symposium and seminar publications edited by F. R. Fosberg,[18] F. M. Smith,[19] B. Farrell,[20] and J. B. Hardaker[21]; the conference publication edited by J. N. Hurd[22]; and the study by the Development Studies Centre of the Australian National University[23] became available.

In the midst of the decolonization process of the small island territories in the 1960s and 1970s, the United Nations was obliged to investigate the development problems and international roles of these islands. The first UN study on the subject was conducted by its Institute for Training and Research (UNITAR) in 1971 under the title *Small States and Territories: Status and Problems.*[24] The UNITAR study, coupled with the vigorous requests from small developing island economies, prompted a further special study by the UN Conference on Trade and Development (UNCTAD), whose 1972 conference resolution reads:

> Requests that the Secretary-General of UNCTAD, in line with the objectives of the International Development Strategy, and in collaboration with the regional

economic commissions and the United Nations Economic and Social Office in
Beirut, convene a small panel of experts selected in their personal capacity to
identify and study the particular problems of these countries and to make recommendations thereon, giving special attention to the developing island countries
which are facing major difficulties in respect of transport and communications
with neighbouring countries as well as structural difficulties, and which are remote from major market centres, and also taking into account overall prospects
for, as well as existing levels of development.[25]

The 1974 UNCTAD Experts' Report,[26] which became a major source of
study on developing island countries, contains six chapters that include detailed
statistical data on fifty-one islands and archipelagoes: (1) characteristics of developing island economies; (2) problems of small developing island countries;
(3) transport; (4) natural disasters and control of marine resources; (5) regional
policies; and (6) recommendations. The report recommended, among other
things, a study on the viability of small island countries, since very little work
had been done in this field.

A follow-up study of the UNCTAD Experts' Report was conducted by the
UN Economic and Social Council (UNECOSOC) and published in 1975.[27] The
study identified in more detail the special economic problems and development
needs of geographically more disadvantaged developing island countries. A
major contribution of the UNECOSOC study is the systematic analysis of the
economic dependence of small island countries. The study classifies the small
dependent economies into three types according to their mode of externally
generated economic activities: the plantation economy, the mineral economy,
and the tourist economy. It also examines the possibility of reducing their
dependency on external sources of income through diversification of their domestic industrial activities.

Following these overall economic development studies by the United Nations, a number of important studies focusing on specific countries or problems
were carried out by various development organizations. Those dealing with the
South Pacific include the World Bank studies on Papua New Guinea and the
Solomon Islands,[28] the Commonwealth Secretariat studies on trade relations in
the South Pacific[29] and on the balance-of-payments problems, the Asian Devel-
opment Bank (ADB) study on South Pacific agriculture,[30] a study conducted by
C.G.F. Simkin[31] for the Economic and Social Commission for Asia and the
Pacific (ESCAP), ESCAP's unpublished discussion papers on trade instability
in the South Pacific,[32] and the UN Industrial Development Organization's
(UNIDO) detailed *Study of Harmonization of Industrial Incentives in the South
Pacific Region.*[33]

Almost all of these studies and discussions identified the similar problems
faced by small island economies and other developing countries, but they also
emphasized the special development problems pertaining to small islands. As to

the direction of development, there has been an increasing tendency to shift from arguments for trade-led specialization to support for agriculture-based diversification, as is more fully discussed in Chapter 2. The diversification of an island economy has been desired "as a means of lessening external dependence and internal fragmentation of the economy and increasing internal integration and economic transformation."[34] The idea of diversification suggested in these studies, however, is not based on a rigorous analysis of small developing islands whose economies have been increasingly embedded in foreign trade and aid.

In this chapter I discuss the general characteristics and problems of small island economies using statistical data mainly on the South Pacific countries and examine the role of trade in an island economy in relation to land resources, terms of trade, and agricultural diversification.

Definition and General Characteristics and Problems of Small Island Economies

Definition

When discussing the economic development of small island economies, one is always troubled as to the definition and measurement of "island." "Island economy" in itself does not necessarily imply a small economy. Unique development problems having significant economic consequences are apparent when degree of isolation, as well as smallness, is considered. The problems of small economies are intensified if they are located far from their major markets; the South Pacific islands are a good example. This is why the United Nations has identified "geographically disadvantaged developing island countries," along with "least developed" and "land-locked" developing countries, as being in need of special attention.[35]

Smallness can be defined in terms of the physical size (land area), population and GNP (or GDP), or a combination of these variables as attempted by C. L. Taylor,[36] depending upon the purpose of the analysis. S. Kuznets[37] used a population of 10 million as the economically significant dividing line between small and large economies. Most of the arguments, however, favor using the concept of national income as the most appropriate one to measure the size of an economy, particularly in the discussion of "diseconomies of small-scale production in small countries, and the derivative arguments concerning instability and trade dependence in small nations."[38] If we want to see smallness in terms of current productive capacity, GNP or GDP best serves the purpose.

Shand's[39] systematic classification of selected small island economies of the South Pacific and Indian Ocean, however, demonstrates that a small population in general corresponds to a small land area and also to a small GDP, which can be seen in the diagonal distribution of states and territories in Table 1.1 according to small, very small, and microcategories. All three size indicators do not apply in some states; two categories apply in all except New Caledonia, American Samoa, and the Maldives.

Of course, as Shand warns, these size indicators are more or less arbitrary, and there is no economically significant cutoff point for "small," "very small," and "micro." However, by using these size indicators, we may be able to identify these countries' stages of economic development as well as similarities in their development problems. If we take into consideration other factors such as isolation, migration, and external sources of income, the usefulness of the classification is greatly enhanced.

The UNITAR study lists ninety-six small states and territories with populations of less than 1 million and makes a distinction between thirty-nine mainland territories and fifty-seven islands or island groups. Table 1.2 shows the approximate number of islands, land area, and population in each island group. Though, as the study admits, information with regard to number of islands and population is incomplete, rather out-of-date, and, to a large degree, inaccurate, Table 1.2 shows the geographical distribution and some important characteristics of small island states and territories.

Of the fifty-eight small island states and territories, twenty are in the Pacific, seventeen in the Caribbean, eleven in the Atlantic, eight in the Indian Ocean, and two in the Mediterranean Sea. The small Pacific islands, the main concern of this investigation, are not only the most numerous but also the most scattered and varied islands in the world.

General Characteristics and Problems

Keeping in mind again that smallness is a relative and not an absolute idea, we can summarize the general characteristics and problems of small island economies, vis-à-vis large ones, as follows:

1. Economic activities are less diversified and more specialized in small island economies, due mainly to their narrow range of human and nonhuman economic resources and markets. The narrow resource base and domestic market, coupled with high transport costs, severely limit what C. P. Kindleberger calls the "capacity of transformation" of the economies.[40]

2. Because of the small domestic market, there are not many options available for economic development. Thus, under the constant population pressure on the limited arable land and the "revolution of rising expectations," almost all small island countries have had to open their economies to world markets. Many years ago, A. Marshall stated that a small country often had a relatively large foreign trade not only because of limited production resources but also because it "has a larger frontier in proportion to [its] area than a larger country of the same shape."[41]

The degree of openness to or dependency on world markets is customarily measured by the trade to GDP ratio, as is shown for the South Pacific islands in

Table 1.3. The smallest trade (exports + imports) to GDP ratio was 54 percent in 1980 for French Polynesia. For economies such as Vanuatu and American Samoa, the ratio is nearly 200 percent. Although these trade data are rather outdated, the picture has not changed significantly in recent years (see Chapter 7). Considering the fact that the trade to GDP ratio for large island economies such as Indonesia and the Philippines is typically less than 30 percent, we can see that these small economies are vitally dependent upon foreign trade. Small island economies' heavy dependency on external factors creates the problem of economic instability and vulnerability, which has been a challenging topic for discussion.[42]

3. As a direct result of the narrow range of their resource bases and production conditions, small island economies depend upon a few primary products for their export earnings while importing a wide range of consumer as well as capital goods. One export commodity, such as fish in American Samoa and copra in Kiribati and Tokelau, accounts for nearly all of each country's export income (Table 1.3).

The exports of small developing island economies are also characterized by their high geographical concentration. This characteristic may be easily inferred from the fact that island countries, whose politico-economic ties with former colonial governments are still strong, produce more or less similar primary products in relatively small quantities that can never influence the world market. The large percentages of South Pacific exports are directed toward a few developed countries (Table 1.4). Nearly all exports of Niue and the Cook Islands are directed to New Zealand, as are American Samoa's to the United States. Close to 60 percent of exports in French Polynesia and New Caledonia are destined for their sovereign country, France. Imports also tend to be geographically concentrated, but they are more diversified than exports.

It may be worthwhile to note that intraregional trade among the Pacific islands accounts for only 4.3 percent of exports and 1.5 percent of imports (Table 1.4). In terms of the number of trading patterns within the region, Fiji is the most diversified, exporting to seven and importing from eleven South Pacific countries (Figure 1.1). Guam and the Trust Territory of the Pacific Islands (TTPI) are the least diversified within the region. The poor trade interrelationships among the regional countries are a natural outcome of the meager complementarity of their economic activities. Economic diversification within the South Pacific islands is the most important prerequisite for achieving an economically viable regionalism, a subject that has been much discussed for many years.[43]

Not only does these islands' dependency on a few export products and markets make them vulnerable to the fluctuations of world markets, they are also susceptible to natural hazards such as cyclones, floods, drought, and disease.

4. Most of the small island economies have been suffering from chronic deficits in trade balances, which have largely been financed by growing inflows of

foreign aid. With the exception of Papua New Guinea and American Samoa, where exports bring in sufficient income to pay for imports, all South Pacific islands registered deficits in 1980 (Table 1.5). In the countries with trade deficits, the amount of imports paid for by exports ranged from 99 percent for the Solomon Islands to less than 10 percent for French Polynesia, Tuvalu, Niue, and Wallis and Futuna, whose huge deficits—with the exception of French Polynesia—were more than offset by the inflows of Official Development Assistance (ODA).

In addition to ODA, tourism income, remittances from emigrated workers or families, and capital inflows were considered to be the major sources of income to pay for imports. This is illustrated by the data in Table 1.6, which shows the balance-of-payments statistics for selected South Pacific countries. It is worthwhile to note that only Fiji, due to its large tourist income, had a favorable balance in invisible (or service) trade. The invisible trade deficits for Papua New Guinea and the Solomon Islands were much greater than their trade deficits. Though a large part of the trade deficits was financed by government transfers or aid flows, all covered countries incurred deficits in current-account balances, which were largely offset by inflows of long-term capital.

5. Small island economies suffer from diseconomies of scale in production, investment, consumption, transportation, education, and administrative services. The problem of diseconomies of scale becomes intensified where the island countries or territories are fragmented into "mini" islands and located far from large foreign markets. In the South Pacific, Fiji alone consists of nearly 100 inhabited islands, and most of the South Pacific islands are located more than 1,000 kilometers from the nearest continent (Table 1.7).

Diseconomies of scale are probably the most-discussed subject in the development of small island economies. Yet except for some fragmentary evidence, there has been no systematic empirical study on the subject.[44] I once calculated the scale effect of unit cost in generating electricity in the islands of Okinawa. The unit-cost curve in generating electricity decreases dramatically as the size of the islands in terms of population increases (Figure 1.2). The cost per hour of generating electricity in such neighboring small islands as Miyako and Yaeyama, which account for 87 percent of the total population of Okinawa, is more than 196 and 58 percent, respectively.[45]

6. The heavy burden of transportation costs may be the single most important barrier to the socioeconomic development of small islands. The UNECOSOC report,[46] Brookfield,[47] and A. Proctor[48] analyzed in detail the external transport problems of small islands. The UNECOSOC report states that the transportation problem is due not only to the high cost of shipping resulting from extremely small-scale operations but also to "the irregularity of supply which leads, even in the absence of any balance of payments constraints on imports, to periodic shortages and erratic price movements."[49]

7. Many small island economies have experienced more rapid population

growth and urbanization than have other developing economies, which have aggravated unemployment problems. The total population of French Polynesia, Nauru, New Caledonia, and TTPI doubled during the 1950–1980 period; Niue and Pitcairn Island experienced depopulation (Table 1.8). The increasing population pressure on the limited land is reflected in a rising population density in most South Pacific countries.

One of the striking features of small island economies is a persistent net migration to neighboring mainlands, which helps to ease population pressure. The data on net emigration for the selected South Pacific countries were obtained by subtracting the natural rates of increase from the rates of population increase (Table 1.9). Though one might question the reliability of the data, they confirm the general belief concerning migration from the South Pacific. Table 1.9 shows that all South Pacific countries, more or less, experienced net migration during the 1972–1981 period. The Cook Islands and Niue, for example, recorded depopulation during this period that was due to a substantial net migration to New Zealand. Though "migration is particularly important in island countries or territories with a population of below 150,000 inhabitants,"[50] it is worthwhile to note that since 1977 Tonga has recorded net in-migration.

The per capita GNP of the South Pacific countries is generally higher than that of other island groups of the world. Nevertheless, a high population pressure coupled with slowed economic growth rates has in past decades had a detrimental effect on the standards of living in terms of real per capita GNP for some countries (Table 1.10).

It should also be noted that there was ample evidence of a serious unemployment problem in most South Pacific countries, though unemployment statistics were available for only a few of the countries and were often difficult to interpret because of inadequate coverage.[51]

8. Another characteristic of island economies, which is more or less related to the aforementioned problems, is their heavy dependence on government activities as a major source of income and employment and probably as a symbol of prestige. It is astonishing that government expenditures in some years in the Cook Islands, Niue, TTPI, Wallis and Futuna, and Western Samoa accounted for more than 80 percent of their respective gross national products.[52]

Some small island countries are also dependent on the monetary authorities of industrial countries in the sense that "they do not have an independent currency and/or do not follow autonomous monetary policies."[53]

We should also note that one or more large multinational corporations dominate foreign trade in a number of small island economies.[54] "The policies and decisions of these companies have a determining influence on the island's development."[55] These characteristics are a vestige of the colonial heritage of other developing countries.[56]

So far, I have discussed the special problems of small island economies that discourage sustainable economic development. There are, however, a number of characteristics of small islands that can be considered to be economically advantageous over larger economies, such as "the importance of being unimportant in external commercial policy, more unified national markets, greater flexibility, and perhaps greater potential social cohesion."[57] The huge expanse of ocean surrounding these island masses may also provide rich marine resources and natural energy that can be tapped for future economic development.

The Role of Trade in Small Island Economies

The Resource Expansion Effect of Trade

In classical and neoclassical trade theories, the role of foreign trade in economic development has been succinctly expressed in the Robertsonian term "engine of growth":

> The specializations of the nineteenth century were not simply a device for using to the greatest effect the labours of a given number of human beings; they were above all an engine of growth. Their most spectacular effect was to hold at bay for a century the devil which Malthus had unchained, so that, just as the Red Queen was five times as rich as Alice and five times as clever, so the inhabitants of these islands in the pre-war decade managed, according to a commonly quoted though obviously not very reliable computation, to be four times as well off as their ancestors of a hundred years before and four times as numerous.[58]

Classical economists in particular—for example, Smith[59] and Mill[60]—hinted that foreign trade would be more beneficial to a small and poor nation than to a large and rich one simply because the latter's reciprocal demand for trading goods is much stronger than the former's. This classical proposition was further expanded and elaborated by F. D. Graham,[61] whose trade model, according to Lloyd, is "particularly important because it is the only many-country, many-good model of comparative advantage in which the (pre-trade) size of countries has been introduced as a variable, and it yields significant results."[62]

Graham's model reveals that small countries tend to gain more from trade than large countries because they can specialize exclusively in a few goods whose international terms of trade, under which all other goods can be obtained, differ greatly from their domestic terms of trade, under which they can produce all goods themselves.

The dictum of such pure trade theory, however, has been rather overly emphasized by neoclassical development economists to the extent that for a small nation, trade is not only an "engine of growth" but also an "engine of survival."[63]

The gains from trade are tantamount to an increase in real income, even if the economy operates under the constraints of given amounts of resources and production technology. As is shown in Figure 1.3, with the conventional production possibility curve (PP') for two commodities (E = exportable good and C = consumption good) under the usual assumptions, trade produces exactly the same effect as the expansion of productive resources by shifting the production frontier from PP' to P''P'''.[64] Given the pretrade domestic terms of trade (Td), the economy will produce both goods at A on the transformation curve and will consume all of them domestically. But if the international terms of trade (Tw) are more favorable for the exportable good than for the consumption good, the economy will respond to the difference in the price ratio by moving from A to B on the transformation curve, thereby producing more of E and less of C.

If we assume that the economy will export all of its exportable good (BCI), as is nearly the case for Fiji's sugar product or the copra products of many Pacific islands, it can obtain the CIP''' volume of the consumption good according to the international exchange ratio (Tw). Thus, in terms of the maximum availability of the consumption good, which is OP', the economy is now better off by a volume of P'P''' after trade. If the gain from trade expressed in terms of the consumption good increases more rapidly than the population growth (P/P), trade may provide a powerful engine for a continuous prosperity, as shown by the rising trend line of per capita consumption (C/P), starting from the pretrade level in the lower part of Figure 1.3. For most small island economies with extremely limited productive resources combined with a higher rate of population increase, foreign trade may be the only way to enlarge their economic capacities so as to sustain or improve their standards of living. But if the population growth rate is continuously greater than the trade growth rate, the standard of living will inevitably deteriorate.

Though this is a highly simplified model under highly unrealistic assumptions, it does explain why a small country, in particular, tends to specialize in foreign trade. Table 1.11 provides some empirical evidence of the resource expansion effect of trade on the Fijian economy. As we have seen, Fiji has increasingly specialized in producing sugarcane, which is its major exportable crop, and imports of the staple food, namely rice, have increased steadily, accounting for 53 percent of Fiji's total rice consumption in 1980. As a result, more and more of the country's productive resources (e.g., land, labor, and capital) have been reallocated to sugarcane production rather than to rice. Of all the scarce productive resources, arable land is considered to be the most constraining factor in expanding agricultural production for a small island economy such as Fiji. Because of the increasing competition for arable land from both within and outside agriculture, the productive use of land has been the major concern of the development program.

Table 1.11 shows the productivity of land in terms of per hectare dollar sales value for Fijian rice production (row F) and sugarcane production (row J). Both products were valued in terms of world prices, namely, the import price for rice and the export price for sugarcane. Although some refinement in computation is needed, a striking fact is that sugarcane production was 2.5 times more productive in resource use than rice production in 1971; 3 times in 1975 and 4.2 times in 1980 (see row K). Row M gives the land area needed to produce all imported rice domestically; row N gives the land required for sugarcane production to just pay for all imported rice by exporting sugarcane.

The land-resource expansion effect from specializing in sugarcane, shown in row O of Table 1.11 or in Figure 1.4, increased from 3,938 hectares in 1971 to 7,744 hectares in 1980, or from 1.8 to 3.3 percent, respectively, of the total Fijian arable land (see row Q in Table 1.11). The result seems to be less dramatic than the theoretical gains from trade claimed by many neoclassical economists. We should, however, note that the effect of specialization in trade should also be discussed in terms of economic security and stability, employment, and income distribution.

A Development Path Through Trade

There is no doubt that many island people used to live in an autarchic subsistence economy before they came into contact with the outside world. According to an exciting document unveiled by archaeologist P. S. Bellwood, "The Peopling of the Pacific,"[65] the Pacific islands were settled by migrants of the modern Australoids and Mongoloids. Long before the European "discovery" of these islands, the Pacific islanders were engaged in sophisticated trading systems through feasts and gift-giving. The reciprocal transfers of goods "often evolved on the basis of resource complementarity, so that a dry island might trade yams for the taro of a wet island, or an island people might trade fish for the sago and vegetables of the mainlanders on larger land bodies."[66]

It is interesting to note that the dependency on trade, which has often been considered by modern development economists to be a major source of economic instability, was considered to be a practical wisdom of the ancient islanders not only to complement each other's scarce resources but also to keep peace and cohesion in social intercourse among different islanders. As stated by A. Couper, "When a community was called upon to trade with another it could readily refuse, so that islanders were able to exchange their craft products for foodstuffs in distant islands in times of natural catastrophe, such as hurricanes and drought. In this way, the quasi-oligopolistic nature of production in particular goods was transformed through the social pressure to conduct trade into a system of natural support."[67] B. H. Quain[68] and A. M. Hocart[69] have also demonstrated that specialization in a few trading goods, which has also been claimed by modern antitrade exponents[70] as a legacy of colonialism and an exploitation device, was often practiced by small islanders long before the European colonial powers appeared in the Pacific region.

There is no doubt, however, that most of the people in the South Pacific lived in autarchic subsistence, or probably what Fisk has termed "primitive affluence,"[71] before the European navigator-traders introduced various cash crops into these islands, along with new goods such as tobacco, cloth, iron goods, and Western foodstuffs that could be exchanged for cash. J. C. Furnas cited the following amusing conversation from the writing of the Reverend James Chalmers, who visited New Guinea in the nineteenth century "Have you coconuts in your country?" "No." "Have you yams?" "No." "Have you breadfruits?" "No." "Have you sago?" "No." "Have you plenty of hoop iron and tomahawks?" "Yes in great abundance." "We understand now why you have come." "You have nothing to eat in Beritani; but you have plenty of tomahawks and hoop iron with which you can buy food."[72]

This state of "subsistence affluence" in the past made E. C. Hald, a UN economic adviser, question whether "the peoples of the southern part of this vast ocean might be better off if left alone to live their lives in the traditional ways."[73] This somewhat nostalgic longing for a subsistence life annoys a realistic economist like Fairbairn: "Images of this kind could adversely influence official policy. It could, for example, divert attention away from the tackling of urgent social and economic problems that are sometimes present in the rural-subsistence sector, e.g., high infant mortality rates, low life expectancy, malnutrition and lack of adequate protection against the danger of periodic droughts, storms, and the like."[74]

Since it is too late for Pacific islanders to go back to their villages and since, at the same time, the capitalist aspects are in direct conflict with their traditional life-style,[75] we should attempt to find some appropriate mixture of a subsistence-cash production system for small island economies. As S. M. Mark has correctly pointed out, "Most islanders want neither a return to a primitive life-style nor an advance into high-technology society that is beyond their means to sustain, but rather, they want to go forward in ways that improve their well-being without destroying their self-reliance and culture."[76]

H. Myint has defined "subsistence economy" in terms of self-sufficient economic units such as the family, the village, or the tribe that produce only for their own consumption with little or no systematic exchange relationships among them.[77] Myint's definition coincides with R. G. Ward's "integral subsistence system"[78] and Hald's "pure subsistence economy."[79] In this analysis, however, "subsistence economy" is defined as that portion of production activities that is directed solely toward the producer's own consumption, since there is ample evidence that a pure form of subsistence economy vanished long before the arrival of the European traders. Today, island economies of the South Pacific are more or less mixed cash-subsistence systems of production.[80]

To identify the stages of development without the constraints of neoclassical assumptions, I will use a diagrammatic model, which starts from inside the production possibility curve, and trace the dynamic growth path of a small island economy through trade (Figure 1.5). Point A on the diagram indicates the pure subsistence stage, where all produced goods are consumed within the subsistence economy. In this primitive stage of economic development, there is no incentive for peasant farmers to produce more than they consume because the value of surplus products (output − consumption) is zero unless these products are stored for a feast or anticipated gifts. Initially, as is often documented, it was the external demand for the peasants' products that gave an incentive to farmers to produce surplus products for export, which in turn served to satisfy new wants through imports. The expansion of imports was a major dynamic force facilitating the further expansion of exports.[81]

Given commodity terms of trade (T_1), the economy will produce at B, where OE_1 of the exportable goods is exchanged for C_1T_1 of the imported consumption goods. One possible hypothesis is that, as the international terms of trade improve from T_1 to T_2 and T_3, the economy not only expands its exports but can also claim more imports for a given amount of exports.

Although the overall commodity terms of trade for developing countries worsened from the 1950s through the 1960s, the unit prices for export commodities from the South Pacific, such as sugar, copra, and coffee, have fluctuated considerably (Table 1.12).

When discussing the terms of trade for Pacific islands, where trade specialization is limited to a few agricultural products and where a wide variety of other agricultural products, especially rice and wheat, are imported, we should pay much attention to the relative productivity of sugar or copra compared with rice or wheat. Even though the terms of trade deteriorate vis-à-vis manufactured goods, it may still be better for Fiji to export sugar or for Tonga to export coconut products as long as they possess comparative advantages over rice and other products in producing these commodities. This is particularly so if the islanders continuously prefer imported foodstuffs to sweet potatoes, taro, or yams despite the convincing warning from R. R. Thaman[82] and many others about the deteriorating nutritional status of the people.

An important thing to be emphasized in the growth path depicted in Figure 1.5, is that both exportable goods and subsistence goods have expanded. This type of growth is possible only under the conditions of surplus arable land and labor, as has been documented by Myint in his celebrated "vent-for-surplus"[83] theory of international trade. The essential lubricant that pushed the peasants so smoothly and rapidly into export production and the money economy was the existence of a considerable margin of surplus productive capacity in the form of both surplus land and surplus labor over and above their minimum subsistence requirements.

Aided by foreign traders and the improved transportation system, peasant farmers ventured into producing rather risky export crops on a part-time basis because they could fully secure their minimum subsistence food. In the early phase of export expansion, therefore, farmers could obtain extra cash income simply by cultivating more unused land for export crops and by using surplus labor—without endangering their "subsistence affluence."

A basic characteristic and problem of this type of growth path is that expansion in production has been made possible through extending cropland without changing the traditional mode of production. Therefore, the productivity of land remains unchanged or decreases due to the cultivation of marginal land over a long period of time. M. Moynagh's[84] painstaking study of the Fiji sugar industry and recent statistical data on selected crops, though fragmentary, support the relevancy of the vent-for-surplus theory to the export-led growth path of the South Pacific island economies (Table 1.13). As Table 1.13 indicates, even under the technological innovation of modern times, the land productivity in cash crops, such as sugar and cocoa, and subsistence foods, such as sweet potatoes and yams, has essentially remained unchanged. This lag in technological innovation in the primary export industry was a major reason that the expansion in exports in many developing countries did not bring about "spread effects," that is, the impact of export activity on the diversification of the domestic economy as had been explained by the staple theory of export-led growth.[85]

Under this pattern of growth, it is not difficult to see that further expansion in both cash and subsistence crops is possible up to point D in Figure 1.5, where all arable land is cultivated. From this neoclassical world of the production frontier, further improvement in terms of trade (T_4) will expand exports only at the cost of subsistence production. It seems to be quite important to identify where an island economy is located on the depicted growth path when we map possible development options for small island economies. As is fully discussed in Chapter 2, it is particularly important, as Fairbairn has pointed out, to identify the role of subsistence agriculture quantitatively as well as qualitatively in order to "provide a more complete basis for national planning purposes, including the formulation of a soundly conceived development policy and strategy."[86]

If we assume that subsistence economic activities as previously defined are concentrated in the rural sector, the urbanization ratio of population (i.e., urban population divided by total population) is considered to be a rough indication of the extent of the remaining subsistence economy; urbanization will be inversely related to the share of subsistence production. If we also assume that the commercialization or monetization of an economy is positively related to per capita GDP and food imports, the degree of subsistence production would also be inversely related to the level of per capita GDP and food imports.

As can be seen in Table 1.14, there are fairly good correlations between the two indicators and urbanization; and they also seem to confirm that there is some common sense in the degree of subsistence production of these economies. Guam, New Caledonia, French Polynesia, and American Samoa are considered to be the most commercialized economies in the South Pacific region; Western Samoa, Papua New Guinea, and the Solomon Islands are still deep in the subsistence mode of production.

Terms of Trade, Trade Imbalance, and Import Substitution of Foodstuffs

It has been widely accepted by many development economists, such as R. Nurkse,[87] R. Prebisch,[88] H. W. Singer,[89] and G. Mydral,[90] that the countries exporting primary products have generally suffered from a deteriorating trend in the terms of trade. The theory of worsening terms of trade prompted the idea of "export pessimism" or "immiserizing growth,"[91] which meant that the growth in output of a developing country was more than offset by the loss from adverse terms of trade; the result was lower real income after growth. This pessimistic view of foreign trade as an "engine of growth," an idea that had strong early support from the United Nations, persuaded many developing countries to adopt inward-looking or import-substituting development strategies. I am not prepared to discuss this issue further; at this point, it suffices to say that the most convincing counterarguments against export pessimism have been presented by Myint[92] and Ian Little.[93]

Let us assume, as many development economists believe, that the long-run commodity terms of trade for the South Pacific have in general worsened, except probably during the recent past.[94] Figure 1.6 depicts the impact of worsening terms of trade on trade balance. Let us assume that there is a considerable degree of downward rigidity in export production and import consumption for a small island economy due to the narrow range of resources and markets. Then, though the terms of trade deteriorate from T_1 to T_2 and T_3, the economy may try to maintain the same quantity of exports or it may even try to expand exports in order to offset the lost purchasing power of its export product as opposed to the neoclassical reversibility assumption of economic behavior. The quantity of import to be exchanged for a given volume of export will become smaller and smaller as the terms of trade deteriorate. The difference between the constant export line (E) and the line of decreasing imported consumption goods (C) indicate growing trade deficits, which must be financed through other means such as aid and tourism income in order to prevent the standard of living from falling. If we assume, however, that economic resources, including labor mobility, are easily reversible in their use, as has been suggested by Fisk[95] and R. Bedford,[96] the worsening terms of trade may stimulate the economy to produce more subsistence foods at the expense of export goods; this is shown on Figure 1.6 as a shift of the production point from D to D' if resources are fully employed.

There are two approaches to producing more domestic goods at the expense of exportable goods. One approach is "import displacement," substituting domestic production for imported goods. The other approach is "import replacement," substituting traditional products for imported foods. The two approaches will be more fully discussed in Chapter 2.

Finally, a brief remark on development plans is warranted. Almost all development plans in the South Pacific are designed to achieve one clear objective, namely, the increase of real per capita income through the self-reliant mobilization of domestic resources.[97] To achieve this objective, all these plans explicitly or implicitly adopt the strategies of export promotion, import replacement, and import displacement without careful examination of their internal consistencies and feasibilities under the limited availability of domestic resources. This problem will be discussed in Chapter 3.

Conclusions

The development problems pertinent to small island economies have become an increasing concern among development economists as well as various development organizations since the decolonization process of small island territories began in the 1960s. In this chapter I have reviewed the growing literature on these issues and discussed the socioeconomic characteristics of the small island developing countries.

As analyzed here, island economies, particularly in the South Pacific, are facing compound problems of development; in addition to facing the general problems of developing countries, they have economic and political disadvantages stemming from their insular nature, that is, smallness, isolation from major markets, and fragmentation within their own markets. We can, of course, argue that there are advantages to smallness and isolation, such as greater potential for social and political cohesion and greater ability to monitor and motivate the economy for the betterment of the people.[98] So far, however, the disadvantages of smallness and isolation have outweighed their possible advantages, at least in terms of economic development.

In the South Pacific, trade was not only the vehicle of peaceful coexistence among the islands, it was also the powerful engine of growth for most of the island nations. A rapid rise in real per capita income was largely made possible by exporting advantageous primary products, including mineral and agricultural products. In the process of export-led growth, resources were rapidly transferred from the subsistence sector to the monetized sector. Though there are great variations in the degree of monetization that has occurred, island economies such as Nauru, New Caledonia, French Polynesia, and Tuvalu are now almost totally monetized.

The monetization of island economies and the attainment of political independence inevitably brought about the "revolution of rising expectations" to the island people. The deeper specialization in primary export goods, which were susceptible to the vagaries of price fluctuations in the international market, meant greater dependency on imports, which in turn generated new wants through the demonstration effect. The result was growing trade deficits that have largely been financed through foreign aid. Every conscientious planner now recognizes that this process of economic development is not only sustainable in the long run but also inconsistent with the strategy of self-reliant economic development that has been incorporated into all development plans in the South Pacific nations.[99]

Self-reliant development is easy to talk about but difficult to pursue. We can find South Pacific countries' development plans in virtually all development strategies proposed in the various international forums, such as import-substituting industrialization, trade-oriented development, collective self-reliance through regionalism, zero-growth strategies based on a mixed subsistence-plantation mode,[100] and basic human needs strategies. Although we can fully expect that development strategies should differ according to the stage of development and the natural and human resource endowments of each island economy, there seems to be consensus among development economists and planners that regional cooperation through coordinated planning and specialization among the South Pacific nations is a long-term viable solution to the problems.

I also believe that economic integration is the right direction despite the enormous difficulties and a number of unsuccessful examples of such attempts in other developing areas. Meanwhile, all planners of the South Pacific should seriously think of how to prevent some of the resource-poor island nations from falling back into what Fisk calls "subsistence poverty."[101]

TABLE 1.1 A Classification of Selected Pacific and Indian Ocean States and Territories by Size of Population, Land Area, and Domestic Economy, 1975

	Land Area								
	Small (10,000–30,000 km²)			Very Small (500–10,000 km²)			Micro (<500 km²)		
	Domestic Economy								
Population	Small (GDP >A$100 million)	Very Small (GDP A$25–100 million)	Micro (GDP <A$25 million)	Small	Very Small	Micro	Small	Very Small	Micro
Small (>250,000)	Hawaii Fiji			Ryukyus Mauritius					
Very small (25,000 to 250,000)		New Caledonia Solomon Islands New Hebrides		French Polynesia Guam	W. Samoa TTPI Tonga Kiribati		American Samoa	Seychelles	Maldives
Micro (<25,000)								Nauru	Cook Is. Wallis and Futuna Tuvalu Niue Tokelau

SOURCE: Based on R. T. Shand, *Island Smallness: Some Definitions and Implications* (Paper presented to the Development Studies Centre Conference of the Australian National University, May 1979), p. 4.

TABLE 1.2   Small States and Territories: Islands or Groups of Islands, 1966

	Number of Islands	Number of Inhabited Islands	Total Land Area (km²)	Estimated Population
Islands in the Atlantic Ocean				
Bermuda	300	20	53	50,000
Cape Verde Islands	14	10	4,033	228,000
Channel Islands	16	11	195	115,000
Falkland Islands	200	12	11,961	2,000
Faroe Islands	21	17	1,399	37,000
Iceland	1	1	103,000	195,000
Isle of Man	1	1	588	50,000
St. Helena, Ascension,				
Tristan da Cunha	3	3	314	5,815
St. Pierre-et-Miquelon	8	2	242	5,000
São Tomé and Principe	(2	2	964	59,000)
(Fernando Po: part of				
Equatorial Guinea)	(2	2	2,034	74,000)
Islands in the Caribbean				
Antigua	3	2	442	60,000
Bahamas	700	30	11,406	140,000
Barbados	1	1	430	245,000
Cayman Islands	3	3	259	9,000
Dominica	1	1	751	68,000
Grenada	2	2	344	97,000
Guadeloupe	7	7	1,779	319,000
Martinique	1	1	1,102	327,000
Montserrat	1	1	98	14,000
Netherlands Antilles	6	6	961	210,000
St. Kitts-Nevis-Anguilla	4	4	357	61,000
St. Lucia	1	1	616	103,000
St. Vincent	6	6	388	90,000
Trinidad and Tobago	3	3	5,128	1,000,000
Turks and Caicos	30	6	430	6,000
British Virgin Islands	40	11	153	9,000
U.S. Virgin Islands	50	3	344	50,000
Islands in the Mediterranean Sea				
Cyprus	1	1	9,251	603,000
Malta	5	3	316	317,000
Islands in the Indian Ocean				
British Indian Ocean Territory	25	?	74	2,000
Cocos (Keeling) Islands	27	3	14	1,000
Comoros	7	4	2,171	225,000
Christmas Island	1	1	135	3,000
Maldive Islands	2,000	220	298	101,000
Mauritius	4	4	2,096	780,000
Reunion	1	1	2,510	408,000
Seychelles	89	4	404	49,000 ·
Islands in the Pacific Ocean				
American Samoa	7	6	197	27,000
Cook Islands	15	14	234	21,000
Fiji	300	100	18,160	478,000
French Polynesia[a]	125	100	4,000	90,000

	Number of Islands	Number of Inhabited Islands	Total Land Area (km²)	Estimated Population
Gilbert and Ellice Islands[b]	37	31	886	54,000
Guam	1	1	549	79,000
Nauru	1	1	21	6,000
New Caledonia	40	5	19,000	93,000
New Hebrides	80	30	14,763	70,000
Niue	1	1	259	5,000
Norfolk Island	1	1	36	1,000
Pitcairn	4	1	5	92
Ryukyu and Bonin	100	90	2,196	944,000
Solomon Islands	100	90	29,785	140,000
Timor (Indonesia)	4	4	18,990	560,000
Tokelau	3	3	10	2,000
Tonga	200	40	699	75,000
Trust Territory of the Pacific Islands[c]	2,100	96	1,770	94,000
Wallis and Futuna	25	3	200	8,000
Western Samoa	8	8	2,842	130,000

[a]Ocean area: 4 million km².

[b]Ocean area: 5 million km².

[c]Ocean area: 7 million km².

SOURCE: J. Rappaport, E. Muteba, and J. J. Therattil, *Small States and Territories: Status and Problems* (New York: Arno Press for the United Nations Institute of Training and Research, 1971), pp. 34–35.

TABLE 1.3   Relative Importance of Foreign Trade of the Pacific Islands, 1980

Country	GDP (US$ millions)	As Percentage of GDP		Share of Exports (%)	
		Exports	Imports	Of One Commodity	Of Three Commodities
American Samoa	111.5	100.0	74.9	96.0	96.7
Cook Islands	17.4	15.0	95.0	36.3	59.0
Fiji	922.9	35.6	83.4	57.0	65.0
French Polynesia	931.8	2.9	51.3	24.0	29.6
Kiribati	20.8	11.6	81.0	90.0	99.9
New Caledonia	931.1	34.3	34.3	72.2	72.6
Niue	2.8	12.3	68.7	36.8	72.6
Papua New Guinea	2257.3	39.8	39.4	46.4	78.4
Solomon Islands	123.6	51.8	52.4	38.1	81.7
Tokelau	0.9	1.8	32.3	100.0	100.0
Tonga	38.5	17.6	78.3	45.0	66.6
Tuvalu	3.7	6.9	49.6	77.9	82.6
Vanuatu	53.6	78.3	120.0	24.2	31.3
Wallis and Futuna	8.9	0.0	67.5	na	na
Western Samoa	43.5	35.7	129.7	53.1	77.6

Note: Dates of GDP and trade ratios are 1978 for Cook Islands; 1979 for New Caledonia, Tuvalu, Vanuatu, and Wallis and Futuna; 1978–1979 for Niue; 1979–1980 for Tonga; and 1977 for Western Samoa; na = not available.

SOURCE: South Pacific Commission, *South Pacific Economies: Statistical Summary* (August 1982).

TABLE 1.4   Trade of the Pacific Islands with the Industrialized Countries, 1979 (percent)

	South Pacific Islands	Australia	New Zealand	France	United Kingdom	Other Europe	United States	Japan	All Others	TOTAL
						Exported to				
American Samoa		0.1			0.0		99.5	0.2	0.0	100.0
Cook Islands			99.8				0.2			100.0
Fiji	5.2	9.2	9.6		37.0	0.3	15.1	1.3	22.2	100.0
French Polynesia	8.5	0.1	0.3	60.5	0.0	20.8	7.8	1.1	0.9	100.0
Guam	49.4	0.0	0.0				26.1	1.6	22.9	100.0
Kiribati	0.2	47.5	37.1		14.5		0.3	0.2	0.1	100.0
New Caledonia	3.5	0.0	0.0	59.8	0.0	1.5	13.9	21.1	0.6	100.0
Niue	1.8	0.6	97.7							100.0
Papua New Guinea	1.9	8.1	0.6	0.7	5.6	27.2	8.7	31.3	7.6	100.0
Solomon Islands	15.9	1.6	0.7	3.2	17.7	18.7	5.7	23.8	13.3	100.0
New Hebrides	2.9	0.1	0.1	40.2	0.0	22.2	26.9	5.0	2.7	100.0
Tonga	15.1	37.2	32.6	0.2	0.1	0.1	1.5	4.6	8.7	100.0
Tuvalu										
TTPI										
Nauru										
Wallis and Futuna		48.5	3.0			20.4	0.0	0.0	1.4	100.0
Western Samoa	12.1	1.2	21.4		0.7	55.4			9.2	100.0

Imported from

	South Pacific Islands	Australia	New Zealand	France	United Kingdom	Other Europe	United States	Japan	All Others	TOTAL
American Samoa	2.6	2.0	7.4		0.1	0.0	69.8	16.2	1.9	100.0
Cook Islands	0.5	6.6	62.3	0.3	4.7	2.3	3.7	10.8	8.8	100.0
Fiji	0.2	35.3	15.0	0.5	8.9	2.2	5.7	14.3	18.0	100.0
French Polynesia	0.4	3.3	4.5	50.4	1.8	11.0	19.1	2.7	6.8	100.0
Guam	0.6	1.4	0.4				32.4	7.0	58.2	100.0
Kiribati	9.7	59.0	6.3	0.0	8.1	1.0	4.5	5.5	6.3	100.0
New Caledonia	4.3	10.8	4.1	40.5		10.8	4.1	4.3	21.0	100.0
Niue	14.0	0.3	80.0		0.2		0.4	3.2	1.9	100.0
Papua New Guinea	0.0	46.6	1.4	0.2	5.3	4.2	7.0	14.4	20.9	100.0
Solomon Islands	3.8	30.0	6.3	0.3	13.5	2.8	3.6	18.0	21.8	100.0
New Hebrides	9.6	30.0	4.0	25.1	5.1	8.3	2.6	7.8	10.0	100.0
Tonga	5.3	27.3	34.3	0.0	8.7	1.5	3.5	8.1	11.2	100.0
Tuvalu	20.6	48.1	9.7	0.1	10.5	0.3	1.1	3.7	6.0	100.0
TTPI	13.2	6.4	0.0				35.9	26.1	21.8	100.0
Nauru		91.2	8.8							100.0
Wallis and Futuna		47.3	14.1						38.6	100.0
Western Samoa	3.0	16.6	24.7	0.0	2.5	2.2	0.3	11.0	19.7	100.0

SOURCE: South Pacific Commission (SPC), "Overseas Trade, 1979," *Statistical Bulletin of the South Pacific*, 18 (December 1981): pp. 18–19.

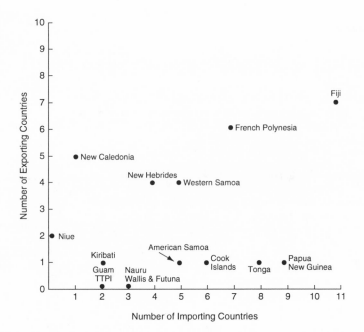

FIGURE 1.1   Intraregional Trade in the Pacific Islands, 1979
SOURCE: South Pacific Commission (SPC), *South Pacific Economies: Statistical Summary*
(April 1981), pp. 15–20.

TABLE 1.5   South Pacific Islands: How Trade Deficits Are Financed, 1980
(in thousands of Australian dollars)

	A	B	C	D	E	F
			Balance			
	Exports	Imports	of Trade	ODA	A/B	D/C
American Samoa	111,533	83,491	28,042	35,351	1.34	1.26
Cook Islands	3,612	20,353	−16,741	8,726	0.18	0.52
Fiji	328,557	493,284	−164,727	41,479	0.67	0.25
French Polynesia	26,589	477,617	−451,028	139,800	0.06	0.31
Kiribati	2,407	16,851	−14,444	19,056	0.14	1.32
New Caledonia	350,060	398,191	−48,131	173,404	0.88	3.60
Niue	266	2,916	−2,650	3,189	0.09	1.20
Papua New Guinea	898,338	888,536	9,802	257,054	1.01	26.20
Solomon	64,000	64,784	−784	30,269	0.99	38.60
Tokelau	32	318	−286	1,466	0.10	5.12
Tonga	6,764	30,135	−23,371	20,121	0.22	0.86
Tuvalu	86	3,147	−3,061	4,929	0.03	1.61
Vanuatu	31,397	63,804	−32,407	47,673	0.49	1.47
Wallis and Futuna	0	6,136	−6,136	7,300	0.06	1.19
Western Samoa	15,525	56,421	−40,896	21,849	0.28	0.53

SOURCES: South Pacific Commission (SPC), *South Pacific Economies: Statistical Summary*
(April 1981); and Asian Development Bank, *Key Indicators of Developing Member Countries of
ADB* 13 (April 1982).

TABLE 1.6 The Balance of Payments for Selected South Pacific Countries, 1981

	Trade Balance	Services (net) (travel)	Private Transfers (net)	Government Transfers	Current Balance	Long-term Loans (net)	Direct Investment	Others	Short-term Capital (net)	Errors and Omissions	Overall Balance
Fiji	-277.5	74.2 (142.8)	-8.8	25.8	-186.3	88.0	35.6	17.1	-1.1	24.2	-22.5
Papua New Guinea	-296.1	-422.8 (14.1)	-129.1	280.6	-567.4	301.1	86.3	-1.9	14.7	126.5	-40.6
Western Samoa	-19.9	0.0 (3.2)	3.0	3.9	-13.0	6.6	—	3.0	-2.2	3.6	-2.0
Solomon Islands	-11.1	-27.4 (2.8)	2.4	17.6	-18.5	12.2	0.2	0.4	0.0	0.1	-5.8
Tonga	-32.7	1.2 (7.0)	19.1	n.a.	n.a.	12.0	6.0	-10.5	n.a.	n.a.	12.9

SOURCE: Computed from the United Nations Conference on Trade and Development, *Handbook of International Trade and Development Statistics,* 1983.

TABLE 1.7   Classification of Developing Island Countries and Territories by Population Category, Income Level, and Distance from Nearest Continent, 1970

Population Category (1970)	Income Level: per Capita GNP (in dollars) 1970	Distance from Nearest Continent		
		Near (less than 200 km)	Medium (200 to 1000 km)	Far (more than 1000 km)
Large and medium (over 1 million inhabitants)	Under 250	Indonesia L Sri Lanka L	Madagascar L Haiti M	
	250 to 399		Philippines L Dominican Republic L Papua, New Guinea L	
	400 to 1,000	Hong Kong S Singapore VS Trinidad and Tobago M	Cuba L Jamaica M	
	Over 1,000		Puerto Rico M	
Small (150,000 to 1 million inhabitants)	Under 250	Macao VS	Portuguese Timor M Comoro S Cape Verde Islands M	Mauritius S British Solomon Islands M
	400 to 1,000		Cyprus M Martinique S Guadeloupe S Malta VS Barbados VS Bahrain VS	Fiji M Réunion S
	Over 1,000		Ryukyu Islands S Netherlands Antilles S Bahamas M	
Very small (under 150,000 inhabitants	Under 250		Maldives VS St. Vincent VS Seychelles VS	Western Samoa S
	250 to 400		St. Lucia VS Grenada VA Dominica VS St. Kitts-Nevis-Anguilla VS São Tomé and Principe S Antigua VS	Trust Territory of the Pacific Islands S Tonga VS Gilbert and Ellice Islands VS
	400 to 1,000			New Hebrides M American Samoa VS
	Over 1,000		Virgin Islands VS	Brunei M French Polynesia M New Caledonia VS Guam VS Bermuda VS

Note: Land area: VS = very small − below 1000 km².
S = small − 1000 to 3999 km².
M = medium − 4,000 to 39,999 km².
L = large − 40,000 km² and more.

SOURCE: United Nations Conference on Trade and Development, *Developing Island Countries: Report of the Panel of Experts* (New York, 1974), p. 5.

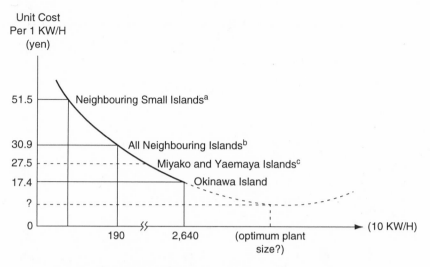

a The amount of electricity generated is not available.
b Includes Miyako and Yaeyama Islands.
c Shows only unit cost.

FIGURE 1.2   Unit Cost Curve for Generating Electricity in the Islands of Okinawa, 1979
SOURCE: H. Kakazu, "Okinawa Keizai Jiritsu eno Michi" (A Direction Toward Self-Reliant
Economic Development of Okinawa), *Shin Okinawa Bungaku,* 56 (1983): p. 23.

TABLE 1.8 Population Trends and Density of the South Pacific, 1901–1980

	Population (persons)				Population Density (per km²)			
	1901[a]	1921[b]	1951[c]	1980[d]	1901	1921	1951	1980
American Samoa	5,767	8,056	18,937	32,400	29	42	96	197
Cook Islands	8,213	9,459	15,079	17,900	34	39	63	240
Fiji	120,124	157,266	345,737	634,100	7	9	19	35
French Polynesia	30,600	31,600	62,678	148,100	9	10	37	45
Guam	9,676	13,275	59,498	105,800	18	25	193	196
Kiribati	n.a.	23,318	31,513	58,600	n.a.	34	46	85
Nauru	2,066	2,641	3,473	7,300	98	126	165	348
New Caledonia	54,400	47,505	65,500	139,400	3	3	3	7
Niue	4,051	3,761	4,553	3,400	16	15	18	13
Papua New Guinea (PNG)	n.a.	n.a.	2,184,986	2,996,300	n.a.		5	6
Pitcairn Island	n.a.	200	136	100	n.a.	40	27	20
Solomon Islands	n.a.	94,066	124,076	225,200	n.a.	3	4	8
Tokelau	875	989	1,580	1,600	87	99	158	160
Tonga	20,700	24,937	51,838	97,400	30	36	81	139
TTPI	n.a.	52,222	54,843	116,200	n.a.	29	30	85
Tuvalu	n.a.	3,457	4,487	7,500	n.a.	133	173	288
Vanuatu	n.a.	n.a.	n.a.	117,500	n.a.	n.a.	n.a.	10
Wallis and Futuna	n.a.	n.a.	8,546	10,800	n.a.	n.a.	34	42
Western Samoa	n.a.	36,343	84,909	156,400	n.a.	12	29	53

[a] American Samoa and Tokelau for 1900; Cook Islands and Niue for 1902.
[b] American Samoa, Guam, and TTPI for 1920; Solomon Islands, 1931.
[c] American Samoa, Guam, and TTPI for 1950; Fiji, 1956; Kiribati, 1947; Nauru, 1954; PNG, 1966; Pitcairn Island, 1954; Solomon Islands, 1959; Tonga, 1956; Tuvalu, 1947; and Wallis and Futuna, 1969.
[d] Mid-year estimates.

SOURCES: South Pacific Commission, "Population 1978," Statistical Bulletin of the South Pacific no. 15; South Pacific Economies: Statistical Summary (April 1981).

TABLE 1.9 Population Changes in Selected South Pacific Countries, 1972–1981 (in thousands of persons, percent)

	1972	1973	1974	1975	1976	1977	1978	1979	1980	1981
Cook Islands										
Population[a]	21.3	20.5	19.2	18.1	18.4	18.4	18.5	18.5	17.9	17.4
Rate of growth	0.9	-3.8	-6.3	-5.7	1.7	0.0	0.5	0.0	-3.2	-2.2
Natural rate of increase[b]	2.8	2.7	2.3	2.0	1.9	2.0	1.9	1.9	2.0	2.1
Rate of net emigration	-1.9	-6.5	-8.6	-7.7	-0.2	-2.0	-1.4	-1.9	-1.2	-0.1
Fiji										
Population	540.0	560.0	570.0	580.1	588.1	590.1	600.1	619.1	634.1	
Rate of growth	2.1	2.2	1.6	1.9	1.6	1.9	1.8	2.0	2.4	1.9
Natural rate of increase[c]	2.3	2.3	2.4	2.2	2.4	2.3	2.4	2.6	2.3	
Rate of net emigration	-0.2	-0.1	-0.8	-0.3	-0.8	-0.4	-0.6	-0.6	0.1	
Kiribati										
Population		51.9	52.8	53.6	54.5	55.3	56.5	57.3	58.6	59.9
Rate of growth	1.6	1.6	1.9	1.7	-10.0	2.0	2.2	2.0	2.3	0.7
Natural rate of increase	1.8	1.8					2.1			
Rate of net emigration	-0.2	-0.2					0.1			
Nauru										
Population						7.0		7.3	7.3	7.3
Rate of growth	1.5	1.5	1.4	1.4	1.4	1.4	0.0	0.0	0.0	
Natural rate of increase				1.5	1.5					
Rate of net emigration				-0.1	-0.1					
Niue										
Population	4.8	4.4	4.0	4.0	3.9	3.8	3.7	3.6	3.3	3.2
Rate of growth	-5.9	-8.3	-9.1	0.0	-2.5	-2.6	-2.6	-2.7	-8.3	-3.0
Natural rate of increase[d]		1.9	2.0	1.8				2.1	2.3	
Rate of net emigration		10.2	11.1	-1.8				4.8	10.6	

(continues)

TABLE 1.9 (continued)

	1972	1973	1974	1975	1976	1977	1978	1979	1980	1981
Papua New Guinea										
Population	2540	2600	2650	2700	2760	2820	2880	2940	3000	3010
Rate of growth	2.0	2.4	1.9	1.9	2.2	2.2	2.1	2.1	2.0	0.3
Natural rate of increase[e]	2.8	2.9	2.9	2.9	2.9	2.9	3.0	3.0	3.0	3.0
Rate of net emigration	-0.8	-0.5	-1.0	-1.0	-0.7	-0.7	-0.9	-0.9	-1.0	-2.7
Tonga										
Population	86.5	87.5	88.0	88.0	89.0	91.5	93.5	95.7	97.1	98.9
Rate of growth	1.8	1.1	0.6	0.0	1.1	2.8	2.2	2.4	1.5	1.9
Natural rate of increase	2.4	2.2	2.2	2.4	2.2	2.0	2.0	2.0		
Rate of net emigration	-0.6	-1.1	-1.6	-2.4	-1.1	0.8	0.2	0.4		
TTPI										
Population	11.0	11.0	11.0	12.0	12.0	12.0	13.0	13.0	14.0	14.0
Rate of growth	10.0									
Natural rate of increase	3.9	3.1	3.0	3.0	2.8	2.6	1.9	2.5		
Rate of net emigration	6.1									
Western Samoa										
Population	147.0	148.0	149.0	150.0	151.0	153.0	153.7	154.8	155.8	156.9
Rate of growth	1.4	0.7	0.7	0.7	0.7	1.3	0.5	0.7	0.6	0.7
Natural rate of increase	2.4	2.8	2.4	1.8	2.0	1.8	1.8	1.5	1.3	
Rate of net emigration	-1.0	-2.1	-1.7	-0.9	-1.3	-0.5	-1.3	-0.8	-0.7	

a Mid-year estimates for all countries.
b Rate of population growth = natural rate of increase (birth rate − death rate) + rate of net emigration (= net social increase).
c Fiji: data tabulated by year of registration rather than occurrence for 1978–1980.
d Niue: data refer to the number of live births and deaths that occurred or were registered.
e PNG: indigenous population for 1972–1974.
SOURCE: Computed from the United Nations, Statistical Yearbook for Asia and the Pacific, 1981 (ST/ESCAP/185).

TABLE 1.10   Average Annual Growth Rates of Population and Per Capita Real GNP for Selected South Pacific Countries, 1960–1969 and 1970–1979

	1960–1969		1970–1979	
	Population	GNP per Capita	Population	GNP per Capita
American Samoa[a]	5.5	8.9	1.5	n.a.
Fiji	2.8	2.7	2.0	3.0
French Polynesia[a]	3.1	9.1	2.4	n.a.
Guam[a]	4.9	3.4	1.2	n.a.
Kiribati[a]	n.a.	n.a.	1.6	n.a.
New Caledonia[a]	2.6	3.9	2.2	n.a.
TTPI[a]	2.7	3.7	3.0	n.a.
Papua New Guinea	2.4	2.0	2.3	0.3
Solomon Islands	2.9	1.9	3.5	2.3
Tonga[a]	3.1	−3.3	1.3	n.a.
Vanuatu[a]	n.a.	n.a.	3.2	n.a.
Wallis and Futuna[a,b]	2.0	−1.5	n.a.	n.a.
Western Samoa[c]	2.6	−1.1	1.1	n.a.

Note: n.a. = not available.

[a]Estimates of GNP per capita and its growth rate are tentative.

[b]GNP per capita refers to 1978.

[c]Australian National University estimates its gross domestic product per capita for 1980 at US$650.

SOURCE: International Bank for Reconstruction and Development, *World Bank Atlas,* 1970 and 1981, pp. 8–19.

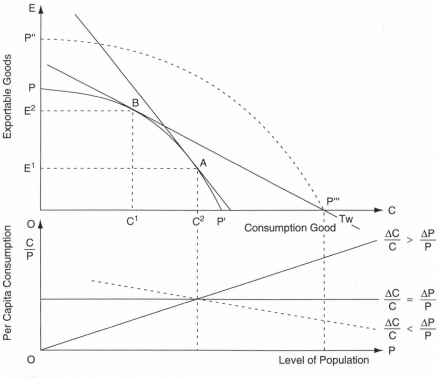

FIGURE 1.3   Trade and Economic Development

TABLE 1.11   Resource Expansion Effect of Foreign Trade: The Case of Fiji, 1971–1980

	1971	1972	1973	1974	1975	1976	1977	1978	1979	1980
Rice										
A. Area harvested (1,000 ha.)	9.0	9.0	9.0	9.0	10.0	9.0	9.0	9.0	9.0	9.0
B. Production (1,000 m.t.)	16.0	17.0	16.0	17.0	23.0	21.0	18.0	16.0	19.0	14.0
C. B/A (m.t./ha.)	1.8	1.9	1.8	1.9	2.3	2.3	2.0	1.8	2.1	1.6
D. Unit value (F$/m.t.)[a]	156.4	114.9	207.2	337.8	304.1	286.1	298.0	382.3	348.2	393.5
E. Total value (F$1,000)[b]	2,502.4	1,953.3	3,315.2	5,742.6	6,994.3	6,008.1	5,364.0	6,116.8	6,615.8	5,509.0
F. Value per ha. (F$)[c]	278.0	217.0	368.4	638.1	699.4	667.6	596.0	679.6	735.1	612.1
Sugarcane										
F. Area harvested (1,000 ha.)	47.0	44.0	45.0	45.0	45.0	47.0	52.0	54.0	62.0	67.0
G. Production (1,000 m.t.)	2,545.0	2,238.0	2,495.0	2,151.0	2,160.0	2,283.0	2,674.0	2,849.0	4,058.0	3,360.0
H. B/A (m.t./ha.)	54.1	50.9	55.4	47.8	48.0	48.6	51.4	52.8	65.5	50.1
I. Total value (F$1,000)[d]	32,851.0	34,319.0	34,280.0	67,023.0	94,718.0	67,704.0	93,576.0	83,273.0	116,960.0	174,170.0
J. value per ha. (F$)[c]	699.0	780.0	761.8	1,489.4	2,104.8	1,440.5	1,799.5	1,542.1	1,886.5	2,599.6
K. J/F	2.5	3.6	2.1	2.3	3.0	2.2	3.0	2.3	2.6	4.2
L. Total value of imported rice (F$1,000)	1,818.0	1,351.0	3,572.0	5,525.0	4,366.0	3,543.0	5,236.0	6,379.0	5,950.0	6,200.0
M. Required area to produce[f] imported rice above (ha.)	6,538.5	6,224.9	9,697.2	8,659.0	6,242.2	5,307.3	8,785.2	9,385.8	8,094.3	10,128.9
N. Required area to produce[g] imported rice in terms of sugarcane (ha.)	2,601.0	1,732.1	4,689.0	3,709.5	2,074.3	2,459.5	2,909.6	4,136.6	3,154.1	2,385.0
O. M − N (ha.)	3,937.5	4,492.8	5,008.2	4,949.5	4,167.9	2,847.8	5,875.6	5,249.2	4,940.2	7,743.9
P. Arable land (1,000 ha.)	225.0	228.0	228.0	230.0	230.0	231.0	233.0	234.0	234.0	236.0
Q. O/P (%)	1.8	2.0	2.2	2.2	1.8	1.2	2.5	2.2	2.1	3.3

[a]Unit import value has been used as a proxy.

[b]B × D.

[c]E/A.

[d]Total value of sugar exports has been used as an imputed value of sugar production.

[e]I/F.

[f]L/F.

[g]L/J.

source: Computed from the United Nations, *Statistical Yearbook for Asia and the Pacific, 1981* (St/ESCAP/185).

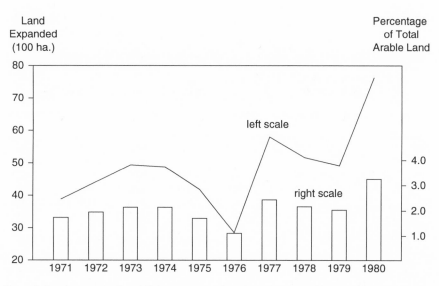

Land
Expanded
(100 ha.)

Percentage
of Total
Arable Land

Rows O (land expanded) and Q (percentage of total arable land) of Table 1.11, respectively.

FIGURE 1.4   Land Resource Expansion Effect from Exporting Sugarcane and Importing
Rice: Fiji, 1971–1980
SOURCE: Computed from the United Nations, *Statistical Yearbook for Asia and the Pacific,
1981* (St/ESCAP/185).

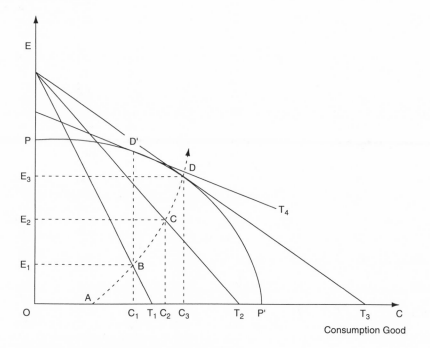

FIGURE 1.5   A Development Path Through Trade

TABLE 1.12   Terms of Trade and Unit Prices for Selected Products, 1950–1982

	Terms of Trade (1975 = 100)[a]		1982 Constant Unit Prices (US cents)				
	Developing Countries	Industrial Countries	Sugar[b] (kg)	Copra[c] (m.t.)	Coffee[d] (kg)	Rice[e] (m.t.)	Petroleum[f] (barrel)
1950	100	100	48 (100)	1,101 (100)	511 (100)	594 (100)	7 (100)
1951	105	96	46 (96)	1,068 (97)	474 (93)	529 (89)	6 (84)
1952	95	98	33 (69)	677 (61)	449 (88)	558 (94)	6 (82)
1953	95	102	28 (58)	876 (80)	492 (96)	652 (110)	7 (82)
1954	100	100	27 (48)	787 (71)	671 (131)	600 (101)	7 (91)
1955	98	100	27 (56)	696 (63)	531 (104)	528 (89)	7 (91)
1956	96	101	28 (58)	664 (60)	595 (116)	500 (84)	7 (93)
1957	93	100	40 (83)	626 (57)	493 (96)	480 (81)	7 (95)
1958	93	103	26 (54)	681 (62)	382 (75)	471 (79)	7 (95)
1959	95	106	23 (48)	866 (79)	347 (68)	461 (78)	7 (89)
1960	93	108	24 (50)	704 (64)	337 (66)	424 (71)	7 (88)
1961	90	110	20 (42)	575 (52)	326 (64)	463 (79)	6 (82)
1962	88	110	21 (44)	569 (52)	308 (60)	523 (88)	6 (84)
1963	89	109	63 (131)	632 (57)	297 (58)	487 (82)	6 (84)
1964	91	109	42 (88)	648 (59)	359 (70)	459 (77)	6 (84)
1965	89	110	15 (31)	753 (68)	355 (69)	453 (76)	6 (84)
1966	90	110	13 (26)	580 (53)	328 (64)	512 (86)	6 (76)
1967	89	111	13 (27)	630 (57)	285 (56)	635 (107)	6 (76)
1968	90	111	14 (29)	766 (70)	310 (61)	665 (112)	6 (80)
1969	91	111	23 (48)	662 (60)	325 (64)	613 (103)	6 (80)
1970	90	112	24 (50)	665 (60)	368 (72)	426 (72)	6 (72)
1971	94	111	27 (57)	515 (47)	297 (58)	353 (59)	6 (84)

	Terms of Trade (1975 = 100)[a]		1982 Constant Unit Prices (US cents)				
	Developing Countries	Industrial Countries	Sugar[b] (kg)	Copra[c] (m.t.)	Coffee[d] (kg)	Rice[e] (m.t.)	Petroleum[f] (barrel)
1972	92	112	40	351	312	367	6
			(84)	(32)	(61)	(62)	(84)
1973	101	112	43	737	335	731	7
			(91)	(67)	(66)	(123)	(93)
1974	141	98	109	1,102	285	902	16
			(228)	(100)	(56)	(152)	(216)
1975	126	101	66	376	264	532	15
			(136)	(34)	(52)	(90)	(208)
1976	132	100	37	396	501	366	17
			(77)	(36)	(98)	(62)	(224)
1977	130	100	24	534	715	362	17
			(50)	(49)	(140)	(61)	(230)
1978	123	102	19	530	457	414	14
			(40)	(48)	(89)	(70)	(193)
1979	133	100	21	679	411	337	16
			(44)	(62)	(80)	(57)	(236)
1980	152	92	59	423	389	404	27
			(123)	(38)	(76)	(68)	(370)
1981	157	91	37	371	346	473	33
			(77)	(34)	(68)	(80)	(439)
1982	155	93	19	314	323	293	34
			(39)	(29)	(63)	(49)	(459)

Note: Parentheses are indexes; 1982 = 100.

[a]Unit value index of exports divided by unit value index of imports.

[b]From 1950 to 1960, quotations refer to New York World Contract No. 4, f.o.s. Cuba; beginning 1961, International Sugar Council "World" daily price, f.o.b. and stowed Caribbean ports.

[c]1950–1963 quotations are Straits/Borneo, fair merchantable, c.i.f. European ports; Philippines, c.i.f. European ports.

[d]Colombian coffee from Manizales, Armenia, and Medellin.

[e]5 percent broken, milled, f.o.b. Bangkok.

[f]Light crude oil, 34–34.9° API gravity, f.o.b. Ras Tanura.

SOURCE: International Bank for Reconstruction and Development, *Commodity and Price Trends*, 1977 (pp. 5–60) and 1983–1984 (pp. 11–72) editions.

TABLE 1.13 Yields of Selected Crops for Fiji, Papua New Guinea, and Tonga, 1971–1981 (per ha.)

	1971	1972	1973	1974	1975	1976	1977	1978	1979	1980	1981
Fiji											
Sugarcane											
Area harvested (1,000 ha.)	47.0	44.0	45.0	45.0	45.0	47.0	52.0	54.0	62.0	67.0	74.0
Production (1,000 m.t.)	2,545.0	2,238.0	2,495.0	2,151.0	2,160.0	2,283.0	2,674.0	2,849.0	4,058.0	3,360.0	3,810.0
Per ha. yields (m.t./ha.)	54.1	50.9	55.4	47.8	48.0	48.6	51.4	52.8	65.5	50.1	51.5
Papua New Guinea											
Cocoa											
Area harvested (1,000 ha.)	55.0	59.0	62.0	70.0	77.0	75.0	80.0	82.0	75.0	78.0	78.0
Production (1,000 m.t.)	29.0	29.0	23.0	33.0	36.0	32.0	29.0	30.0	27.0	31.0	31.0
Per ha. yields (m.t./ha.)	1.9	2.0	2.7	2.1	2.1	2.3	2.8	2.7	2.8	2.5	2.5
Sweet potatoes											
Area harvested (1,000 ha.)	83.0	85.0	87.0	90.0	93.0	93.0	94.0	95.0	98.0	98.0	99.0
Production (1,000 m.t.)	360.0	380.0	388.0	400.0	420.0	422.0	425.0	430.0	436.0	440.0	450.0
Per ha. yields (m.t./ha.)	0.2	0.2	0.2	0.2	0.2	0.2	0.2	0.2	0.2	0.2	0.2
Tonga											
Sweet potatoes and yams											
Area harvested (1,000 ha.)	5.0	6.0	6.0	6.0	6.0	6.0	6.0	6.0	6.0	6.0	7.0
Production (1,000 m.t.)	73.0	75.0	76.0	77.0	78.0	78.0	79.0	79.0	79.0	80.0	80.0
Per ha. yields (m.t./ha.)	0.1	0.1	0.1	0.1	0.1	0.1	0.1	0.1	0.1	0.1	0.1

SOURCE: Computed from the United Nations, *Statistical Yearbook for Asia and the Pacific, 1981* (ST/ESCAP/185), pp. 161–603.

TABLE 1.14   The Rate of Urbanization and Per Capita GDP and Food Imports as Indicators of the Level of Subsistence Activities for Selected South Pacific Countries, 1980

	Rate of Urbanization[a] (percent)	Per Capita GDP[b] (A$)	Per Capita Food Imports (A$)
New Caledonia	61	6,699	434
French Polynesia	59	6,292	558
American Samoa	43	3,442	373
Fiji	37	1,465	110
Kiribati	36	354	93
Tuvalu	30	504	123
Cook Islands	27	941	254
Tonga	26	395	73
Western Samoa	21	304	77
Papua New Guinea	11	750	58
Solomon Islands	9	549	31

[a]Share of urban population to total population.

[b]Dates of GDP and trade ratios are 1978 for Cook Islands; 1979 for New Caledonia, Tuvalu, Vanuatu, and Wallis and Futuna; 1978–1979 for Niue; 1979–1980 for Tonga; and 1977 for Western Samoa.

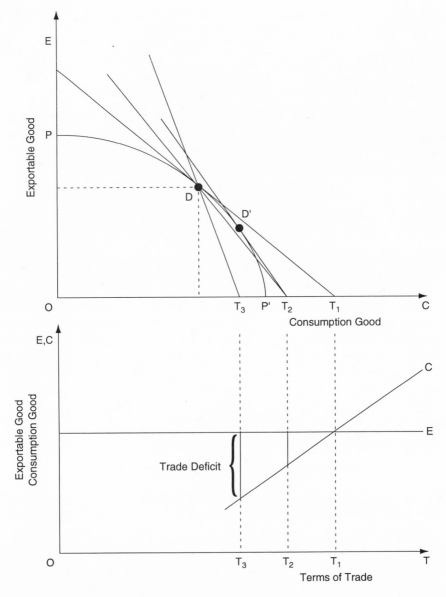

FIGURE 1.6   Terms of Trade and Trade Imbalance

2

Trade and Diversification
in the South Pacific Islands

The development problems pertaining to small island economies have become an increasing concern among development economists as well as various development organizations since the 1960s, when the decolonization process of small island territories started. Although there has been an increasing tendency to shift from arguments for trade-led specialization to support for agriculture-based diversification in order to prevent these economies from possible collapse into what Fairbairn and Fisk[1] call "subsistence poverty," a clear-cut approach for diversification has not been satisfactorily developed.

In this chapter, I shall (1) analyze two possible ways the export-led island economies might collapse into subsistence poverty, (2) examine two feasible approaches to the viable diversification of the economies, (3) describe the nature and roles of subsistence economy, and (4) derive some policy implications from the analysis.

Two Possible Collapse Cases of Trade-Led Growth

The Exhaustion of Natural Resources

For the South Pacific island economies, where diversification of the economic base is severely limited mainly because of small domestic markets, external trade was not only the vehicle of peaceful coexistence among the islanders but also the powerful engine of growth (see Chapter 1). A steady rise in real per capita incomes for these island economies was largely made possible through exporting a few comparatively advantageous agricultural and mining products. Some of the island countries rely heavily on one or two export products, as for example, American Samoa on processed tuna, Kiribati on copra, Nauru on phosphate, and New Caledonia on nickel products; in Fiji and Papua New Guinea, sugar and copper concentrates, respectively, dominate export earnings (Table 2.1).

The small countries' reliance on copra and other coconut products, supplemented by one or two other items, is notable. However, whilst specialization is undoubtedly an important explanatory factor for current levels of per capita income, very high in a number of instances, it is not necessarily the major influence in all cases. Foreign aid has been significant, as in French Polynesia, New Caledonia, and Papua New Guinea; the spending as well as personal remittances from overseas kin must also be taken into account.

Specialization in a few primary export products in the South Pacific has been intensified both by colonial economic policies and by new demands created through imported goods. In the process of export-led growth, resources have been transferred from the subsistence sector to the monetized sector. The nature of a subsistence economy will be fully discussed later. Although there are great variations in the degree of monetization, island economies such as Nauru, New Caledonia, French Polynesia, and Tuvalu are now highly monetized. The key question that has been raised by Fisk, Doumenge, and Fairbairn and Tisdell[2] is whether such export-led growth is sustainable. There are two possible ways that a small export-oriented economy with relatively high per capita income might collapse into subsistence poverty. One is the exhaustion of natural resources. A good possible case is the phosphate of Nauru, which estimates indicate will be exhausted during the next few years.[3]

The possible case of Nauru is shown in Figure 2.1 using the conventional production possibility curve (PP') with two commodities (E = exportable good and C = consumption good) under the usual assumptions.[4] For illustrative purposes, let us start from point A on the transformation curve where, given the pretrade domestic terms of trade (Td), the economy will both produce goods and consume all of them domestically. But if the international terms of trade (Tw) are more favorable for the exportable good than for the consumption good, the economy will respond to the difference in the price ratio by moving from A to B on the curve—that is to say, by producing more E at the expense of C. In addition to favorable terms of trade, new tastes and a "demonstration effect" induced by imports no doubt have accelerated the economy's movement from A to B.[5] At the production point B, BC_1 quantity of phosphate can be exported in exchange for C_1C_4 quantity of consumption good. The welfare level of the economy in terms of consumption ($OC_1 + C_1C_4 = OC_4$) is much higher than that of the pretrade level (OC_3).

Given the state of technology, the gradual exhaustion of the phosphate resource will push the transformation curve downward, say from PP' to P'P'''. With the terms of trade remaining unchanged, the possible consumption level (OC_2) is even lower than the pretrade level (OC_3). This collapse of the transformation curve may happen gradually depending upon the rate of exhaustion of the phosphate resource, as is suggested in Figure 2.1. The lower part of Figure 2.1 shows that the process of collapse—in contrast to the process of trade expansion, which has brought more real income than population increase—is accompanied by the rapid deterioration of per capita consumption (C/P) unless depopulation greater than the decrease in consumption or massive aid flow takes place. Fairbairn and Tisdell[6] have discussed the same issue within the Ricardian model of population growth and technological change.

This simple model indicates a danger of specializing in one resource-specific nonrenewable export good. According to the theory of comparative cost advantage, the gradual exhaustion of an exportable resource means a gradual increase in the relative cost of exploiting the resource. Before the resource is completely exhausted, exports will be halted through the market mechanism—that is to say, whenever the unit production cost of the exportable good exceeds the world price. We have witnessed the disappearance or new disappearance of a number of resource-specific export goods from some South Pacific countries—such as the phosphate of Kiribati and Makatea, the gold of Fiji, and bananas of Western Samoa—because of their relative disadvantage in international markets.

The theory of comparative advantage has better applied to large economies, where alternative resources for exports can more easily be developed, than to small ones. For the very small economies of the South Pacific such as Nauru and Kiribati, the exhaustion of a nonrenewable exportable resource means the complete collapse of external trade and the return to a subsistence economy. There is a good possibility that the return to a subsistence economy will result in a level of production lower than the pretrade level due to the possible loss of a traditional subsistence skill and other subsistence resources.[7] This is illustrated by Figure 2.2. As the economy becomes more specialized in producing exportable good (E), moving from A to C on the transformation curve, more resources for subsistence production and consumption (C) will be lost, as is indicated by the asymmetric shrinkage of the curve toward the origin.

Deterioration in the Terms of Trade with the Loss of Traditional Skills

The collapse of a small export economy can also result from a deterioration in the terms of trade combined with a loss of subsistence skills, as is shown in Figure 2.3. If we assume a transformation curve similar to that in Figure 2.2, the deterioration in the international terms of trade from T_1 to T_2 shifts the production point, according to traditional trade theory, from B to A on the curve, thereby reducing the consumption level from C_3 to C_2. If, however, traditional production skills were lost in the process of export specialization, the same degree of deterioration in the terms of trade will bring the production point to A' on the transformation curve which will result in a consumption level (C_1) much lower than A. If the population level remains unchanged, then per capita income and consumption must decline to the minimum subsistence level, which may bring significant social and political problems in an island economy. Or if population growth continues at the current high rate, the result may be prolonged starvation.

Actually, however, most South Pacific countries have chosen to increase both export production and foreign capital inflows to compensate for the loss of export earnings induced by the deterioration in the terms of trade. This course has been chosen instead of curtailing the level of consumption (particularly of imported goods) or instead of increasing subsistence production, which is assumed in the traditional trade theory. Specialization in an exportable good in the face of deteriorating terms of trade will be intensified if an island economy has no alternative resource to fall back on, as is suggested by B. Higgins and J. D. Higgins.[8]

Two Criteria for Diversification

The Balance-of-Payments Approach

In order to prevent a small island economy from collapsing into subsistence poverty, we have to find some operational criteria that ensure a stable mix between export and subsistence production. One such simple yet manageable criterion is a balance-of-payments approach.

Figure 2.4 shows three possible growth paths: A, B, and C. Growth path A is considered to be the most conservative in terms of growth rate and is oriented toward subsistence production. The economy will produce rather unstable and risky exportable cash products after securing fully its own food supply through subsistence production. This type of growth path is quite similar to the one expounded in the "vent-for-surplus" theory of international trade.[9]

Imports (M) are limited to essential goods that cannot be produced domestically. Therefore, growth path A ensures a balance-of-payments surplus $(X - M > 0)$, which can be saved for uncertainties or utilized for future economic development.

Growth path B represents equilibrium growth, implying that the economy can just pay for what it consumes. This growth path is consistent with a strategy of "self-reliant economic development," which is now a catchword of all South Pacific island countries.[10] From the standpoint of current chronic trade deficits in the South Pacific, this growth path may provide the most desirable mixture of trade and subsistence production.

Growth path C is what neoclassical development economists have been recommending for a number of years based upon the classical notion that foreign trade is more beneficial to a small and poor nation than to a large and rich one.[11] Actually, this growth path has, more or less, been vigorously pursued by South Pacific countries. The result, however, has been growing trade deficits that cannot be sustained in the long run.

Table 2.2 highlights the trade deficits experienced by almost all island countries during two previous periods and the levels of official development assistance that helped support their balance of payments. Large trade deficits in absolute terms are noticeable in several cases, for example, Fiji, French Polynesia, New Caledonia, and Papua New Guinea; but beyond these, the trade deficit in relation to export earnings is most substantial for small countries such as the Cook Islands, Kiribati, and Western Samoa. (American Samoa and Nauru escaped only because of substantial exports based on mining and tuna processing, respectively, in relation to import demand.) The change in the trade position of Kiribati (formerly the Gilbert Islands) and New Caledonia is of interest; both moved from trade surpluses to deficits over the period, reflecting the exhaustion of phosphate supplies in the former and rapid import expansion in the latter. As was the case in New Caledonia, rapidly rising import demand coupled with generally static export performance faced by most Pacific countries was the underlying reason for deteriorating trade conditions, though the effects of a global recession on terms of trade also played a part.

In addition to foreign aid, invisible trade receipts such as tourism, personal remittances from overseas kin, and financial services have become increasingly important sources for financing the trade deficits in the South Pacific. Due to a lack of detailed and reliable data, the importance of these invisible trade receipts in Pacific island economies is not easily determined, but there is no doubt that these sources are substantial in a number of cases. In Western Samoa, net foreign exchange earnings from tourism, including hotels, transport, and shopping, were estimated at $2.5 million in 1981, an amount exceeded only the return on copra and taro among the traditional export products.[12] In Tonga in 1980, gross foreign exchange earnings from tourism were estimated at $6 million, only $1 million less than the island's total export earnings for that year. Although no reliable information is available, tourism earnings were probably similar for New Caledonia, French Polynesia, and Vanuatu. Many Pacific island countries have enormous potential to develop a tourism industry, and they look upon it as an important source of foreign exchange earnings. The tourism industry, however, is in many ways beyond the control of these small island economies. It depends not only on economic conditions of industrialized countries but also on various imported inputs such as transportation, hotels, sales promotion, raw materials, souvenirs, and even foodstuffs, all of which consist of leakages from the economies. Even in Fiji, one of the largest Pacific island economies, more than 70 percent of tourist expenditures leak out of the country in the form of imports, profit expropriation, and expatriate salaries.[13]

Other important sources of invisible trade incomes for the Pacific islands are remittances and services that are even more difficult to account for than those of tourism. But fragmentary evidence suggests that Western Samoa's income from foreign remittances amounted to $13 million in 1984, which was nearly one-half of the country's trade deficit for that year.[14] We can expect that other small island economies such as American Samoa, Tonga, the Cook Islands, and Vanuatu will also depend heavily on remittances. With respect to service incomes, Vanuatu, the Cook Islands, and Western Samoa have offered tax havens and off-shore banking facilities. Vanuatu has operated an off-shore banking facility since 1970, and it is now one of the largest in the Southeast Asia and Pacific region, making the facility the country's third-largest foreign exchange earner.[15]

As we have seen, export expansion in the South Pacific island economies has usually proceeded not through the relative change of international price, as the traditional trade model assumes, but to a large extent through trade concessions from their former colonial masters and the necessity to finance the increasing demands for imports, which have been accelerated by both the demonstration effect and rising expectations. This is why the slope of imports in Figure 2.4 is greater than that of exports. Export expansion has created the greater demands for imports.

Thus, these small island nations have tended to expand their exports beyond the limit permitted by the market mechanism in order to finance ever-growing import demands. Excessive export-biased policies may be more damaging to these small resource-poor island economies than excessive inward-looking policies, which have been denounced by many development economists, such as H. Myint and I. Little, T. Scitovsky and M. Scott.[16]

These growth paths can be expressed in the following simple macromodel. If we assume that investment is zero for convenience,

$$C = Y + (M - X)$$
$$= Y + F$$

Growth path A: $X > M$ or $Y > C$
Growth path B: $X = M$ or $Y = C$
Growth path C: $X < M$ or $Y < C$,

where C = consumption, Y = gross national product, M = imports, X = exports, F = net foreign capital inflows. Currently almost all South Pacific nations are in the positions of $X - M < 0$, or $C > Y$. That is to say, they are spending beyond their means and the differences are financed largely through inflows of foreign aid (Table 2.2).

The balance-of-payments approach suggests that consumption should be kept within the limit of domestic productive capacity (Y) or that subsistence production should expand to ensure $C = Y$ or $M = X$. This approach will be more easily implemented in relatively resource-rich and subsistence-oriented economies such as the Solomon Islands, Papua New Guinea, Fiji, and Western Samoa than in those smaller, highly export-oriented economies such as Nauru and Kiribati.

The Safe-Minimum-Standard Approach

The safe-minimum-standard (SMS) approach, originally conceived by S. V. Ciriacy-Wantrup[17] and recently highlighted by Hiroshi Yamauchi and H. Onoe,[18] suggests another possible criterion for finding a socially optimum balance between export and subsistence production. The concept, which was developed in the field of conservation economics, rests upon the idea that for certain classes of renewable resources in ecosystems where production is an important consideration, there are potential critical zones in their use that might lead to irreversible losses.

Critical zones are those biophysical conditions brought about by human actions that would make it uneconomical to halt or reverse depletion. If use beyond the critical zone involves social uncertainties, an assessment must be made of the possibilities of suffering immoderate losses that might threaten the continuity of a social group.[19]

The SMS approach to the production system of the South Pacific island economies provides policymakers with a simple yet potentially powerful tool to achieve development balanced between the export-oriented cash sector and the subsistence food sector. The quantification of such a standard is not an easy task and must depend upon the specifics of each situation. Institutional rules that define performance standards in terms of practices and results are typically involved. The conceptual framework can be adapted to economic development and food security strategies. For example, to obtain a numerical standard, we can begin with a "safe minimum self-sufficiency" rate of foodstuffs for an island economy. Such a rate might be derived from a minimum caloric requirement for survival of the population on the island. An effort along this line is being developed by the Japanese. The essence of the procedure is illustrated by Yamauchi[20] as follows:

$$\text{minimum caloric intake for survival} = 1,800 \text{ cal/day}$$
$$\text{current average caloric intake} = 2,500 \text{ cal/day}$$

Thus, the Japanese people currently consume 2,500/1,800 calories, or 1.39 times as many calories as necessary for theoretical survival. But if the overall food self-sufficiency rate is 30 percent, this is 1,050 calories, or 58 percent short of ensuring human survival in case of emergency.

$$\text{i.e.,} \quad \frac{1,800 - 0.3(2,500)}{1,800} = 58\%$$

There are many technical problems involved in translating such a figure into rules governing production for domestic consumption versus exports, and a major interdisciplinary effort is necessary.

The previous procedure cannot currently be applied by Pacific island countries owing, among other things, to a lack of data. Food-import statistics are generally good, but reliable quantitative indicators of local food production, consumption, and nutrition are absent. Evidence on average dietary intake is available in a few cases, but it is invariably too aggregated to be of practical value. Thus, R. Taylor, G. Koteka, and M. Mokoputua[21] cite figures of adult dietary intake for the Cook Islands for 1962: 3,350 calories in Rarotonga and 2,355 in Atiu-Mitiaro (two outer islands). In a 1984 study, the Asian Development Bank[22] quoted a corresponding figure of 2,280 calories for Western Samoa. The operational application of the minimum-caloric-requirement approach among Pacific island countries therefore awaits refinement of food-consumption and dietary data, and the hiatus may be remedied by ongoing research efforts in this field.

The minimum-calorie-requirement concept of food security has much more practical meaning for the small South Pacific countries than for large ones because of their isolation and unstable export incomes and because of frequent cyclones, droughts, earthquakes, and tsunamis.[23] This approach can also be defended from the standpoint of improving the nutritional standards of the South Pacific, where malnutrition, due mainly to the increasing consumption of imported foodstuffs at the expense of subsistence foods, has been the recent major developmental issue.[24]

The Importance of the Subsistence Sector
and Policy Implications

The Subsistence Sector

The direction of economic development derived from the foregoing analysis is quite clear. In order to prevent their economies from collapsing into subsistence poverty, these island countries should steer their development policies away from an export-led strategy to the revitalization of the subsistence economy, which was defined in Chapter 1.

The main role of a subsistence economy is to reduce the increasing heavy dependency on imported foods, which has aggravated the balance-of-payments positions and lowered the nutritional standards of these islands. Subsistence activities, however, are not limited to food production. According to Fairbairn,[25] they can be classified into broad categories: for example, foodstuffs as well as their processing, building activity, capital works, furniture, and traditional crafts. They also include village councils, the local government rule of village elders and chiefs, indigenous medicine, the entrepreneurial role of family heads, the maintenance and upkeep of village facilities and utilities, and family funerals and religious services.

Specific subsistence-based activities with employment potential are handicrafts production, dressmaking, carpentry, and the production of a range of agricultural products such as cassava, taro, coconut, breadfruit, fish, pork, and poultry. Other possibilities are the production of capital items such as traditional houses, canoes, and bridges. Processing and household manufacturing activities are also important in many countries; some examples are the processing of cassava flour, rice, tapioca powder, homegrown tobacco, and coconut oil; home brewing; and food preservation (e.g., breadfruit in Samoa and babai in Kiribati and Tuvalu).

Contributions of these subsistence activities to the social and economic life of island countries are summarized as follows:

1. They provide many categories of goods and services that form basic and highly valued ingredients of contemporary village life. These often have no direct substitute in the modern trade sector.
2. They provide a source of livelihood for those unable to find secure employment in the wage sector.
3. They constitute a familiar base from which innovations in commercial agriculture and other areas can be carried out by villagers should they desire such changes.
4. Many subsistence foodstuffs are highly nutritious (and cheap), compared with trade store substitutes.
5. Subsistence activities are valued as integral elements of what many Pacific islanders conceive of as the sort of life-style they wish to maintain and encourage.

Most Pacific island economies are hybrids, or dual systems, where the monetary sector coexists with a substantial subsistence sector. Subsistence activities have remained strong despite long contact with the modern trade economy, and A. C. Walsh[26] suggests that "semi subsistence involvement should . . . be regarded as at least a semi-permanent feature of Pacific island society, and policy makers should operate within this term of reference."

Table 2.3 provides estimates of the subsistence component of national incomes for Pacific island countries that compile such estimates. Caution needs to be exercised in the interpretation of these estimates because of differences in the estimating techniques used and the areas and activities covered. A common deficiency is a failure to cover the range of major subsistence activities (e.g., construction of village houses and canoes and production of capital tools and handicrafts). The estimate for Western Samoa, for example, applies only to agricultural production. It is apparent, therefore, that in many cases subsistence production is significantly underestimated.

The real importance of subsistence production is probably best represented by "employment" data. N. V. Lam[27] reports that approximately 620,000 (57%) of the total work force of Papua New Guinea in 1981 was almost completely dependent on the "nonmarket" sector. In Western Samoa in 1976 it was estimated that 47,906 (76%) were occupied predominantly in the subsistence sector,[28] and in Tuvalu those aged fifteen years and above who were "active in village employment" primarily for subsistence totaled 3,456 (70%).[29]

The continuing importance of subsistence production in the Solomon Islands is due to such factors as limited contact with the cash economy by a large section of the population, the often unusually productive nature of the traditional rural sector, and continually strong preferences for traditional foods and other goods. Where subsistence income is relatively low, as in Fiji, this is probably due to high levels of cash incomes made possible by a strongly growing monetary sector and strong preferences for trade goods built up over time (one also suspects significant underestimation of subsistence production).

Policy Implications

Although there are great variations in degree, the subsistence sector of the South Pacific has been gradually eroded due mainly to the foreign-trade-induced monetization of economies, high population growth, and the loss of production skills in the sector. It will become more difficult for these economies to redirect their resources from export-oriented production to domestic consumption-oriented production as the subsistence activities become less important. Fisk[30] argues that subsistence affluence should be seized "as early as possible" because the larger the subsistence sector, the more unused resources of land and labor concealed in the sector may be mobilized in order to diversify the economic base without reducing the level of subsistence consumption.

For most South Pacific islands, there are two qualitatively different ways to produce domestic goods at the expense of exportable goods. One direction, suggested by W. G. Demas,[31] is "import replacement," namely substituting domestic production for what is imported such as rice, canned fish, and soft drinks. The other direction is "import-displacement," or substituting traditional food products such as taro, yams, sweet potatoes, tapioca, paw paw, coconut juice, and fish for imported rice, flour, beer, coke, and canned fish. The former direction may be more realistic than the latter if it is true that the people may become so accustomed to the taste and convenience of imported foodstuffs that they do not want to return to a diet of traditional root crops.[32]

Judging from the experiences of other developing countries, however, there is a good probability that the import-replacement approach will not only bring higher food prices, which may be resisted particularly by urban dwellers, but it also may worsen trade deficits through reduced export earnings and increased import requirements such as fertilizer inputs and capital goods for domestic production.[33] Traditional foodstuffs, at which import-displacement is directed, are problematic not only because some find them distasteful and because they are inconvenient and nonmarketable but because some of them are more expensive than imported foods in terms of cost of calories and protein, as is revealed by G. T. Harris.[34] It is clear, however, that given available resources, the import-displacement approach is generally more effective than import replacement in reducing the heavy burden of trade imbalances and improving the nutritional standards of the South Pacific countries.

Though the dependency on imported foodstuffs has been generally high for all South Pacific countries, there has been a great deal of variation in the states of dependency from country to country. For example, the per capita food imports of French Polynesia, American Samoa, and New Caledonia were more than eleven times higher than those of Papua New Guinea and the Solomon Islands in 1980.[35] Since production and marketing conditions are also significantly different from country to country, there must be different approaches to reducing the dependency on food imports. For relatively resource-rich and subsistence-oriented countries such as Fiji, Papua New Guinea, the Solomon Islands, and Western Samoa, the import-displacement approach may be more successful than for much smaller and resource-poor countries. R. E. Ward[36] has concluded that under the present environmental conditions in Kiribati, import-displacement through the local production of starchy root is virtually impossible. The same conclusion can also be drawn for Nauru, the Cook Islands, and Tuvalu.

In order for these countries to succeed in import-displacement strategy, other interrelated questions must be answered. Contrary to the general belief that arable land is extremely scarce and labor is underemployed in the subsistence sector of the South Pacific, A. B. Desai and B. A. Ponter[37] reveal some convincing evidence that the chief scarcity factor is not land but labor. Young male laborers, who are most needed in subsistence food production, are the most likely members of the population to migrate to the urban centers. Despite serious unemployment problems in the urban centers, these workers are most likely to stay there or migrate further to the overseas urban centers.[38]

It should also be noted, as S. M. Mark[39] has pointed out, that foreign aid, particularly U.S. surplus-food aid, has discouraged subsistence food production from both the supply and demand sides; aid made these countries able to spend far beyond their means on imported foodstuffs, which inevitably depressed the domestic food supply through adverse terms of trade. Although foreign aid in the South Pacific is, to a large extent, considered to be payoffs by political and strategic interests of donor countries, there has been a legitimate fear among concerned economists about the cumulative effects of foreign aid on rising urban and consumption levels, which might destroy the entire socioeconomic fabric of these small island nations.[40]

Further development of tourism is an important alternative for earning foreign exchange for a number of Pacific island countries. Much effort, however, should be directed to maximize its potential and make actual gains for the local economy through improving transportation and local support services, undertaking promotional work overseas, and promoting local tourism-related industries.

Conclusions

Using simple analytical models, I have analyzed in this chapter two possible ways in which the highly export-oriented small island economies in the South Pacific might collapse into subsistence poverty. Collapse may be brought about by the exhaustion of nonrenewable natural resources such as the phosphates of Nauru and Kiribati and the nickel of New Caledonia. It may also be brought about by the deterioration of terms of trade, or the disappearance of demand for exportable goods. Collapse will be accelerated by deliberate specialization in exportable goods, population growth, and the loss of traditional production skills.

Two clear-cut approaches for diversification may prevent these economies from collapsing into subsistence poverty or severe deprivation. One approach is to conduct the development policies so as to maintain the balance-of-payments equilibrium. This approach would be particularly effective in the South Pacific, where growing trade deficits are a source of alarm among policymakers. The other approach is based upon the concept of the SMS, which is designed to secure the minimum caloric requirement for survival of the island people through domestic food production. Although this approach is particularly relevant for small island economies, we need more conceptual refinement as well as a reliable database for a successful application of the concept to the South Pacific.

Policy implications of the two approaches are mutually reinforcing; they require a resource shift from the export sector to the subsistence sector, which is a mainstay of many South Pacific island economies and which has great potential for development. In order to diversify the economic base through revitalizing the subsistence sector, an import-displacement approach may be much more effective than an import-replacement or import-substitution approach.

I should caution, however, that policy prescriptions derived from the present analysis may differ according to the stage of socioeconomic development, natural resource endowments, and the importance of the subsistence sector. The best available policy mix for each island economy cannot be found without considering interrelated issues such as possible changes in technology, demographics, and decisionmaking processes at all levels.

TABLE 2.1 Population, per Capita Income, and Main Export Products of South Pacific Countries

Country	Population 1982 (000)	Per Capita Income ($)	Main Export Products
American Samoa	33.9	4,060	Tuna
Cook Islands	16.9	1,110 m	Fresh fruits and vegetables, clothing, processed fruit and copra
Federated States of Micronesia	82.4	830	Copra, fish
Fiji	658.0	1,630 m	Sugar, gold, coconut oil, fish
French Polynesia	153.8	4,600 m	Coconut oil, vanilla
Guam	108.4	4,860 m	n.a.
Kiribati	59.3	420 m	Copra
Marshall Islands	32.8	n.a.	n.a.
Nauru	8.4	n.a.	Phosphate
Niue	3.2	620 p	Fruit products, copra
Northern Marianas	18.4	4,000	Vegetables
New Caledonia	145.0	7,900 m	Nickel and products
Palau	12.4	n.a.	n.a.
Papua New Guinea	3,126.6	820 m	Copper and concentrates, cocoa, coconut products
Solomon Islands	243.0	670 m	Fish and fish preparations, copra, timber, palm oil
Tokelau	1.5	650	Copra, handicrafts
Tonga	99.5	460 f	Coconut oil, dessicated coconut, fruit and vegetables
Tuvalu	7.7	590 m	Copra
Vanuatu	125.6	550	Copra, fish, frozen meat
Wallis and Futuna	11.9	1,030	Copra
Western Samoa	157.0	605	Copra, cocoa, taro, timber

Note: Based on official estimates for either 1979 or 1980 except for Fiji and Western Samoa, which are for 1982 and 1983, respectively. National income figures are GDP except for Guam, Vanuatu, and Western Samoa, which are GNP. GDP at factor cost is denoted by f; at market prices, by m; and at producer prices, by p.

SOURCES: South Pacific Commission Unit, Noumea (for population figures); I. J. Fairbairn, *Island Economies: Studies from the South Pacific* (Suva: University of the South Pacific, 1985) pp. 87–89; Asian Development Bank, *Economic Survey of Western Samoa* (Manila, 1984), p. 111.

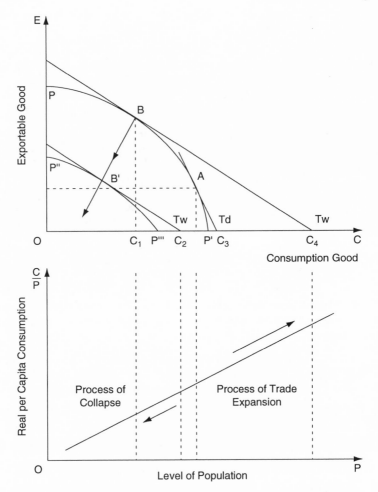

FIGURE 2.1   The Case of Possible Collapse as a Result of Natural Resource
Exhaustion

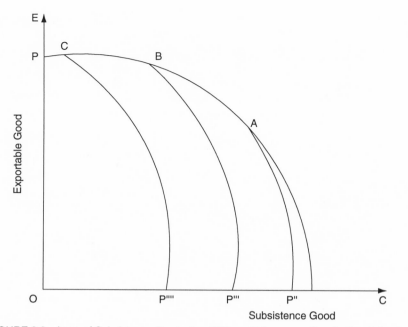

FIGURE 2.2   Loss of Subsistence Production Skills and Resources Due to Specialization in Export Crops

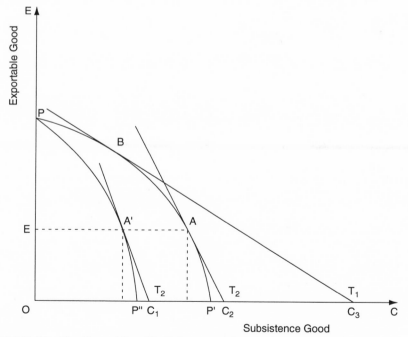

FIGURE 2.3   The Case of Possible Collapse as a Result of Deterioration of Terms of Trade and Loss of Subsistence Production Skills

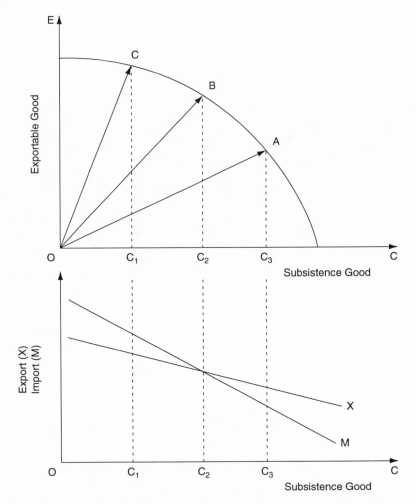

FIGURE 2.4   Three Possible Growth Paths in Terms of the Balance-of-Payments Positions

TABLE 2.2   Trade Deficits and Foreign Aid of Selected South Pacific Islands, 1975–1976 and 1982 (US$1,000)

Country	Trade 1975–1976			Official Development Assistance 1975–1976	Trade 1982[b]			Official Development Assistance 1982
	Exports[a]	Imports	Trade Balance		Exports	Imports	Trade Balance	
American Samoa	61,190	48,790	12,400	23,620	131,680	98,580	33,100	n.a.
Cook Islands	2,460	5,470	−3,010	5,730	3,850	22,430	−18,580	10,400
Fiji	94,720	252,110	−157,390	19,790	281,230	501,390	−220,160	35,400
French Polynesia	4,770	293,350	−288,580	69,450	(28,000)	563,390	−535,390	173,200
Gilbert Islands/Kiribati	32,250	10,810	21,440	5,840	2,860	19,890	−17,030	15,100
Nauru	43,480	27,360	16,120	nil	135,340	(12,000)	123,340	nil
New Hebrides/Vanuatu	15,920	33,640	17,720	20,430	22,890	58,910	−36,020	26,000
Niue	200	2,160	−1,960	2,350	310	3,440	−3,130	4,400
New Caledonia	274,100	265,730	8,370	51,410	413,240	470,140	−56,900	158,700
Papua New Guinea	468,980	366,670	102,310	268,500	758,280	1,004,340	−246,060	310,600
Solomon Islands	21,940	25,460	−3,520	19,430	54,270	70,520	−16,250	27,900
Tokelau	23	n.a.	n.a.	660	36	n.a.	n.a.	1,900
Tonga	4,110	15,080	−10,970	3,520	7,800	35,580	−27,780	16,900
Tuvalu[c]					100	3,710	−3,610	6,200
Western Samoa	6,700	32,120	−25,420	9,600	10,940	45,250	−34,310	21,900

[a] Exports for 1975–1976 refer to domestic products

[b] Trade figures apply to 1982 for Fiji, Papua New Guinea, the Solomon Islands, Vanuatu, and Western Samoa and to 1979 for the remainder except for the Cook Islands (1981) and Nauru (1978). Figures within brackets are estimates.

[c] Included in estimates for the Gilbert Islands in 1975–1976.

SOURCES: South Pacific Commission *South Pacific Economies: Statistical Summary* (Noumea, 1978); OECD aid computer printouts; I. J. Fairbairn, *Island Economies: Studies from the South Pacific* (Suva: University of the South Pacific, 1985), chapter 4; Asian Development Bank, *Economic Study of Western Samoa* (Manila, 1984), p. 111; government of Vanuatu.

TABLE 2.3   Subsistence Output and National Income (US$ million)

Country	Year	National Income		Subsistence Output	% Subsistence to National Income
Fiji	1982	740.2	GDPf	490	6.6
Kiribati	1978	44.1	GDPm	7.0	15.7
Papua New Guinea	1981	2,473.7	GDP	426.5	17.2
Solomon Islands	1981	152.1	GDP	54.2	35.6
Tonga	1979–1980	54.9	GDPm	12.4	22.6
Tuvalu	1977	2.7	GDP	0.5	18.5
Western Samoa	1983	85.8	GDPp	30.1	35.1

Note: GDP   = gross domestic product
     GDPm = gross domestic product at market prices
     GDPf = gross domestic product at factor cost
     GDPp = gross domestic product at producers' prices

SOURCES: Fiji, government of Fiji; Western Samoa, Asian Development Bank, *Economic Survey of Western Samoa* (Manila, 1984), appendix 2, p. 24; Kiribati, Papua New Guinea, the Solomon Islands, Tuvalu, I. J. Fairbairn, *Island Economies: Studies from the South Pacific* (Suva: University of the South Pacific, 1985), pp. 87–89.

3

Aid and Self-Reliant Development
in the South Pacific Islands

Some observers cite the widening gap of real per capita income between rich and poor countries, as evidence that world economic development has been essentially uneven. Resource transfers from rich to poor countries have been justified on politico-economic, strategic, and moral grounds. Official Development Assistance (ODA) resource transfers from developed countries (DCs) to the less developed countries (LDCs) is a much-discussed subject. Many economists, however, have argued that ODA has become "official dependency assistance" because it intensifies dependency and vulnerability instead of "assisting" viable economic development of the recipient countries.[1]

The problem of resource transfers is particularly relevant to small island economies, where domestic resources are severely limited and levels of consumption are far beyond productive capacities. In this chapter I discuss the role of resource transfers in the Pacific island economies and offer a new "rent-seeking" approach to address the so-called aid-dependency dilemma of these economies.

The term "rent-seeking" was first introduced by Ann Krueger[2] in connection with the cost of corruption of import quotas; the concept has since been broadened to "directly unproductive profit-seeking" (DUP) by J. Bhagwati[3] and Bhagwati, R. Breacher, and T. Hatta.[4] Rent-seeking in this broader context includes highly profitable activities that do not directly result in real output but nevertheless have the potential for ultimately yielding beneficial results. The approach adopted in this chapter draws on this literature and also refocuses attention back to the original Ricardian concept of rent to see how it can be used to reassess the aid-dependency issue within the modern macroeconomic analytical framework for small open economies.

What Is Rent?

The Classical Ricardian Concept of Rent

Since Adam Smith's *Wealth of Nations,* the definition of "rent" has been a controversial issue. Classical economists, notably David Ricardo,[5] defined rent in terms of the surplus value of output over its cost of production or, as illustrated in Figure 3.1, in terms of the difference between the commodity price of marginal land (P_3) and the commodity price of fertile land (P_1). Since the commodity price of marginal land (P_3) is equal to the marginal cost (MC_m) and the average cost (AC_m), rent initially accrues to the fertile land as indicated by the area P_1P_3ab. If, however, the landlord of the fertile land wants to maximize its rental income, he will insist that cultivators produce up to Y'_f where $P_3 = MC_f$ and the new rent is equal to the shaded area P_2P_3cd. The landlord's income is maximized where the marginal revenue (equivalent to average revenue in this case) is equal to MC_f given P_3, which is determined by the marginal land. In the Ricardian model, the rent of corn land depended on the price of corn, which in turn was determined by the demand for and supply of corn. Unlike neoclassical economists, however, Ricardo regarded rent as the only source of transfer income from a cultivator to a landlord who did not labor to obtain real income.

The Modern Macroeconomic Concept of Rent

Our next step is to see how this Ricardian concept of rent can be used to reinterpret the notion of international transfer of resources in the modern macroeconomics context. Assume that there are only two economies: a large, highly productive, rich economy (r) with relatively abundant resources and a regional economy of small Pacific islands (Pacific island economies, or PIEs) (p) with relatively limited insular resources. Rents from international trade generated by traders in the rich economy accumulate as savings that supply the capital for investments in the macroeconomy. But the supply of savings and the demand for investments are seldom equal, and the difference is eventually accounted for in the net surplus trade balance. In the simplest macroeconomic accounting framework, the current-account surplus in the balance of payments can be interpreted as a proxy for aggregate rent as follows.

$$Y_r = E_r + X_r - M_r = E_r + R_r,$$

where Y_r = GNP or productive capacity of rich economy
         E_r = domestic demand or domestic absorptive capacity
         X_r = exports of goods and services
         M_r = imports of goods and services
         R_r = $X_r - M_r$ (a proxy for aggregate rent)

In this framework, international transfer income is drawn from R_r, which includes net gifts and unilateral transfer payments as well as net foreign investment. From this equation, a condition for the rent- or surplus-generating economy is $Y > E$, and a condition for the rent- or surplus-seeking economy is $Y < E$. In other words, the rent-generating economy is a "surplus" economy in the sense that its productive capacity, as indicated in the equation, is much greater than its domestic demand. The rent-seeking economy is a "deficit" economy because its domestic demand cannot be met by its own productive resources. Of course, a "deficit" economy such as the United States at the present time can be a "rent-giving" economy at the same time. But this double role cannot, in principle, be sustained for the long run. The United States is a special case under the present key currency system in that it does not need to generate surpluses to help finance the deficits of foreign countries. Since there are only two economies in our model, whenever $Y_r > E_r$, $Y_p < E_p$. Or $Y_r + Y_p = E_r + E_p'$ and $Y_r + Y_p = (E_r + R_r) + (E_p + R_p) = E_r + E_p$, since R_r is exactly offset by R_p. The rich economy's rent (R_r) is always equal to the transfer income (R_p) of the PIEs. In recent years, some of the East Asian economies of the Pacific have been among the largest rent-generating economies; the PIEs have constituted a growing rent-seeking regional economy.

Structure of the Rent-Seeking Pacific Island Economies

From the previously shown relationships, it is obvious that rent is an integral part of the international transfer of resources from a "surplus" country to a "deficit" country. The rent-seeking economy is an economy whose consumption level is being sustained by continuous inflows of rent generated in foreign countries. Although the rent-seeking economy need not be a small island economy, it typically exhibits the structural characteristics of an economy that cannot meet its domestic demand through its own productive resources.

First, as discussed in Chapter 1, island economies are generally less-diversified in their production and export structure than large economies due mainly to a narrow range of human and nonhuman economic resources and markets. For instance, as is evident in Table 3.1, economic activities are concentrated in agriculture (Wallis and Futuna, Western Samoa), mining (Nauru), and services (Guam, Niue, Kiribati, French Polynesia, and Tuvalu). These activities depend heavily on government expenditures that are much greater than the respective GNP of Niue, Tokelau, and Wallis and Futuna.

Exports are concentrated in a few commodities for a few industrialized markets. Typically, one export commodity, such as phosphates in Nauru, fish in American Samoa, and copra in Kiribati and Tokelau, accounts for nearly all export income. Production and export concentrations not only make these small economies vulnerable to the fluctuations of world markets, but they also make them susceptible to natural hazards such as cyclones, floods, droughts, and disease.

Second, island economies suffer from diseconomies of scale in production, investment, consumption, transportation, research and development, and administrative services. It has been estimated that in building additional thermal capacity power generation, for instance, several small countries face a cost

disadvantage averaging 65 percent.[6] Scale diseconomies are particularly intensified in the production of goods whose input costs are also subject to scale
economies. A typical example is integrated circuits (ICs), which are widely
used as inputs in a variety of industrial products. The unit price of ICs halved in
the 1973–1982 period as production and sales increased (Figure 3.2).

Because of these structural weaknesses, Pacific island economies, except for
American Samoa and Nauru, have experienced growing deficits in their trade
balances. These deficits have been financed mainly by ODA and remittances.
ODAs alone more than offset the trade deficits in Kiribati, New Caledonia,
Papua New Guinea (PNG), the Solomon Islands, Tokelau, TTPI (former Trust
Territories of the Pacific Islands), Tuvalu, and Wallis and Futuna, as was discussed in Chapter 2. Although official figures for remittances are not available,
estimates by G. Bertram[7] indicate that for migration-oriented mini-islands such
as the Cook Islands, Niue, Kiribati, Tokelau, and Tuvalu, remittances are more
or less of comparable magnitude to their respective export earnings. According
to Bertram, in the first half of the twentieth century, the normal situation for
Pacific island economies was one of equality between exports and imports.
After World War II, however, these island economies gradually transformed into
deficit rent-seeking economies. This is illustrated in Figure 3.3 for the Cook
Islands.

The Roles of Rent in the Context of
Small Island Development

Rent as Complementing Domestic Resources

Accumulated rent is a source of capital, and in an international context, external sources of capital derived from rent may be interpreted in terms of foreign savings. Conventional economic theories, particularly neoclassical and
Harrod-Domar types, regard external sources of capital (i.e., from foreign savings) as complementary to scarce domestic resources. An increase in foreign
capital is often the cheapest way to obtain additional resources. Particularly,
grants-in-aid are the most desirable if the recipient country need not incur any
opportunity cost, that is, if it need not sacrifice any scarce domestic resources to
obtain additional resources from outside.

The Harrod-Domar (H-D) model has been used to justify external sources
of capital (in the form of ODA), based on the idea that foreign savings can be
used to complement domestic savings. The simplest version of the model is as
follows.

$$G = (s_d + s_f)/v,$$

where   G   = GNP growth rate
       s_d = rate of domestic savings (S_d/GNP)
       s_f = rate of foreign savings (S_f/GNP)
       v   = marginal capital-output ratio

From this model, it is obvious that savings generated from domestic sources (S_d) complement foreign savings (S_f). The formula implicitly assumes that domestic investment (I_d) is greater than domestic savings (S_d), as is the case for most developing countries; therefore, domestic savings must be supplemented with foreign capital inflows. Of course, in the ex post sense, I_d is always equal to $S_d + S_f$. The H-D model has been used particularly to justify the import-substitution strategy for industrialization in the Third World. In developing economies, what is lacking is not necessarily demand but rather a productive capacity that can be expanded through importing foreign capital, such as machinery and intermediate goods, that cannot be produced domestically.

The H-D approach to industrialization has been challenged by many economists[8] who argue that dependency on foreign capital encourages overly capital-intensive industrialization. This, in turn, discourages exports and exacerbates balance-of-payments problems. Based on the previous model, if the capital-output ratio (v) increases more than the increase in foreign capital inflows (s_f), the growth rate (G) will be lower than that which prevailed prior to the capital inflows. According to Toshio Watanabe and Ann Krueger[9], the Asian newly industrialized economies (NIEs)—Hong Kong, Singapore, South Korea and Taiwan—have followed the H-D model of development through dynamic complementarity between scarce domestic savings and foreign capital. The NIEs have escaped the "dependency trap" by transforming rent into a vital growth component.

Rent as Substituting for Domestic Resources

Some economists argue that for small island economies of the Pacific, there is a trade-off between domestic savings (S_d) and foreign savings (S_f) that argues against the potential for complementary relationships.[10] According to their arguments, people save less when they expect a large portion of their savings to be supplemented by foreign savings. Usually two routes of substitution have been pointed out. One is through production (or costs) and the other through consumption (or revenues). An example of the production route is the transfer of U.S. agricultural surplus products in the name of food aid under PL480, which, according to some economists, has discouraged production and viable agricultural development.[11]

Let us assume for simplicity, as in Figure 3.4, that resources are given and that the transformation (TT') between PL480 goods and domestic products (Qd) is linear. Additional inflows of the former from an original level of PL_1 to PL_2

will reduce the production of the latter from $A(Qd_1)$ to $B(Qd_3)$ which will accelerate the rent-seeking character of an economy. This trade-off between PL480 and domestic production is usually accompanied by a loss of indigenous production technologies as indicated by the shift to TT".[12] Thus, it is impossible to return to the original production point (Qd_1) even after aid is reduced to its original level (PL_1).

In the other route, one of substitution through consumption, there are two influencing factors. One is the price effect and the other, an income-preference effect. Consumer prices of PL480 commodities, if sold, are usually much lower than international market prices. In this case, the trade-off between PL480 and Qd proceeds much faster than otherwise, as shown in tt'. Even though domestic production is the same (Qd_3) for B and B', the demand for foreign goods is much greater at $B'(PL_3)$ than at $B(PL_2)$. It is also reported that the price per unit of protein from PL480 or imported commodities is much higher than that of many indigenous foodstuffs.

Another consumption route of substitution is through a change in consumer preference. The consumers' indifference curve (I) shifts from A to B' in Figure 3.4 as indigenous consumers acquire new tastes for foreign goods. This has typically been the case with coconut juice (considered an inferior good) and Coca-Cola and with breadfruit and bread. Newly acquired tastes are spreading very fast, and these shifts in preferences are to a large degree irreversible.

If we think of rent in terms of possible changes in total resources, three stylized relationships between external rent (R) and output (GNP) may be depicted, as in Figure 3.5. The classical case, where rent is a pure transfer that does not result in net additions to wealth, may be taken as the baseline B. Case C is the dependency case, where increases in foreign aid compete with domestic resources, resulting in a decline in output relative to the baseline. Case A is the Harrod-Domar case, where increases in external capital (rent) represent additional productive resources that can be employed to produce increasing output, again relative to the baseline. As we have already seen, these relationships may vary depending upon the stage of development, available domestic productive resources, and the degree of dependency. As noted earlier, the Asian NIEs are considered to have followed the H-D path, and many of the small island economies of the Pacific appear to have followed the dependency (trade-off) path.

Suggested Interpretations of Rent-Seeking Activities

Rent-Seeking as a Productive Activity

Among a number of planning goals, all rent-seeking economies in the Pacific have consistently selected two seemingly contradictory goals: (1) economic growth or an increase in the standard of living and (2) self-reliance or economic independence (Table 3.2). If the intents of these goals are to achieve economic growth based upon the use of the economy's own productive resources in the conventional sense, then past experiences of these island economies have been unmistakenly a trade-off between the two goals. If we, however, define "rent-seeking activities" as an alternative way for a country to use its own economic and noneconomic resources and advantages such as political ties, strategic location, international security, and goodwill, then economic growth and rent-seeking can be consistent. In the words of Bertram,[13]

> We shall argue that what many people call "dependence" is a positive rather than a negative feature of these societies, and that policy prescriptions based upon the supposed goal of "reducing dependence" are misplaced. The standard formulations of "dependency" textbooks are as inapplicable in the Pacific as are those of the modernization school; in analyzing the political economy of the small island societies, one has to start from scratch, and not from continental "Third World" models. One contributory reason for this is the nationalist fallacy of assuming that Island societies are bounded geographic national entities, rather than organic parts of wider economic systems from which on balance they derive substantial benefits.

If we regard self-reliance as an economic development strategy based upon the economy's own resources and rent-seeking as an alternative strategy making use of foreign economic resources, the best economic or political choice could well be a combination of both that gives maximum benefits to all the people. This is depicted in Figure 3.6 under the conventional assumptions on production possibility and indifference curves. If the rent-seeking activities could expand production by shifting the production frontier to the right, then the use of foreign economic resources (FR) in new combinations with domestic resources (DR) moving along DR_0 to FR_1 could improve the level of living standards from I_A to I_B even to the extent of conserving domestic resources.

This interpretation of rent is further illustrated in Figure 3.7, which is an extension of Figure 3.5: The large rich economy (r) now produces in excess of its domestic demand ($Y_r > E_r$) and the regional PIEs absorb more than their domestic output ($Y_p < E_p$). The shaded area is the rent generated by the former (R_r) and absorbed by the latter (R_p). Both economies are complementary to each other in the sense that the former's productive capacity can be sustained only through "exporting its rent" to the latter. The latter's standard of living can be sustained only through "importing or acquiring the rent."

We can now integrate the microeconomic approach to rent into the macroeconomic approach. The earlier Ricardian rent model (Figure 3.1) suggests that rent can be generated only when there are marginal producers. By the same token, a relatively rich country can generate rent because there are marginal producers who, in effect, become rent-takers. Rent-generators and rent-takers are in a symbiotic relationship, since their economic statuses depend on each other. This approach is similar to a "principle of profit-sharing" from international trade that has been advocated for the Pacific islands. "The basic view is that a country which exports to another profits thereby, and that a proportion of that profit should be shared (in the form of aid) with the country to which the exports are sent. The principle seems reasonable but I have not yet seen anyone propose a specific formula to provide a realistic basis for negotiation."[14]

Strategies of Rent-Seeking

If complementary rent-seeking activities are to be viewed as potentially useful economic pursuits, then we need to map strategies to maximize the benefits from such activities. In an interesting article on establishing principles for providing aid to meet international responsibilities, Y. Matsui[15] mapped (see Figure 3.8), largely from a Japanese perspective, the positions of various entities with aid-related interests according to perceived purposes and actual outcomes. It is worth noting that Japanese conservative groups such as the Ministry of International Trade and Industry (MITI), the Federation of Economic Organizations (Keidanren), and the Ministry of Foreign Affairs are more favorably inclined toward increasing aid on the grounds of export expansion and security than are reformist groups such as the Japan Socialist Party, the Japan Communist Party, and the radical economists, who would put more emphasis on improving the effectiveness of aid for such purposes as furthering humanitarianism and economic development and meeting basic human needs.

An important rent-seeking strategy is to "politicize" the trade imbalance between two economies, as has been successfully done by the United States against Japan. Recent international rent-seeking activities in the deficit U.S. economy are reflected in a host of political activities that result in financing trade and federal deficits with foreign savings while lobbying to protect domestic industries and pressuring surplus countries such as Japan to assume greater responsibilities in ODA programs. As mentioned earlier, the United States is in the unique position of being a rent-seeker and rent-generator at the same time because of the role of the U.S. dollar as the principal international reserve currency. Japan, for example, cannot be a net rent-generating country unless its current-account balance is in surplus, and it cannot assume the dual role of a rent-generator and rent-seeker as long as the yen is not the main international reserve currency.

Since the PIEs have also been in deep trade deficits with Japan, they may have good reasons to claim the rents that can help them offset their deficits. It is important to recognize that a rent-generating economy can benefit from potential scale economies that become possible when the rent-seeker expands the market. This is illustrated in the relationship between unit cost and profit in Figure 3.9. If, for example, Japan were to produce only for its domestic market (OY_1), its unit cost of production would be at C_1. But if Japan could expand its market to the PIEs who face the same demand curve (PP') for $Y_1 Y_2$, the unit cost would be reduced to C_2 as a result of scale economies. The profits from Japan's domestic market would expand from A to A + B, and there would be an additional net profit, as indicated by the shaded area C. The ODA rents received by the PIEs from Japan could be considered as a share of this gain in net profit that was made possible by the expanded markets.

Another important rent-seeking strategy is to "sell their strategic value and historical ties" to major external powers, as suggested by Crocombe:[16] "This is most strikingly evident in the U.S. controlled territories north of the equator (Marshall Islands, Federal States of Micronesia, Palau, Northern Marianas) and the French territories of the South Pacific (New Caledonia and French Polynesia particularly) where strategic value to the metropolitan power is much the largest factor income."

As a matter of fact, "selling strategic value and historical ties" explains a large portion of bilateral aid flows in the PIEs (Table 3.3). American Samoa, Guam, and the former Trust Territories of the Pacific Islands obtained substantially all their aid flows from the United States. Australia has the greatest interest in PNG and Fiji; New Zealand, in the Cook Islands and Niue; France, in French Polynesia, New Caledonia, and Vanuatu; Britain, in Kiribati and the Solomon Islands; Japan and Germany, in Western Samoa.

The promotion of out-migration, claims on the Exclusive Economic Zone (EEZ), and the use of political wisdom in the international arena are also important rent-seeking strategies that should be discussed elsewhere.

Conclusions

An eighteenth-century French physiocrat, Francois Quesnay, demonstrated that an "unproductive" landlord class was absolutely necessary to sustain a nation's scale of economic activity. Quesnay's observation can be applied to the modern-day unbalanced growth of the world economy. Economic growth inevitably proceeds with regional imbalances and generates surplus economies such as Japan and the Asian NIEs in the Pacific Basin, at the same time necessitating deficit economies such as the United States and the PIEs and other less-developed economies. Although rent-generating surplus countries must share in the responsibility for the global economic performance, as do the rent-seeking deficit countries, these external imbalances are an inevitable part of the dynamic growth process as long as international economic development proceeds in a competitive environment.

It is, therefore, important to recognize the symbiotic relationship between rent-seekers and rent-generators. Contrary to conventional wisdom, rent-seekers play a positive economic role in absorbing the surpluses of rent-generating countries and in contributing to the productivity of the latter by offering larger markets and associated scale economies. In this sense, rent-seeking activities need not be considered as merely generating unproductive resource transfers with adverse effects on economic growth. It is economically logical for small island rent seekers to shift their limited resources from producing costly and uncompetitive products to rent-seeking activities as long as there are opportunities for income gain.

Rent-seeking activities are not cost-free. But the conventional arguments against rent-seeking activities need to be carefully reexamined from the viewpoints of both donor and recipient countries. The former may be concerned about the proliferation of activities that will distort the efficient allocation of international resources. The latter's concern is the unsustainability of growth in rent-seeking economies and further encroachment on their politico-economic independence. In reality, however, the ministates of the Pacific will have serious difficulties in maintaining their current standards of living unless they make full productive use of the resources made available through their rent-seeking activities. They can mobilize both domestic and foreign resources for productive purposes.

The politico-economic issues of dependency and rent-seeking are particularly important for the Pacific island economies, especially those that are being increasingly impacted by external macroeconomic changes in the region. The analytical approach adopted here is offered as a step toward the eventual resolution of these issues and also raises some fundamental questions on the effectiveness of conventional national income accounting concepts in dealing with current issues regarding the international redistribution of income.

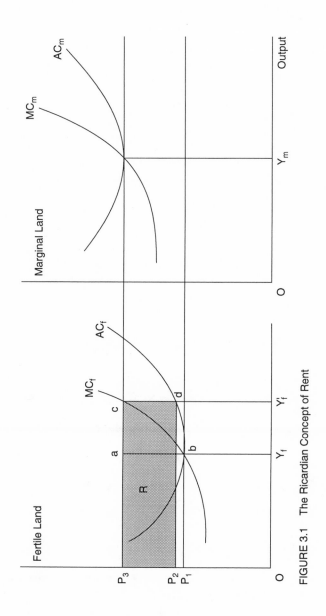

FIGURE 3.1   The Ricardian Concept of Rent

TABLE 3.1 Economic Structure of the Pacific Islands, 1980

Country	Percentage of Employment by Sectors			Percentage of Contribution to GDP (or GNP) by Sectors				Government Expenditure of GDP/GNP (%)	Government Employment (%)
	Agriculture	Industry	Service	Agriculture	Industry	Service	Subsistence Sector		
American Samoa	n.a.	n.a.	n.a.	n.a.	n.a.	n.a.	n.a.	47.7	40.3
Cook Islands	22	18	53	17.4	9.8	72.8	n.a.	94.8	43.9
Fiji	44	16	34	25.3	20.2	54.5	6.6	30.4	32.2
French Polynesia	17	19	64	n.a.	n.a.	n.a.	n.a.	44.5	30.0
Guam	1	23	76	n.a.	n.a.	n.a.	n.a.	44.4	40.7
Kiribati	7	21	67	n.a.	n.a.	n.a.	15.7	63.9	n.a.
Nauru	0	76	23	n.a.	n.a.	n.a.	n.a.	n.a.	n.a.
New Caledonia	28	28	44	n.a.	n.a.	n.a.	n.a.	37.8	n.a.
Niue	10	10	74	n.a.	n.a.	n.a.	n.a.	136.4	n.a.
Papua New Guinea	57	9	22	36.5	25.8	36.9	17.2	39.2	n.a.
Pitcairn Island	n.a.	n.a.	n.a.	n.a.	n.a.	n.a.	n.a.	n.a.	n.a.
Solomon Islands	45	14	41	n.a.	n.a.	n.a.	35.5	40.1	n.a.
Tokelau	n.a.	n.a.	n.a.	n.a.	n.a.	n.a.	n.a.	262.5	n.a.
Tonga	51	9	30	43.3	13.5	43.2	22.6	39.2	n.a.
Tuvalu	4	24	62	16.0	13.6	70.4	18.5	52.0	n.a.
Vanuatu	n.a.	n.a.	n.a.	n.a.	n.a.	n.a.	n.a.	37.4	n.a.
Wallis and Futuna	78	6	30	n.a.	n.a.	n.a.	n.a.	114.9	n.a.
Western Samoa	61	9	30	50.9	12.2	36.9	35.1	44.4	n.a.
TTPI	n.a.	n.a.	n.a.	n.a.	n.a.	n.a.	n.a.	n.a.	n.a.

Note: n.a. = not available; inconsistencies in data are due to the lack of a single standardized source.

SOURCES: South Pacific Commission, *South Pacific Economies: Statistical Summary* (Noumea, 1982), pp. 3–15; the subsistence sector size is from I. J. Fairbairn, *Island Economies: Studies from the South Pacific* (Suva: University of the South Pacific, 1985), p. 33.

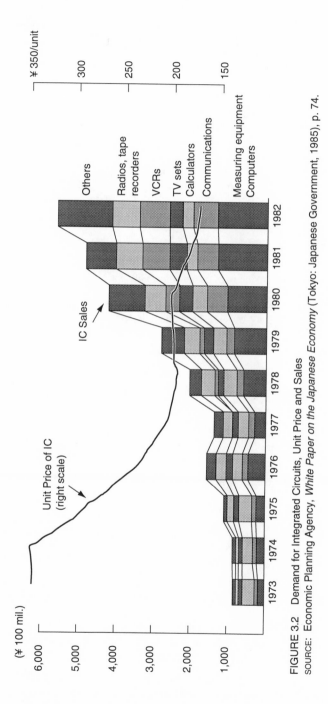

FIGURE 3.2   Demand for Integrated Circuits, Unit Price and Sales
SOURCE: Economic Planning Agency, *White Paper on the Japanese Economy* (Tokyo: Japanese Government, 1985), p. 74.

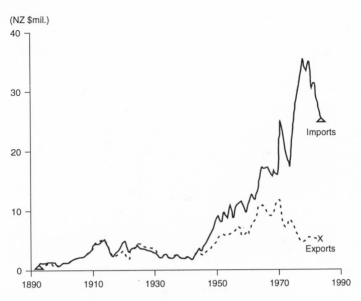

FIGURE 3.3   Historical Trend of Cook Islands Imports and Exports
(Deflated to 1982 NZ dollars)
SOURCE: G. Bertram, "Development, Dependence and Viability," unpublished mimeograph
(Victoria University, Wellington, New Zealand, 1984), p. 22.

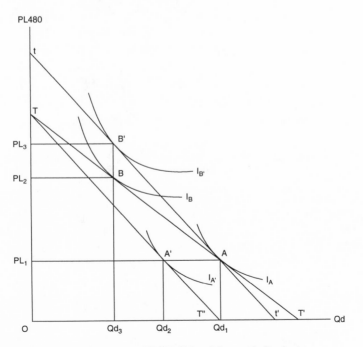

FIGURE 3.4   Relationship Between PL480 Aid and Domestic Products

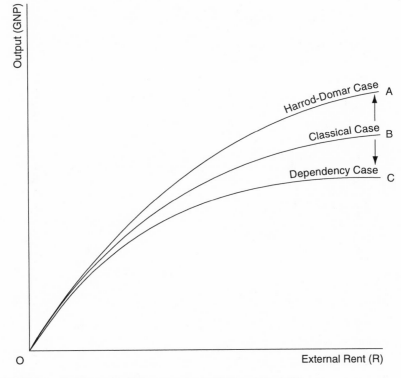

FIGURE 3.5   Relationships Between Output (GNP) and Rent (R)

TABLE 3.2 Planning Goals of the Pacific Island Nations

Planning Goals	PNG	Fiji	Tonga	Solomon Is.	Tuvalu	Niue	Western Samoa	Kiribati
Growth/increase standard of living	X	X	X	X	X	X	X	X
Self-reliance/economic independence (revenue)	X	X	X	X	X	X	X	X
Redistribution to meet PIN's goals	X	X	X	X	X	X	X	
Diversification (export base)	X	X	X	X	X			
Employment generation	X	X	X	X		X		
Increase private foreign investment	X	X	X	X		X		
Industrialization or agriculture	X	X	X	X				
Preservation (culture & environment)	X	X	X				X	
Indigenization	X	X	X		X	X	X	X
Rural-urban or ethnic balance	X	X	X	X				
Constitutional/territorial integrity and sovereignty	X			X	X			X
Regionalism	X	X			X			X

SOURCE: Neil D. Karunaratne, "Development in the Pacific," in Benjamin Higgins, ed. *Regional Development in Small Island Nations* (Nagoya: United Nations Center for Regional Development, 1982), p. 62.

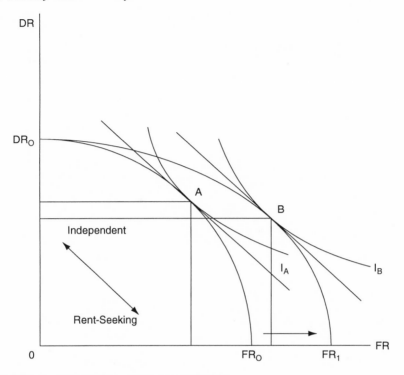

FIGURE 3.6   Rent-Seeking and Economic Welfare

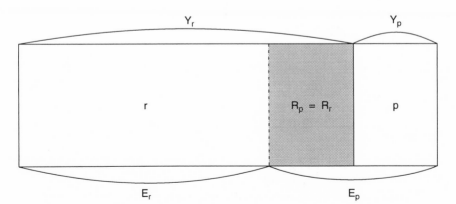

FIGURE 3.7   A Complementary Macrorelationship Between Rent-Seeking and Rent-Generating Economies

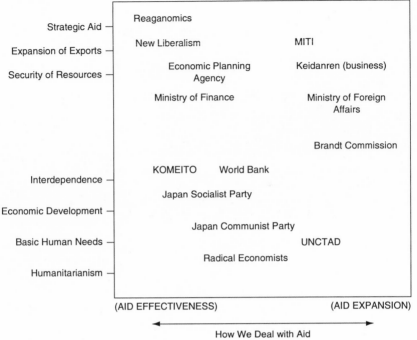

FIGURE 3.8   Coordinate Axes of Views on Aid

SOURCE: Y. Matsui, "Kokusaiteki Sekinin e Enjo Rinen no Kakuritsu o" (Establishing Aid Principles to Meet International Responsibility), *Economisuto* (April 13, 1987): pp. 74–75.

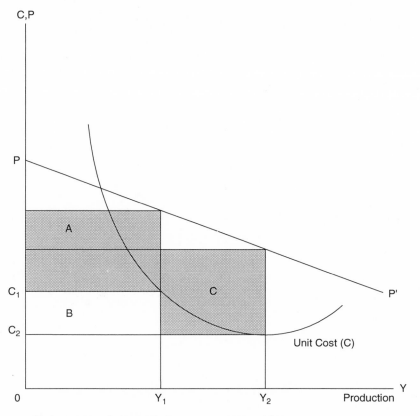

A = profits from domestic market before rent-seeking activity.
A + B = profits from domestic market after rent-seeking activity expands foreign market.
A + B + C = profits from domestic market plus foreign markets after rent-seeking activity expands foreign market.

FIGURE 3.9   Relationship Between Unit Cost and Profit

TABLE 3.3   ODA to the South Pacific by Major Powers, 1982 (percent)

	AUS	CAN	FRG	FR	JPN	NZ	NETH	UK	US	ADB	EEC	UNDP[a]	Bilateral	Total (US$1,000)
American Samoa	–	–	–	–	–	–	–	–	100.00	–	–	–	100.00	48,292
Cook Islands	7.26	0.22	0.24	–	–	73.29	0.97	–	–	13.32	–	4.70	81.98	10,995
Fiji	16.24	0.13	–	–	3.73	4.21	–	25.42	1.87	5.89	40.36	2.14	51.60	64,742
French Polynesia	–	–	–	84.71	–	–	–	–	–	–	15.29	–	84.71	21,980
Guam	–	–	–	–	–	–	–	–	100.00	–	–	–	100.00	111,138
Kiribati	9.64	0.55	–	–	16.38	1.93	–	58.49	2.45	–	9.43	1.12	89.44	17,096
Nauru	81.36	–	–	–	18.64	–	–	–	–	–	–	–	100.00	65
New Caledonia	–	–	–	100.00	–	–	–	–	–	–	–	–	100.00	72,655
Niue	22.20	–	–	–	–	59.30	–	–	0.30	–	–	18.20	81.80	1,099
Papua New Guinea	81.85	0.08	0.04	–	0.21	0.41	0.16	2.02	0.35	3.47	10.78	0.64	85.12	360,727
Solomon Islands	18.40	–	–	–	–	2.08	–	41.59	2.08	8.08	25.50	2.27	64.15	28,932
Tokelau	–	–	–	–	–	100.00	–	–	–	–	–	–	100.00	1,710
Tonga	24.07	0.40	–	–	10.05	12.37	–	6.29	6.48	1.04	37.18	2.11	59.66	21,427
TTPI	–	–	–	–	–	–	–	–	99.86	–	–	0.14	99.86	188,944
Tuvalu	9.32	0.58	0.35	–	12.86	3.54	–	53.17	–	–	16.41	3.78	79.82	6,837
Vanuatu	69.99	–	–	–	4.84	10.86	–	–	–	4.59	–	9.71	85.69	5,625
Wallis and Futuna	–	–	–	100.00	–	–	–	–	–	–	–	–	100.00	10,098
Western Samoa	16.99	0.36	–	–	–	15.54	–	–	–	8.81	58.90	–	32.89	19,452
Reg. Inst./Proj.[b]	10.97	–	–	–	–	3.00	–	1.30	3.34	–	75.87	5.53	18.61	75,682
Total (%)	31.39	0.06	0.02	9.50	0.87	2.28	0.06	4.85	33.30	2.08	14.55	1.03	82.34	
(US$1,000)	335,100	690	207	101,373	9,295	24,336	688	51,747	355,509	22,255	155,324	10,973	878,944	1,067,497

Note: The original data are in Australian dollars. The 1982 annual average exchange rate with the U.S. dollar (0.91) was used as the conversion factor.

[a]United Nations Development Program.
[b]Regional Institutions/Projects.

SOURCES: South Pacific Commission, South Pacific Economies: Statistical Summary, various issues; and Kiyoko Nitz, "The Data for Agricultural Policy Decision Making" (Honolulu: Department of Political Science, University of Hawaii, 1990), mimeo.

4

Absorptive Capacity and Diversification of a Small Tourist Economy: The Northern Mariana Islands

The Commonwealth of Northern Mariana Islands (CNMI), which consists of three major islands (Saipan, Tinian, and Rota) with a total land area of 457 square kilometers and a 1988 resident population of 22,346, became a self-governing commonwealth of the United States in 1986. It had been ruled for nearly 300 years by the Spanish (1668–1899), Germans (1899–1914), and Japanese (1914–1944) and had existed as the UN Trust Territory of the Pacific Islands under the administrative rule of the United States from 1947 to 1986. "It has been said that the Spanish brought Christianity to the islands; the Germans—copra commerce; the Japanese—agricultural and industrial development; and the Americans—the concept of self government."[1]

Approval of the CNMI constitution, followed by the self-governing election in 1978 prior to the acquisition of the new commonwealth status, has given the sagging CNMI economy a vigorous push in attracting private business, particularly tourism investment from Japan. The number of tourists increased nearly threefold from in 1980 (119,000) to 1989 (318,000), or to about ten times CNMI's resident population. The rapidly growing tourism industry has not only transformed CNMI's industrial structure, but it has been accompanied by various developmental problems such as severe infrastructure bottlenecks, increasing migrant workers, and declining self-sufficiency in agricultural food production.

The main purpose of this chapter is to (1) analyze structural characteristics of the CNMI economy, (2) construct a balance-of-payments table for CNMI, (3) attempt to measure the absorptive capacity of the economy, and (4) construct a broader model for diversifying the CNMI economy. Some policy conclusions will also be derived from the analysis.

Structure of the CNMI Economy

There are several important characteristics of the CNMI economy, some quite different from other typical island economies. First, unlike neighboring mini-island economies such as the Federated States of Micronesia (FSM), the Marshall Islands, and Palau, where net out-migration is a common phenomenon, CNMI has experienced a substantial population increase, mainly through net inflows of alien workers during the 1980s (Table 4.1). The resident (U.S. citizens) population increased 39 percent from 17,400 in 1980 to 23,500 in 1989; nonresident workers (figures for the nonresident population are available only for 1987 and 1989) increased 6.5-fold, from 2,900 to 18,800, during the same period. Noteworthy is the fact that the nonresident population slightly outnumbered the resident population in 1989. The sharp increase in the nonresident population was due to an influx of migrant workers, mainly from the Philippines, Korea, and China, attracted by a booming tourism industry and an export-oriented garment manufacturing industry since the mid-1980s. It is important to note here that the supply of labor required for rapid economic growth has been met by importing labor from neighboring labor-surplus countries. This will be analyzed in greater detail later. The labor-supply pattern is strikingly similar to that of the prewar Japanese sugar plantations on CNMI, for which farm laborers were brought in from Japan's rural areas. In Saipan, for example, the Japanese migrant population (20,578) far outnumbered the native population (3,222) in the prewar years. The influx of migrant workers has been creating socio-economic imbalances and tensions in CNMI.

Second, unlike other independent island economies in the Pacific region, CNMI has been enjoying benefits arising from its status as a U.S. commonwealth. The Marianans are not only guaranteed a minimum standard of living under the U.S. welfare program but also a large amount of federal grants for capital investment, which has been flowing into the CNMI economy. In 1989 federal grants accounted for about half of CNMI's total budget resources. The CNMI government absorbed more than 50 percent of the total resident wage earners, and their wage and salary levels are comparable to those of the newly industrialized economies (NIEs). It is very important to note here that the increasingly heavy proportion of the public sector, supported by federal grants, has encouraged locals to seek the relatively high-paid and more prestigious government jobs and has naturally discouraged them from engaging in agricultural development.

CNMI farmers rapidly lost their interest in farming, and as a result, during the 1980s commercial agriculture almost disappeared, particularly in Saipan. Although recent land-use data are not available, even before the tourism boom began, total crop acreage had sharply declined, from 8,071 acres in 1963 to 1,105 acres in 1977. Unused arable land accounted for 60 percent of the total agricultural land, which is far higher than the percentage for Yap (12%), the Marshalls (14%), and Palau (20%).[2] This is not only because farmers have abandoned their farmland for more pleasant, higher-paying jobs but also because land prices have risen so rapidly that the opportunity cost of owning land has become too high for growing commercial crops. It is also reported that revenues from land sales or leases to commercial developers have created a nouveau riche whose conspicuous consumption discourages frugality and savings.

Third, land prices increased sharply as a result of foreign investment, mainly from Japan, in the tourism industry, which expanded five times in terms of tourism expenditures during the 1980s (Table 4.1). In 1988 the industry accounted for 55 percent of CNMI's gross island product (see Appendix A.1 for estimated GIP). CNMI's economic growth can be expressed by the following simple formula:

$$GIP.R = f(TN, DUM)$$
$$TN = f(NW, DUM),$$

where the level of real gross island product (GIP.R) is determined by the number of tourists (TN), which in turn depends on the number of nonresident workers (NW). The dummy variable (DUM) has been introduced to get rid of outliers for 1986, the year in which there was an unusual fluctuation in the statistical data due to the political change occurring as a result of the new commonwealth status. Following are the results of a least-squares estimation:

$$GIP.R = -27.63 + 1.09TN + 25.12DUM$$
$$(-3.47) \quad (20.62) \quad (3.98)$$

$$R = 0.983 \quad S = 5.92 \quad DW = 2.43$$

$$TN = 94.26 + 7.15NW - 19.45DUM$$
$$(14.76) \quad (10.06) \quad (-1.63)$$

$$R = 0.926 \quad S = 10.85 \quad DW = 2.49,$$

where R = coefficient of determination, S = standard deviation, DW = Durbin-Watson test, and the parentheses are t-statistics. All t-values, except −19.45DUM, are significant at the 1 percent level. As expected, about 98 percent of CNMI's changes in GIP are explained by changes in the volume of tourists, and 93 percent of changes in the number of tourists are explained by nonresident workers. This demonstrates that a simple model is sufficient to explain the mechanism of the CNMI economy.

The rapid development of the tourism industry was mainly due to (1) CNMI's positive foreign investment policy after attaining its new self-government status in 1978 and its U.S. commonwealth status in 1986; (2) easy access to the huge and growing Japanese tourist market; (3) the stable and secure sociopolitical environment; (4) a substantial appreciation of the Japanese yen after the Plaza Accord in 1985, which stimulated Japanese spending on the attractive tropical islands where Japan has historical ties as well as geographical proximity; and (5) the availability of cheap service labor from Asian and Pacific neighbors, particularly from the Philippines. The booming tourism industry has many side effects, which will be discussed later.

Fourth, CNMI's monetary system is completely different from those of independent island nations due to its U.S. commonwealth status, which has enabled CNMI to use the U.S. dollar as its legal currency. Since seigniorage belongs to the U.S. government, the CNMI government has no power to control the money supply. The supply of "growth currency" has been provided only through the balance-of-payments surplus. Thus the CNMI government cannot adjust the money supply according to business fluctuations. This monetary mechanism is more or less similar to the classical gold standard system, whereby net money supply is completely determined by net inflow of gold. Net inflow of dollars as a result of net export of goods and services (i.e., tourist receipts), federal grants, foreign investment, and so on has increased CNMI's dollar currency reserves and thus its capacity to import. These external sources of money supply will be discussed in greater detail in the balance-of-payments section.

Fifth, CNMI has been experiencing a critical shortage of local (or indigenous) labor to accommodate the growing service sector. In the 1985–1988, the CNMI economy grew by 66 percent; the local resident labor force increased only 18 percent during the same period. Furthermore, it is estimated that only a small portion of the increased local labor force has been absorbed by the newly established garment industries.[3] Only 18 percent of the total employed in the garment factories in 1988 were locals. This is because the local people are not willing to work for low-paying "sweat industries" and also because wages and salaries in those industries are much lower than in the government, where most locals are gainfully employed (Table 4.2). As has already been mentioned, the gap between the local labor supply and the (increasing) demand for tourism-related labor has been filled by importing alien workers. This interesting dichotomy is illustrated in Figure 4.1.

The employment market can be dichotomized: one sector is the resident (indigenous) labor market (Lr), which is determined by autonomous government action, and the other is the market for nonresident (alien) labor (Ln), which is largely determined by tourist-industry demand. The resident labor market is highly inelastic, reflecting both an inelastic supply (SLr) of and an inelastic demand (DLr) for labor. The nonresident labor market (Ln) is highly elastic, reflecting an unlimited supply of alien workers (SLn) and the relatively labor-intensive character of the tourism industry.[4] In the case of the resident (government) sector, the wage rate (Wr) is mostly determined by institutionalized civil service rules not necessarily related to the marginal productivity of labor. Wage rates in the nonresident sector (Wa) are determined by the perfectly elastic marginal productivity of labor (DLn), assuming an unlimited supply of alien labor (SLn). It would be interesting to see if the CNMI tourism industry could be sustained if the alien labor supply were highly inelastic; that is to say, if wages increased as a result of immigration restrictions.

Sixth, despite CNMI's booming economy, inflationary pressure has been minimized due mainly to (1) free entries of goods and services from the United States and neighboring Asian countries and (2) almost unlimited imports of service- and construction-related labor from Asian countries and neighboring Pacific islands. If local industries were protected through high import barriers such as quotas and tariffs, CNMI's overall price level would be significantly higher than the current 4–5 percent annual increase. Furthermore, if cheap imported labor were not available, there would be an increasing cost-push pressure, which would easily be translated into a wage-push inflation. Therefore, about 99 percent of the changes in the CNMI consumers' price level (PNMI) can be explained by the changes in the U.S. consumers' price level (PUS) as follows:

$$PNMI = -293.63 + 2.79PUS$$
$$(-8.24) \quad (25.28)$$

$$R = 0.985 \quad S = 5.41 \quad DW = 1.81$$

A higher correlation can be expected if we take the price level of Guam, which has been the largest transshipment supplier of consumer goods to CNMI.

Seventh, CNMI's tourism industry has been heavily dependent upon Japanese investment and the tourist market. The increasing concentration of Japanese land-intensive tourism has not only discouraged agricultural development and lowered work incentives for the local people, but it has also made it increasingly difficult for the locals to acquire land for housing and public facilities.

Finally, because of the nature of small islands, development impacts can be immediately felt through the common use of public goods (infrastructure) and utilities such as transportation; communication; electricity; water, sewage, and solid-waste disposal systems; and hospitals. CNMI has been facing a particularly serious water shortage caused mainly by the booming tourism industry, which requires a high per capita consumption of water.[5]

Construction of CNMI's Balance of Payments

It has been argued that it may not be meaningful to construct a balance-of-payments (BOP) account for an island economy such as CNMI where the monetary system is completely integrated into that of the United States and there is no independent monetary policy for the CNMI authority to resolve balance-of-payments problems. Nevertheless, the construction of a BOP table for the economy, however crude, is essential to understand the working mechanism of the CNMI economy and also to help solve various development issues raised in the previous section. The construction of a BOP account is particularly important for an open, small island economy such as CNMI where external trade and various sources of capital transactions determine the course of an island's economic development. A reliable BOP table is also essential for estimating the gross island product (GIP).

A BOP table (Table 4.3) has been constructed for CNMI based upon available data and my own estimations.[6] The table should be read cautiously because of the poor quality of the data and estimates. There are no published export figures. However, data on garment exports, which were extracted from a computer printout from the Division of Custom Services, should account for most of the exports from CNMI. The garment industry has flourished in CNMI since 1985 due mainly to its easy access to the U.S. market. If the local content is greater than 50 percent, the CNMI garments (except sweaters) can be exported to the United States free of duty and quota restrictions. To take advantage of this preferential treatment given to the commonwealth, twenty-four garment manufacturers from Taiwan, China, South Korea, and Thailand have invested in plants and facilities employing about 6,000 workers and exporting $154 million in products in 1989.

Published import figures are greatly underestimated, since they cover only those imported items subject to import duties. Imported items sold at duty-free shops are not recorded in the customs statistics. Based upon government sources, published import values are increased by 30 percent for the BOP estimates in order to correct for the obvious underestimation. As expected for a trade-dependent economy such as CNMI, the trade balance shows an increasing deficit, amounting to $199 million in 1989.

Tourist receipts (travel expenditures) in Table 4.3 are primarily based on the average length of stay (four days) for the visitor with an average expenditure of $239 per day for those arriving by air.[7] It is quite possible the figures may be underestimated considering the changing spending habits of Japanese tourists, who account for nearly 80 percent of the total visitors to CNMI. Tourist receipts increased from $122 million in 1985 to $319 million in 1989, or 2.6-fold. According to a survey conducted by the School of Travel Industry Management at the University of Hawaii in 1989, $1 million of tourist expenditures directly and indirectly created seventy-five jobs, $1.2 million in total sales, $0.6 million in household income, $0.1 million in government revenue, and $0.3 million in imports. If we apply these figures to 1989, the tourism industry generated about 24,000 jobs, $380 million in sales, $32 million in government revenue, and $170 million in imports.[8] Tourism receipts are the only available data recorded in the service trade of BOP. Estimates of tourism expenditures, which should be recorded on the debit side of the BOP account, are not available. Therefore, the surplus in the travel balance is, no doubt, overestimated.

As I have already noted, CNMI has increasingly been a net importer of alien workers. There are no official figures available for the net labor income of nonresident (alien) workers. The net labor income of those workers in Table 4.3, which is equivalent to remittances (total earnings minus local expenditures and local savings) of the nonresident workers has been estimated under the assumptions that an average alien worker earns the average wage of the private sector and that such workers remit 40 percent of their average wage earnings. These assumptions can be challenged because they are based upon a small and informal sample survey in CNMI. Remittances of nonresident workers more than doubled, from $15 million in 1985 to $36 million in 1989, due to a sharp increase in the number of workers during the period. It is interesting to note that the average estimated annual earnings of these workers declined from $5,682 in 1985 to $4,781 in 1989, reflecting an influx of cheap labor, mainly from the Philippines.

Trade, service, and income balances including goods, services, and income are important components of GIP (see Appendix A.1 for relationships between GIP and balance of payments). As we have already seen, surpluses in the service balance have more than offset the deficits in merchandise trade and income balances. Therefore, the foreign trade sector of CNMI, unlike in many small island economies, has contributed positively to CNMI's economic growth.

Due to a lack of data, only unrequited official transfers, namely the U.S. federal grants-in-aid, are recorded in the BOP table. Federal grants, however, are the single most important source of transfer receipts. Although the amount of grants increased from $59 million in 1985 to $80 million in 1989, the relative weight of grants in the external receipts declined considerably. The private transfer balance (net unrequited transfers of residents) is likely to be negative, considering the fact that there have been increasing remittances from CNMI for education abroad.

As can be seen from Table 4.3, CNMI's estimated current-account-balance surplus increased from $87 million in 1985 to $163 million in 1989. This means that CNMI was a net exporter of capital during this period. Although no capital-account data, including direct foreign investment in CNMI, are available, the net deposit positions of CNMI's four banks with non-CNMI banks showed sizable positive figures of $128 million in 1988 and $168 million in 1989, which roughly correspond to the respective current-account surpluses (see a consolidated bank report in Appendix A.2). If we assume that all external financial transactions of CNMI were conducted through financial institutions, the surpluses in net deposit positions indicate net capital outflows from CNMI.

CNMI's development-strategy prospectus has observed that "within the booming economy of the CNMI where construction projects are everywhere evident that bank deposits exceed their lending activity to the extent that the above sum ($168 million in 1989) was placed in off-island banks to be invested outside the Northern Marianas."[9]

Absorptive Capacity of the CNMI Economy

The CNMI economy has been rapidly losing its structural balance due largely to the rapid development of the tourism industry. The tourism industry is basically an externally driven development force. Therefore, it is important to realize that this external growth factor is subject to the vagaries of forces beyond CNMI's control. Development must improve the socioeconomic life of the indigenous Marianans, whose very existence is based on the land and natural environment of CNMI. Thus the absorptive capacity (AC) can be defined as the socioeconomic capacity of CNMI to absorb the development impact meant to improve the net welfare of the Marianans. Measurement of AC is not an easy task, particularly in CNMI, where key data are almost totally lacking. However, the following attempt may be better than no attempt at all.

Absorptive Capacity of the Indigenous Labor Force

A very simple way to measure the absorptive capacity of the indigenous labor force (ACi) is to use the growth rate of the that force. According to this criterion of absorptive capacity, given full employment, as has been the case in CNMI, ACi must be determined by the growth rate of the indigenous labor force and its productivity as follows:

$$GACi = GLi + GPLi,$$

where

GACi = marginal absorptive capacity of indigenous labor
GLi   = growth rate of the indigenous labor force
GPLi = productivity growth rate of the indigenous labor force

This simple formula is particularly applicable to CNMI, where wages and salaries in the tourism industry are much lower than the current full-employment wages of the indigenous labor force. Therefore, additional demand for new employment will not increase the net welfare level of the local labor force. As is shown in Figure 4.2, CNMI's indigenous labor force (Li) grew at an average annual rate of about 4 percent during 1980–1989. However, the total labor force (L) grew 25 percent annually during this period, the difference made up by importing alien workers. This suggests that the pace of economic development was far beyond the absorptive capacity of the indigenous labor force. If alien workers had not been available, the actual growth rate would have been limited by the growth rate of the indigenous labor supply, assuming productivity in the service sector had not changed.

Absorptive Capacity of the Capital Fund

The absorptive capacity of the capital fund (ACc) is defined as CNMI's capacity to absorb capital funds at a given rate of capital utilization. Change in the absorptive capacity of capital funds (GACc) is determined by the growth rate of the labor force (GL) and the capital-labor ratio (k) as follows:

$$GACc = f(GL, k),$$
$$\text{where} \quad GL = GLi + GLa \text{ and } k = K/L$$

If we can reasonably assume that the capital(K)-labor(L) ratio (k), or the capital intensity of the CNMI economy, is constant,[10] a change in ACc is determined by a change in GL. As we have already seen, since CNMI's labor market is dichotomized by indigenous (Li) and alien (La) markets, a change in ACc in the private sector will be almost totally determined by changes in the number of alien workers (GLa). If we assume an unlimited supply of alien labor, additional investment funds will be absorbed into the economy without creating home-made inflation. Therefore, in order to sustain CNMI's absorptive capacity of capital funds, the government must allow alien workers to meet the increasing investment demand. This, however, will pose a real development dilemma for CNMI. In order to improve the real welfare of the indigenous population, technologies and the quality of human resources must be continuously upgraded to match the rising wage and land prices.

As long as CNMI continues to import cheap alien workers to sustain its ACc, and therefore the growth momentum, the net welfare of the indigenous population may not be improved. The tourism industry need not be supported by relatively cheap labor, as is seen in the industries that are continuing to grow in high-cost island economies such as Hawaii, Okinawa, and Singapore (see Chapter 8). If CNMI's comparative economic advantage lies in tourism, as it seems to do, the quality of tourism and related industries must be upgraded so that the additional indigenous labor force and local capital are fully employed in the service sector. As we have already seen in the balance-of-payments section, local capital has been flowing out of CNMI, and foreign capital, particularly from Japan, has financed growing investment demand in the tourism industry.

Absorptive Capacity of Infrastructure

The rate of expansion of infrastructure such as roads, ports, water facilities, sewage, electricity, and solid-waste disposal has not kept up with economic growth, and since these facilities are used in common by residents, nonresidents, and tourists, increasing pressures on these facilities will adversely affect tourism. If the Marianas have to pay, or if the CNMI government has to subsidize that part of the increased infrastructure cost created by the visitor industry, then we can say that CNMI's level of infrastructure is just not sustainable, as is shown in Figure 4.3. Besides looking at the absorptive capacity of infrastructure (ACf), one must consider the absorptive capacity of natural environmental amenities. In order to measure this absorptive capacity, there must be some objectively measurable environmental indicators. Since the CNMI economy is at a full-employment level, additional economic activities must improve the environment rather than damage it.

Diversification of the CNMI Economy

Economic diversification is simply defined as a shift in the productive base from a simple monoculture type to more complex, interrelated production activities. There are two types of diversification. One is horizontal: diversifying from the production of a single or a few products such as sugar and coconuts to the production of multicommercial products such as cocoa, ginger, tropical fruits, rice, maize, and dairy, fishery, and forestry products. The other is vertical: shifting the production process from the upstream activities of raw material production to the downstream activities of manufacturing, thereby generating more intra- or interindustry linkages and value-added production activities. For example, sugarcane can be processed into sugar and molasses, which in turn can be processed into rum and other value-added products. In the case of CNMI, horizontal diversification means structural change from tourism-dominated industrial activities to more agricultural and manufacturing activities. Vertical diversification means promotion of tourism-related activities such as the production of souvenirs, foods, and various services.

As we have already seen, CNMI's specialization in tourism has intensified in recent years at the expense of manufacturing and agriculture. The economic rationale behind this transformation can be easily explained (see Figure 4.4). CNMI, for example, used to produce and export sugar, possibly at point A on the production possibility curve in Figure 4.4, at the given domestic exchange rate $(Pt/Ps)d$ between tourism (t) and sugar (s). As the international exchange rate $(Pt/Ps)i$ for tourism became more favorable than that for sugar, the production possibility curve rapidly moved to point B, which enabled CNMI to import and consume more goods and services, including sugar, than before, as shown by the upward shift of consumption from C_1 to C_2.

The economic gain from specializing in tourism is obvious under these static, timeless assumptions for the production process. However, reversing the production process when the international exchange rate becomes unfavorable for CNMI tourism is difficult to do within a reasonable time horizon due to rigid institutional factors, the availability of factors of production, and, above all, the lack of appropriate technologies and markets. Therefore, if reversing the production process in response to a change in the international exchange rate is costly, risky, and time-consuming, specialization in a few exportable products may be less efficient than diversification.

If domestic resources, particularly land, are not being fully utilized in CNMI, diversification will expand both tourism and sugar production, as is shown in Figure 4.5. Productive capacity for both tourism and sugar can be expanded from A to C. Furthermore, if there are complementarities between tourism and sugar production in terms of inputs, land use, and technology, the production frontier itself can be expanded from SR to SR$'$ as a result of diversification.

Another advantage of diversification is the use of the seemingly underutilized agricultural labor force in CNMI. Due to seasonality and lack of complementary productive activities in CNMI, a large portion of the labor force is not fully engaged in productive activities. The horizontal diversification of agriculture will, in effect, reduce the magnitude of underemployment, as is shown in Figure 4.6. The labor force can be activated as diversification proceeds from tourism (L1) to sugar, rice, ginger, flowers, and so forth until full employment (Lf) is achieved. Furthermore, if we can prove that diversification will result in lower average costs (ACd) than would be the case in specialization (ACs) due to complementary production activities and the ensuing dynamic external economies, as depicted in Figure 4.7, then the shift of resources toward agricultural diversification can also be justified not only from the standpoint of food security and full utilization of domestic resources but also on the more important grounds of economic efficiency, which is the basis of the comparative advantage theory.

In view of the extremely limited resource endowments in an island economy, vertical diversification may have more potential than horizontal diversification. Vertical diversification, however, should be carefully pursued because very often the attempt has resulted in deficit operations due to the cost-escalating effects of high-priced local inputs.[11] The world-renowned Puerto Rican rum, Bacardi, for example, has had sustained international competitiveness because cheap imported molasses is used instead of more expensive local inputs. In such a case, exports of specialized products are more beneficial to the economy than subsidized diversified industries because specialization at least can earn foreign exchange income, which can be used to obtain products that are cheaper and better than subsidized domestic products.

Conclusions

The CNMI economy is now poised at a turning point. CNMI must decide whether to further specialize in its mighty tourism industry or diversify toward more agricultural and manufacturing activities. As pointed out, further specialization in the service-oriented tourism industry must be pursued at the expense of exposing the economy to external vulnerability, since the industry almost totally depends on an external market and on external capital and labor. Once such external factors, which are beyond the control of CNMI, diminish, there is a good possibility that the island economy will collapse into a primitive stage, characterized by a low-level subsistence state with a smaller population.[12]

The excessive specialization in tourism also threatens the very life-style of the indigenous Marianans because of the limited absorptive capacity of foreign capital and workers. CNMI'S infrastructure and public utilities, particularly water and sewage systems, are already overburdened by the current level of tourist activities, and there is no sign that these infrastructure bottlenecks can be removed in the foreseeable future. Furthermore, the influx of migrant workers with different life-styles and living conditions are already causing social and political tensions in some communities.

The expansion of the tourism industry should be controlled within the limits of CNMI's physical and social capacities to absorb the external impacts on the economy. Otherwise CNMI will lose its luster as a "paradise island of the Pacific" for the Japanese tourists, whose tastes are very volatile. It should be remembered in particular that social and political tensions in a small island economy are the most effective deterrents to tourism, as was seen in Fiji some years ago. Although CNMI should conduct a comprehensive study to determine its capacity to support the further expansion of tourism, we tentatively recommend that the industry should be expanded within the limits of the growth of its resident population, namely between 3 and 4 percent annually.

It is easy to speak of economic diversification in CNMI but difficult to implement it, not only because of its extremely small-scale and low-level technology but also because of the rapid expansion of its tourism industry. It should be clearly recognized that in an open economy such as CNMI, both limited human and natural resources, including land, are intensively mobilized in a growing industry at the expense of declining industries. This clear yet simple economic logic indicates that expanding tourism has been directly responsible for the rapid decline in agriculture in CNMI. We know there are complementary relationships among agriculture, manufacturing, and tourism through interindustry linkages. These linkages, however, cannot take effect when one industrial sector is growing much faster than the others given limited resources. In the case of CNMI, linkage effects between agriculture and tourism have weakened, and leakage effects have increased. In other words, local demand created by tourism expenditures has been met by increasing imports of food products instead of by stimulating local agricultural production.

As shown in Figure 4.8, industrial diversification in CNMI means the creation of interindustry linkages or a positive correlation among the industrial sectors. One important prerequisite of creating this positive correlation is to find appropriate elasticity of demand for each sector. For example, if elasticity of demand for agricultural products is 0.6, then agriculture is supposed to grow by 6 percent annually when local demand is growing by 10 percent annually in order to strengthen interindustry linkages. The average annual growth rate of CNMI's tourism demand in the 1980s (17%) far exceeded agriculture's capacity to create viable interindustry linkages.

In the 1980s, CNMI's local resources were increasingly mobilized into the booming import businesses, which effectively siphoned off the growing tourism demand. The diversion of resources from agricultural food production to food imports was a major reason behind the decline of agriculture in CNMI. If tourism demand grows by 3–4 percent annually, as has been suggested, then the agricultural sector would be expected to grow 2–3 percent annually, which may be well under CNMI's supplying capacity for the sector. It should be remembered that even if a positive growth rate in agriculture were realized, the relative weight of the sector would still be declining. But a positive growth rate is necessary in order to ensure a minimal sustainability of the Marianans' life-style if and when the collapse of the tourism industry actually occurs.

In order to diversify the CNMI economy, good indicative planning with strong policy supports is essential. Policy measures must be designed to strengthen the competitive edge of local industries. A basic requirement for effective implementation of these policy measures is to establish a quality database including detailed GIP accounts, balance-of-payments and population statistics, and a detailed study of land and resource uses. CNMI has an advantage in creating a reliable database because of its smallness and isolation.

Appendix:
CNMI's Gross Island Product and Balance of Payments

A rough estimate of CNMI's gross island product (GIP) has been made by the Planning and Budget Office since 1986, as shown in Table 4A.1. Although the full details of estimating methods were not available, the estimates, particularly the balance-of-payments sector, do not seem to reflect the reality of the CNMI economy.

As can be seen in Table 4A.1, GIP is estimated from the factor income (labor, land, and capital) side and the expenditure (or product) side. Employee compensation is the largest item of GIP, representing various incomes earned by both resident and nonresident workers. The income in this category, which amounted to $136 million in 1988, seems to have been estimated from data on W-2 tax forms filed by employees. In 1988, only 19,495 employees including both residents and nonresidents filed W-2 forms totaling $105 million in earnings. Since there were 28,000 employed workers (17,000 nonresidents) in 1988, the income in this category may be grossly underestimated. There are no data available to check the accuracy of estimated items such as proprietor's income, rental income, net interest and profits. It should be noted here that profits account for nearly 30 percent of GIP, an unusually high figure compared to that for other island economies. A large portion of these profits may be generated by foreign enterprises in CNMI and be remitted to their home countries.

The expenditure side (or product side) includes personal consumption, gross private investment, inventory change, and government expenditures. Except for government expenditures, there are no survey data available to estimate these items. There are no consumer-expenditure survey and building permits, which are primary sources for estimating these items.

As has been noted, the balance-of-payments section of GIP also presents serious estimation problems. Table 4A.1 shows that the commodity trade balance of CNMI has been increasingly positive, which is highly unlikely judging from the nature of the economy. My estimates, instead, show increasing trade deficits, which may be underestimated considering the fact that the imports-GIP ratio for CNMI was only 37 percent in 1986 and that for comparable island economies such as American Samoa, the Cook Islands, Palau, Kiribati, and Tonga, the ratio ranged from 158 percent to 69 percent.[13] It is quite possible that imported duty-free goods are not included in imports but are included in exports. Duty-free sales to tourists should be included in the service (travel) trade. Due probably to this conceptual problem, travel balances (net travel receipts) in Table 4A.1 are severely underestimated. Net travel receipts for 1988, for example, were only $48 million, but gross tourism receipts were recorded at $244 million for the same year (see Table 4.3). Net travel receipts should be lower than $244 million but much greater than $48 million. Net services in Table 4A.1, which are supposed to include such items as transportation, insurance, royalties, and various incomes from investment, labor, and property, also shows surpluses, due mainly to investment incomes generated by foreign enterprises operating in CNMI. However, it is not clear how much of profits earned in CNMI is remitted to the investors' home countries and how much is reinvested in the economy. If a large portion of the profits was remitted, the service balance could be negative.

As a result, the recorded balances for goods and services show surpluses. Unlike in other resource-poor small island economies, CNMI's external sector, in net, has contributed to its economic growth. GIP for 1988 can be expressed as follows ($ million):

$$GIP = Cp + Ge + Ip + (X - M)$$
$$446 = 171 + 116 + 107 + (52),$$

where Cp = personal consumption
        Ge = government expenditures
        Ip = gross private investment including inventory change
        $(X - M)$ = exports of goods and services − imports of goods and services including factor incomes

If we assume that U.S. grants are the only unrequited transfer item for 1988, then CNMI's current-account balance should show a large surplus, as follows ($ million):

$$CA = (X - M) + \text{U.S. grants}$$
$$117 = 52 + 65$$

The current-account surplus of $117 million for 1988 is not far from my estimate of $127 million for the same year, as shown in Table 4.3. It is interesting that the current-account surplus of $117 is very close to CNMI's net deposits ($128 million in 1988) of financial institutions with external banks as is shown in Table 4A.2. If we assume that all financial transactions between CNMI and other countries were made through financial institutions, then CNMI's net-deposits position should reflect its overall balance-of-payments position. That is to say, there have been net capital outflows from CNMI, as we have already seen. Both the current-account surplus and the net-deposit position suggest that CNMI has been a net capital exporter.

TABLE 4.1 Main Economic Indicators of CNMI, 1980–1989

Indicator	1980	1981	1982	1983	1984	1985	1986	1987	1988	1989
Population (000)										
Resident population	16.8	17.4	18.0	18.9	19.6	20.4	21.1	21.8	22.3	23.3
Nonresident population								19.8		23.5
Nonresident workers	2.9	3.1	3.6	3.9	4.7	6.7	11.5	15.4	17.2	18.8
U.S. Grants ($ million)	40.7	36.2	38.2	53.1	55.5	58.5	50.8	60.1	64.5	79.6
Covenant	22.1	24.4	25.8	27.3	27.7	28.7	26.2	35.3	34.4	40.1
Federal	18.6	11.8	12.4	25.8	27.8	29.8	24.6	24.8	30.1	39.5
Tourism										
Tourists Incomes ($ million)	60.8	59.0	56.7	66.9	71.2	121.6	134.0	154.0	244.0	318.0
No. of tourists (000)	119.0	118.0	111.0	124.0	132.0	142.0	157.0	186.0	233.0	302.0
Gross island product										
Nominal ($ million)	137.0	151.7	165.0	179.0	195.1	256.3	323.0	387.6	445.7	–
Real (1975 = 100)	96.5	98.1	99.3	105.1	110.5	133.5	168.2	181.1	221.7	–
CPI (1978 = 100)	127.6	155.4	195.6	191.3	197.8	203.6	213.2	228.5	239.7	248.0
Trade										
Exports (000 tons)	7.0	8.0	9.0	9.0	29.0	26.0	13.0	21.0	29.0	–
Imports (000 tons)	77.0	78.0	79.0	90.0	135.0	132.0	227.0	194.0	250.0	–
Exports ($ million)	–	–	–	–	–	108.0	24.8	63.2	131.5	154.0
Imports ($ million)	–	–	–	–	–	88.3	117.5	180.9	285.3	353.0

Note: – = data are not available. Export value figures are garment only; import value figures are estimated by the author.

SOURCE: CNMI government sources.

TABLE 4.2   Wage Structure of CNMI, 1989 ($)

	Average Annual Wage & Salary	Number of Workers
Public sector	12,138	5,190
Federal government	17,459	106
CNMI government	12,027	5,084
Private sector	4,781	30,692

SOURCE: CNMI, Department of Finance.

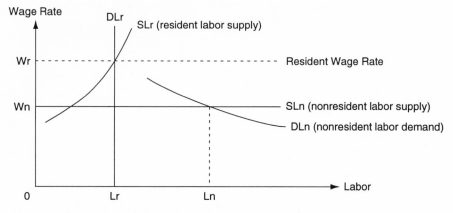

FIGURE 4.1   Dichotomy of CNMI Labor Market

TABLE 4.3   Estimated Balance of Payments for CNMI, 1985–1989 ($ million)

	1985	1986	1987	1988	1989
Merchandise					
Exports	10.8	24.8	63.2	131.5	154.0
Imports	88.3	117.5	180.9	285.3	353.0
Balance	−77.5	−92.7	−117.7	−153.8	−199.0
Service					
Travel	121.6	134.0	154.0	244.0	318.5
Income					
Remittances	−15.2	−20.8	−26.9	−27.8	−36.0
Unrequited transfers					
Official (U.S. grants)	58.5	50.8	60.1	64.5	79.6
Current-Acc. Balance	87.4	71.3	69.5	126.9	163.1
Net deposits of CNMI					
banks with non-CNMI banks	–	–	–	128.1	168.3

Note: See the text for explanations and estimating problems.
SOURCE: CNMI government.

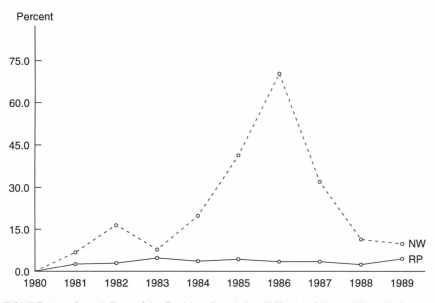

FIGURE 4.2   Growth Rate of the Resident Population (RP) and of Nonresident Workers
(NW), 1980–1989
SOURCE: CNMI government.

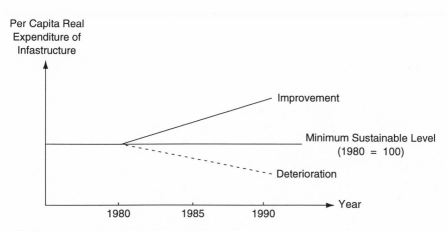

FIGURE 4.3   The Per Capita Level of Infrastructure

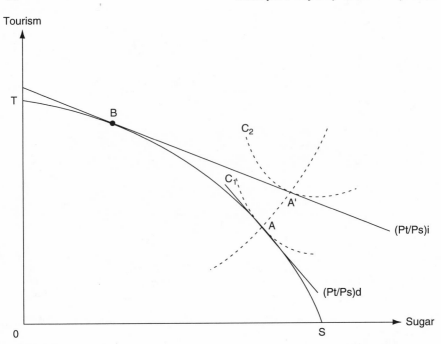

FIGURE 4.4   A Simple Exposition of CNMI's Benefits from Specializing in Tourism

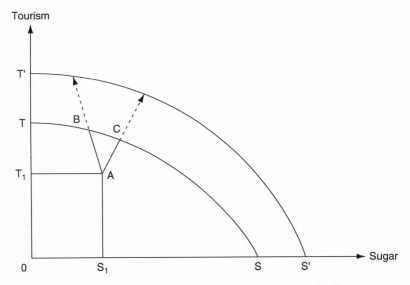

FIGURE 4.5   Full Utilization of Domestic Resources Through Diversification

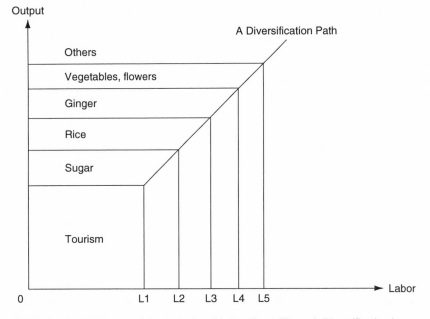

FIGURE 4.6   Full Utilization of the Agricultural Labor Force Through Diversification in a Small Island Economy

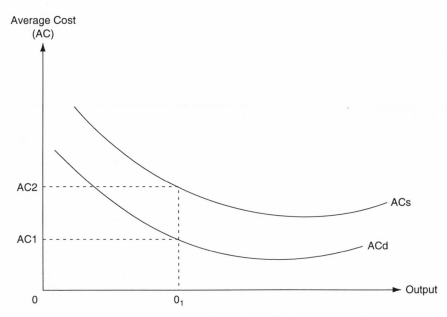

FIGURE 4.7   Expected Cost-Reduction Effect of Diversification in a Small Economy

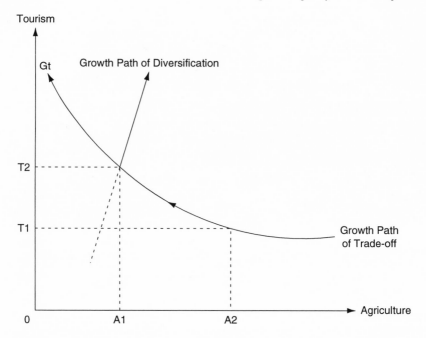

FIGURE 4.8   The CNMI Economy: Two Possible Growth Paths for Tourism and Agriculture

TABLE 4A.1   Estimated Gross Island Product for Commonwealth of the Northern Mariana
Islands, FY1986–1988 ($ million)

	1986	*1987*	*1988*
Income Side			
Employee compensation	100.7	111.6	136.1
Proprietor's income	49.1	59.7	65.0
Rental income	13.3	20.7	35.6
Net interest	12.3	14.8	15.8
Profits	102.4	115.5	126.0
Indirect business taxes	23.6	26.5	28.4
Business transfer payments	8.0	8.9	14.6
Govt. enterprise surplus	0.0	8.9	0.0
Statistical discrepancy	3.6	4.3	4.7
Depreciation	10.0	16.7	19.5
Total	323.0	387.6	445.7
Percentage change	26	20	15
Product Side			
Personal consumption	126.5	142.3	170.5
Gross private investment	67.3	86.9	100.3
Inventory change	4.3	5.4	6.5
Government expenditures	83.8	109.3	116.2
Net Export			
Trade	2.0	2.6	3.2
Travel	38.3	40.2	47.8
Services	0.8	.9	1.2
Total	323.0	387.6	445.7
Percentage Change	26	20	15

Note: 1987 and 1988 GIP revised in 1st quarter, 1988.
SOURCE: Planning & Budget Office, CNMI.

TABLE 4A.2   CNMI Consolidated Report of Conditions of All Banks Doing Business in CNMI (as of December 31, $1,000)

	1988 Totals	1989 Totals
Assets		
Cash & cash items in process of collection	2,404	33,192
Securities		
U.S. Treasury	849	0
U.S. government agencies	0	0
Others	163	5,603
Balances with other banks	473	2,678
Loans (gross)		
Government	2,183	3,821
Consumer	38,870	43,443
Real estate	6,508	2,012
Commercial	40,445	57,434
Nonlocal real estate	730	400
Premises & equipment	3,598	1,815
Other real estate owned	32	0
Due from banks		
Head office or branches	128,076	168,304
Others	950	281,000
Provisions for loan losses/unearned discount	(931)	(1,321)
Other assets	18,809	18,992
Total	243,159	337,654
Interest received from borrowers in 1989	9,058	14,159
Liabilities and capital		
Deposits		
Demand deposits, govt. & govt. agencies	7,392	12,183
Other	47,999	81,788
Regular savings, govt. & govt. agencies	700	1,947
Other	56,805	73,573
TCD,[a] govt. & govt. agencies	31,840	27,208
Other	78,390	130,102
Due to other banks		
Head office or branches	0	0
Others	276	0
Liabilities on acceptances executed & outstanding	0	0
Accrued interest payable & other liabilities	16,398	4,995
Capital stock	1,081	1,251
Capital surplus	1,497	2,562
Undivided profits	291	2,025
Convertible subordinated debt & FSLIC[b] contribution	000,490	000,000
Total	243,159	337,654
Interest paid to depositors	10,114	14,102

[a]Total certified deposits.
[b]Federal Savings and Loans Insurance Corporation.
SOURCE: Banking Division, Department of Commerce and Labor.

5

The Long-Term Strategy for Water Conservation in Saipan's Rapidly Growing Economy

Because of the insular nature of small islands, external demands, as reflected in the influx of capital and labor, impact heavily on the internal resources that must support infrastructure development. Development impacts are immediately felt through the common use of public infrastructure and utilities such as transportation, electric power, communication, solid-waste disposal, water, and sewage systems. Public infrastructure expansion in Saipan has not kept up with the expansion of the private economy, and the impacts on the limited renewable resources of the island have been severe. Water is one of the most severely impacted resources.

With rapid economic development and growth in Saipan, the shortage and depletion of water became a crisis that threatens the political and economic stability of the Commonwealth of Northern Mariana Islands (CNMI), whose capital is Saipan (see Appendix A.1).[1] In the midst of coping with the daily and short-term requirements of the people, officials have not adequately addressed the long-term goal of conserving water to sustain the economic growth and survival of the commonwealth. This chapter addresses the impacts on water resources in the context of the dynamic structural changes that have been occurring in the economy and presents alternatives for designing a long-term strategy for water conservation.

Impacts on Water Resources

To appreciate the impacts of growth on Saipan, it is first useful to gain perspective of the situation relative to other subtropical-tropical islands in the Pacific, such as Oahu, Okinawa, and Miyako, all of which have been facing similar water-scarcity problems due to rapid growth. Table 5.1 shows the general characteristics of these islands (see Figures 5.1 and 5.2 for maps). Saipan is more like Miyako in terms of land area and population, but Miyako is flatter and without any mountains and rivers. Okinawa and Oahu are larger and further along in their economic development and growth than Saipan and Miyako. The contrasts among these islands are useful for our purpose, since their limited insular resources are all heavily impacted by the same types of external economic forces discussed in the previous chapter: tourism, government grants, private investments, and so on.

On the surface, Saipan is blessed with plentiful water. Annual rainfall in Saipan averages 2,039 millimeters,, more than Oahu and less than Okinawa and Miyako. The annual rainfall per capita in Saipan (6132 m³) is more than twice that of Oahu and Okinawa, but less than Miyako's (7232 m³). But the use-rate index, which indicates the relative capture of this natural flow for the water supply, is only about 2 percent for Saipan and Miyako,[2] compared to 4 percent for Okinawa and 22 percent for Oahu. What accounts for such large differences in capture for the water supply? The main factors are storage and distribution (both natural and artificial) and, of course, population.

Hydrogeologic characteristics that result in differences in the natural storage and distribution capacities of these islands make a lot of difference in their abilities to cope with scarcity on the supply side. The hydrogeology of Oahu is characterized by its well-known natural underground Ghyben-Herzberg lens system with limestone caprock along its coastal plain to reduce leakage. Its storage and distribution potential is far greater than the surface-water system in Okinawa, where a network of large national projects in the mountainous northern region supports smaller local waterworks in the populated central and southern regions of the island.[3] This is particularly reflected in the high-use-rate indices for groundwater. Unfortunately, Saipan has neither underground- nor surface-water resources of comparable potential. Low water quality and high leakage rates compound the problem.

Low Groundwater Quality

Groundwater quality in shallow limestone aquifers is poor and getting worse, especially in the low-elevation areas, where the population is concentrated. The available U.S. Geological Survey (USGS) records show average chloride concentrations increasing from 689 parts per million (ppm) in 1980 to 878ppm in 1983. In 1983 half of the total municipal intake was from wells with chloride levels over 1,000ppm. The quality of groundwater is highly sensitive to pumping rates and rainfall, and there has been a very high rate of abandoned wells over the years. From 1946 to 1983, 205 wells were developed, but only 32 of them were used in 1983. Only 4 out of 87 wells drilled from 1946 to 1969 were still being used in 1988. There were several factors behind this high rate of abandonment, but in most cases overpumping of the thin freshwater lens led to saltwater intrusion. The problem of indiscriminate drilling in unplanned sites was compounded by unregulated pumping, so the operational life of wells was short and wells had to abandoned and new ones drilled.

High Leakage Rates

High leakage rates have plagued the aging municipal waterworks systems. In 1988, only about half of the total water intake into eleven separate systems throughout the island reached the customers. Leakage losses may have been even higher; some estimates are as high as 60 percent, since precise meter measurements of all intakes and deliveries are not available. The problem built up over many years; the different systems were typically built over unstable geologic formations and were poorly maintained, often repaired with improper fittings over a long history of changing jurisdictions. Poor water quality contributed to the growth of rust and tuberculosis bacteria in the pipes. Rapid economic development in the 1980s compounded the problem when the crushing weights of construction traffic further damaged already weak galvanized-metal and asbestos-cement pipes. The loss of half of the developed water intakes through leakages prompted the government to give the highest priority to repairing and upgrading the distribution system under a unified system managed by the Water Division of the newly created Commonwealth Utilities Corporation (CUC).

Exploration and Blending Strategy

Reducing leakages and upgrading the distribution system are only a partial solution to the supply problem. Such measures take care of some of the immediate quantity aspects of the problem but do little on the quality side. Nevertheless, the stage is set for addressing the longer-term objective of providing high-quality drinking water to the population. Toward this end, an ambitious program was initiated to explore for and develop high-quality mountain sources and to design a strategy for blending high- and low-quality water into a drinkable product. There are, however, major uncertainties to contend with, including the continuing depletion of the groundwater. Exploratory drillings are finding new high-quality mountain sources, but it is not known how much high-quality groundwater exists. There are optimists and pessimists, and their views have different implications for designing a long-term strategy of water conservation for Saipan.

The alternatives can be discussed in terms of two polar scenarios reflecting extreme depletive versus conservative approaches. We begin with the question of how much high-quality groundwater is required to meet the long-term goal of supplying safe drinking water to the population. The simple equation for blending is

$$Q_b = [(X_l * Q_l) + (X_h * Q_h)]/(X_l + X_h), \tag{1}$$

where X = quantity of water
Q = quality of water
l = low quality
h = high quality
b = blended product

If a unit of low quality groundwater (X_1, Q_1) is blended with a unit of high-quality groundwater (X_h, Q_h), the resultant water is of quantity $X_b = X_1 + X_h$, and quality Q_b. The depletive approach sees no constraint on the future availability of high- and low-quality groundwater and is willing to deplete the present supplies in terms of both quantity and quality. Thus, equation (1) suffices for computations.

The conservative approach is uncertain about the availability of plentiful amounts of high-quality groundwater and is more careful about further depleting the present available sources. In this more cautious approach, the total blended supply is constrained to the present level of supply. This can, in principle, be accomplished in various ways. A simple way is to cut back an equal amount of low-quality water for every new amount of high-quality water produced. Then equation (1) becomes

$$Q_b = [(X_1 - X_h) * Q_1 + (Xh * Q_h)]/(X_1) \qquad (2)$$

For whatever blend quality target Q_b selected, the required amount of high-quality water becomes:

Depletive case: $X_h(d) = [(Q_1 - Q_b)/(Q_b - Q_h)] * X_1 = kd * X_1$ (3)
Conservative case: $X_h(c) = [(Q_1 - Q_b)/(Q_1 - Q_h)] * X_1 = kc * X_1$ (4)

The coefficients kd and kc depend solely on quality differentials in the sources and the blend product. The difference is basically a matter of conservation practices, which will be further discussed later in the context of management options. The following examples illustrate the applicability of these coefficients and respective equations.

Example 1. Waterworks Expansion Requirements (Figure 5.3)

Given: Safe drinking water chloride concentration Q_b = 250ppm
        Available quantity of low-level groundwater X_1 = 10mgd
        Average quality of low-level groundwater Q_1 = 800ppm
        Average quality of high-level groundwater Q_h = 40ppm

Assuming that sufficient capacity exists to blend all the available low- and high-quality water, the amounts of high-quality groundwater, $x_h(\cdot)$, required for blending are as follows.

Depletive case: $X_h(d) = [(800 - 250)/(250 - 40)] * 10$
                           $= 2.62 * 10 = 26.2$mgd

Conservative case: $X_h(c) = [(800 - 250)/(800 - 40)] * 10$
$= 0.724 * 10 = 7.24$mgd.

In the depletive case, the 26.2mgd high-quality water requirement means that the groundwater supply system must expand 2.62 times its present level. In contrast, the conservative requirement of 7.24mgd means that the supply system needs to expand by only 0.724 times its present level. The conservative approach requires only about 27 percent as much high-quality groundwater as the depletive case to upgrade the available low-quality water to the safe level.

Example 2. Alternative Futures

Using the approximate present situation as a baseline, we can compare alternative future scenarios where changes in factors such as population, leakage rates, and per capita consumption can be taken into account. This simple example illustrates the combined effects of alternative blending and immigration policies on the quality of water supply, assuming that leakages can be cut in half (i.e., down to 25%) but that per capita consumption increases by 25 percent.

Future 1 (worst case): depletive approach with uncontrolled immigration leading to a doubling of the population.
Future 2 (best case): conservative approach with no immigration and zero population growth.

The question is, What quality can be expected in the blended product when X_h amount of 40ppm high-quality groundwater is mixed with the available 800ppm of low-quality water?
The results, shown in Table 5.2, indicate that the quality of blended product will not be suitable for drinking in Future 1 but will be quite suitable in Future 2. In addition, the total consumption of this drinkable water will exceed by 0.75mgd the 3mgd of low-quality piped water presently being delivered.
Essentially, Future 1 results in the depletion of groundwater without guaranteeing a drinkable-quality blend, whereas Future 2 conserves on the demand for groundwater while at the same time increasing the per capita supply of drinkable blend through the CUC distribution system. Cutting back on CUC pumping of low-quality groundwater offers potential advantages such as (1) the reversal of the deterioration in groundwater quality and thus a further improvement on the potential for producing a drinkable blend; (2) more low-quality groundwater available as feedwater to self-service reverse-osmosis systems and thereby a substantial reduction in treatment costs (as compared to the present situation of reliance on high-salt water from coastal wells): and (3) a reduction in the growth in per capita water consumption as compared to the depletive case.
In effect, the long-term potential water supply for Saipan depends not only

upon the quantity and quality of available blending sources and the resultant product quality desired but also on the technical and institutional constraints (conservation practices) that can be realistically enforced in the development and use of water. Here we need to consider a more comprehensive demand strategy for water conservation (Figure 5.4).

The stylized scenario in Figure 5.4 shows only the essential features of the present situation as the baseline for considering alternative future management scenarios. The only public purveyor of water in Saipan is the CUC's Water Division. It draws water from various sources. Low-lying groundwater is typically of poor quality and in many places has a high saltwater content because of over-pumping. Recently, higher-quality groundwater was discovered in higher elevations and is now being actively explored for and developed for blending with the lower-quality groundwater. Households, hotels, and garment factories are connected to the CUC distribution mains but are not adequately supplied. Because of the shortage of public supplies, most users are also self-supplied. Drinking water is mainly sold by bottled-water companies that treat relatively high-quality groundwater through their own reverse-osmosis systems. Rainwater catchments are common among most users. Hotels have lower priority than residents, and many of the luxury hotels are self-supplied through private reverse-osmosis systems that draw on high-salt water from wells near the coast.

Alternative Management Scenarios

Alternative future management scenarios can follow different patterns between the two polar extremes illustrated in Figure 5.4. Modern urban systems tend to centralize water-supply management under a single public purveyor, as illustrated in alternative scenario 1. The Honolulu Board of Water Supply (BWS) is a case in point, but this is not necessarily a desirable direction for Saipan. The Honolulu BWS is based on a massive underground storage and distribution system that makes it possible to capture and use more than half (see Table 5.1) of Oahu's natural groundwater recharge. At the present time, this seems hardly possible in Saipan because of its limited known natural storage. Also, it would be depletive to the extent that the alternative sources that have been developed by the various self-supplied users—for example, traditional rainwater catchments and expensive reverse osmosis of high-salt water sources—would be abandoned and greater demands would be concentrated on the fragile groundwater system. The centralized supply system does not offer as much feedback as a diverse system to control demand growth.

The diversity alternative is shown in alternative 2 in Figure 5.4. It takes advantage of more opportunities to capture the natural rainfall of Saipan, through whatever means available, for its decentralized users. They would continue to capture rainwater for their own use and would also have greater incentives to adopt water-saving and recycling practices.[4] Bottled water would continue as a primary source of drinking water. To make high-quality groundwater readily available to all consumers at low costs, it should be used as feedwater to reverse-osmosis (RO) systems. This would help reduce the demand load (in terms of both quantity and quality) on the fragile low-level groundwater lens and, at the same time, help to expand the potential resource base for blending high- and low-quality groundwater.

User conservation consciousness would be kept high with the diversification approach. Overall, diversification of the water-supply system is a more rational management approach for Saipan. The perfection of this approach, however, requires a broader institutional strategy for a safe minimum standard of water conservation[5] that includes demand management to reduce the risks of irreversible saltwater intrusion into the natural groundwater resource base of the island.

Conclusions

Public water agencies are typically concerned with water management on the supply side, since their primary mission is to supply safe drinking water for the sake of public health. This is clearly reflected in the operations of the CUC Water Division, which allocates most of its budget to repair and improve on the distribution systems and explore for and develop new water supplies.[6] Demand management at this operating level is viewed in terms of rationing, metering, and water rates as the potential tools for controlling water consumption. But under the extreme water-shortage conditions of Saipan, these tools have not been effective in coping with the macroeconomic demands originating in the international economy. In the typical financial self-sufficiency framework of public water-supply management, monitoring water consumption (actually deliveries) and collecting revenues are constrained to recovering the costs of the water supply.

A comprehensive strategy of demand management involves more than that. Demand management is concerned with how changes in the economy affect demands on water resources. In this broader context, the allocation of scarce water among competing uses and users is an important component of growth management. It is necessary to understand how the changing patterns and trends of water consumption impose new pressures on alternative sources of water. This means that consumption data need to be carefully separated into functional categories.[7]

Also, comprehensive demand management goes far beyond the scope of water-supply agencies and involves the coordination of various means of control that are within the jurisdiction of other public agencies. In CNMI, for example, various direct and indirect means of controlling water demand (e.g., defining water rights and issuing drilling permits; setting and enforcing drinking-water standards; and controlling land use through zoning and regulations, penalties and subsidies, and development charges) are within the jurisdictions of other agencies. Obviously, the control of demand calls for interagency coop-eration and coordination of the various direct and indirect tools of water conser-vation. But getting the public agencies to act together is not sufficient. The pri-vate sector is just as much a part of the water economy, and its total involvement is also necessary. Institutional rules that provide incentives for adopting conser-vation practices such as rainwater capture and reuse and for investing in water-conserving technology are essential.

In essence, a long-term strategy for water conservation would reduce the de-mands for water use in the present in order to maintain higher levels of use in the future. Reducing present use rates essentially means controlling demands that would deplete the groundwater sources in terms of quantity and quality. In economic terms, a conservative demand strategy means forgoing the benefits of groundwater depletion in those locations sensitive to saltwater intrusions and during those time periods when intrusion is likely in order to increase long-term benefits from the groundwater resource. For the high-demand tourist and gar-ment industries, the implications are to forgo short-term profits from water de-pletion and instead invest in water conservation practices for longer-term profits through higher-quality services and products.

Appendix: Excerpt from *A Report of the Special Joint Legislative Committee on Water Resources for Saipan,* June 1988, 224 pages

The Problem

Water availability on Saipan has now reached a crisis. In many areas of the Island, residents can only collect a few gallons a day from city pipes. As a result, people bathe from buckets, dishes and clothes cannot be washed, toilets remain unflushed. People around the island are taking water from main water stations and hydrants. They leave taps on continuously to catch what little water that does become available.

In at least one area, it's reported that a household has been without public water for three years. Almost without exception, none of Saipan's water can be drunk from the tap. Because water is rationed in water hours around the island, water pipes never re-main full. The cracked and leaking conditions of most transmission lines allow contam-inated groundwater to enter the pipes. Because of the poor water quality and the aging pipes, rust quickly forms in the lining. When city water re-enters the lines, it is often brought to the consumer mixed with contaminated rust and health threatening bacteria.

Saipan's fifty-six (56) overworked wells show a steady, sometimes dramatic, rise in chloride. This indicates over pumping of the basal lens of fresh water aquifer. In other words, brackish seawater is being brought from pockets of underground water to the surface. On top of this, it is estimated that 60% of the water brought up never reaches the consumer. Saipan has clogged and leaking pipes lying decaying throughout the transmission system. Six gallons of water out of every ten pumped are lost back in the ground.

The backbone industries of the Commonwealth's current economic development cannot get enough water. Saipan's booming and water-intensive hotel industry complains of lack of city water. Likewise, Saipan's garment factories have resorted to un-regulated well drilling and construction of rainwater catchment in order to supplement their water needs. A survey of 32 businesses (hotels and garment factories) indicates usage of municipal water at the rate of 580,420 gallons per day (gpd). From privately owned wells, government operated wells excluded, a total of 285,200gpd is pumped out of the ground. For those with rainwater catchments, a total of 35,000gpd is collected. One hotel is processing sea water (reverse osmosis) at a rate of 5,500gpd.

With low water pressure or no water at all, Saipan's schools have faced closure due to unhealthy conditions in their restroom facilities. In some places, first and second graders are expected to hoist buckets to flush the toilet. On March 11, 1988, Marianas High School was ordered closed by the Commissioner of Education and the Chairman of the Board of Education because of a report from Public Health officials saying there was no running water in the toilet facilities and a very unsanitary condition existed. The report states, "We strongly recommend that you close Marianas High School today, March 11, 1988."

Water conditions have forced the Municipality to take emergency measures. Saipan's Mayor (Gilbert C. Ada) uses three water trucks to service 188 households, island-wide, to ease the "critical situation" in the water system.

In short, Saipan faces an acute water shortage. Residences, schools and businesses now experience a clear failure in water services. Except for periods in the aftermath of super typhoons, this degree of failure exceeds that known in the past. Water is worse now than ever before.

Saipan's burgeoning population and unprecedented economic growth has outpaced the limits of water infrastructure. The quantity and quality of Saipan's water service is rapidly failing. No water means: a lack of fire fighting ability, discouragement of indus-try, threatening health plagues, disruption of education, a general lowering of citizen morale, importing expensive potable water and a marked reduction in the confidence in government.

TABLE 5.1   Island Characteristics: Oahu, Okinawa, Miyako, and Saipan, 1988

Characteristic	Oahu	Okinawa	Miyako	Saipan
Location	21°18′N	26°14′N	24°47′N	15°13′N
	158°25′E	127°41′E	125°17′E	145°43′E
Land area (km²)	1,574	1,192	158	124
Geology	volcanic, sedimentary rocks around edges	Ryukyu limestone over rock formation of paleozoic strata	Ryukyu limestone over tertiary strata, "Shimajiri mudstone"	coral limestone over volcanic nucleus
Highest elevation (m)	1,225	498	108	473
	(mt. Kaa'la)	(Mt. Yonaha)	(Mt. Nobaru)	(Mt. Takpochao)
Population, 1988 (1,000)	903	1,069	49.4 (1989)	41.7
Density (persons/km²)	574	897	313	336
Economy	tourism government military sugarcane	tourism government military sugarcane	sugarcane government tourism	tourism government garments
Visitors, 1988 (1,000)	5,800	2,395	132	210
Climate & Water:				
Temperature, mean annual (°C)	25.0	18.1	23.0	25.6
Rainfall, mean annual (mm)	1,850	2,155	2,247	2,039
Water supply:				
Primary	groundwater in basaltic aquifers	surface waters in northern dams	springs	groundwater in limestone
Secondary	surface water reservoirs	groundwater in limestone	groundwater in limestone	rainwater & springs
Annual rainfall per capita (m³/person/yr)	2,890	2,901	7,232	6,132
Use rate index (%)				
Surface water	10.1	6.2	–	–
Groundwater	54.7	16.1	–	–
Total	22.3	3.9	2.1	2.2
Leakage rate (%)	12	21	19.3	49
Per capita consumption (liters/person/yr)	618	307	407	286

SOURCE: Adapted from Nobuya Miwa, "Water Resources Conservation of Saipan, CNMI," *Journal of the Society of Tropical Resources Technologists,* 7, no. 1 (1991).

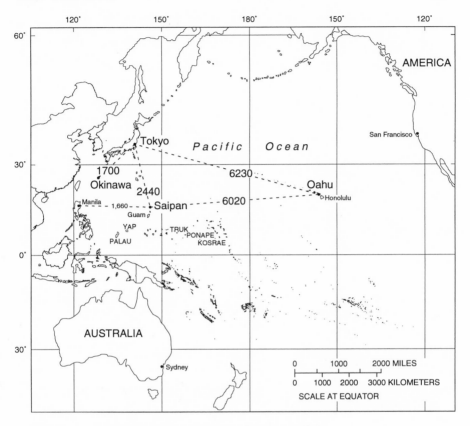

FIGURE 5.1 Location of the Islands: Okinawa, Saipan, and Oahu

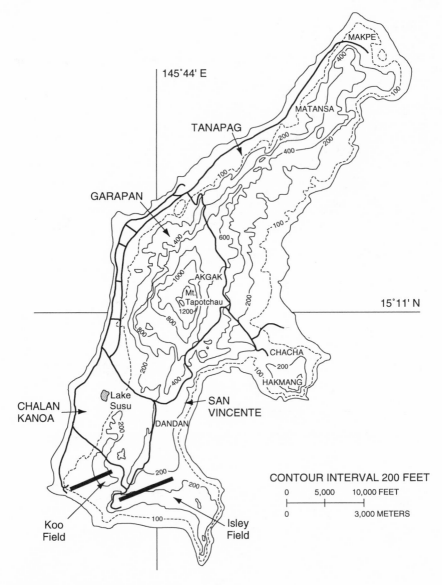

FIGURE 5.2   Map of Saipan Island

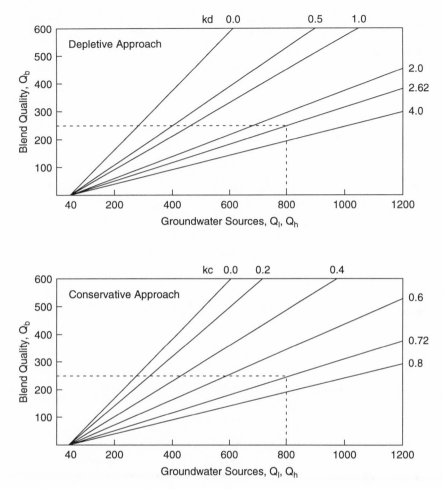

FIGURE 5.3   Waterworks Expansion Requirements

TABLE 5.2 Alternative Future Scenarios

	Present 0 (baseline)	Future 1 (depletive)	Future 2 (conservative)
Population (1,000)	40	double	zero growth
Per capita consumption (gpd)	75[a]	93.75[b]	93.75[b]
Q_l (ppm)	800	800	800
Q_h (ppm)	40	40	40
Total consumption of CUC water (mgd)	3[c]	7.5[d]	3.75[e]
Leakage (%)	50	25	25
Total intake $X_b = X_l + X_h$ (mgd)	–	10	5
X_l (mgd)	6	6	1
X_h (mgd)	–	4	4
Blend quality, Q_b (ppm)	–	496[f]	192[g]

Computations:
[a] 6 mgd * 0.5/40,000 = 75 gpd.
[b] 75gpd * 1.25 = 93.75gpd.
[c] 6mgd * 0.5 = 3mgd.
[d] 93.75 * (40,000) * 2 = 7.5mgd
[e] 93.75 * (40,000) = 3.75mgd
[f] [(6mgd * 800ppm) + (4mgd * 40ppm)]/(6mgd + 4mgd) = 496ppm
[g] [(1mgd * 800ppm) + (4mgd * 40ppm)]/(1mgd + 4mgd) = 192ppm

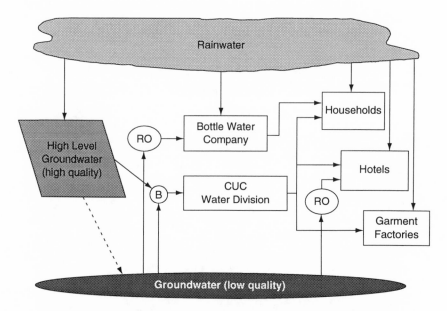

Baseline 0. Present situation (B = business) (RO = reverse osmosis)

FIGURE 5.4 Present and Alternative Future Water-Management Scenarios (*continues*)

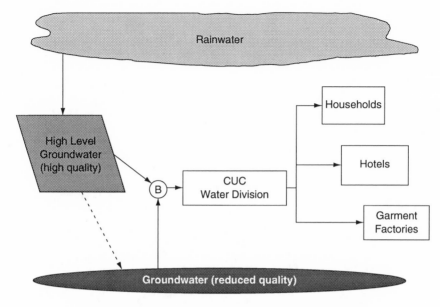

Future Alternative 1. Centralized urban system (depletive)

FIGURE 5.4 (*continued*)

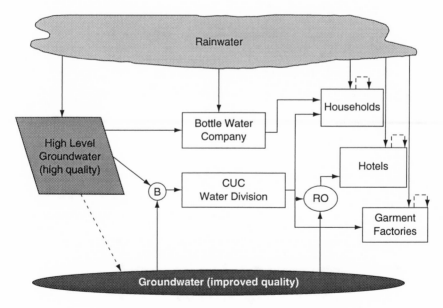

Future Alternative 2. Diversified system (conservative)

FIGURE 5.4 (*continued*)

6

The Role of Agriculture in
Small Island Economies: Hawaii

From time to time in the past, the long-term role of agriculture in the Hawaiian economy has been a subject of analytical interest to economists.[1] In these and other studies, the record of historical changes in the agricultural economy of Hawaii has been analyzed in terms of agriculture's share of total employment, production, and income in the overall economy. The dramatic quantitative and qualitative changes that were experienced in the past have not only continued to the present but are expected to extend into the future.

To understand the historical process of agricultural transformation in a growing and open economy, a macroeconomic development approach is necessary. A wealth of literature has accumulated in this field since the classic works of Simon Kuznets[2], Arthur Lewis[3], and Theodore Schultz[4]. With the aid of this literature, I will examine the major underlying factors and their dynamic interactions that have contributed to the agricultural transformation in Hawaii.

In this chapter, I review and analyze the historical record of agricultural change in Hawaii, focusing on employment, income, product cycles, external trade, and natural resources. I draw upon various documented accounts and statistical sources that sometimes overlap in their periods of coverage. Since the methods and definitions in historical records change with the needs and techniques of the times, it is not always practical to construct continuous data series for econometric modeling. Therefore, in addition to the accepted theoretical wisdom on economic development and growth, relevant practical approaches and experiences are relied on to come up with straightforward economic evaluations and interpretations of the available data on Hawaii. In this manner, I attempt to piece together the essential components of agricultural transformation in the Hawaiian economy and to develop some important analytical concepts and policy implications for the future.

Employment

Structural changes in employment are most closely related to population growth, which has been recorded in official U.S. censuses since 1900, when

Hawaii was annexed as a territory of the United States. As a result of these official censuses, labor force figures by industrial origin are also available going back to that date. Although the statistical precision and continuity of this long-term series are not necessarily perfect, the data are still considered to be sufficiently reliable for describing the changing employment structure of the Hawaiian economy.

Only a rough employment pattern is discernible from the scattered records kept prior to 1900. When Captain Cook first made contact with the Hawaiian Islands in 1778, the population of the islands was estimated to be around 300,000. About a century later, in 1872, the population had declined to its lowest number of 56,900, of which "agriculturists" (apparently excluding much of the indigenous subsistence agriculture) were estimated at 9,670.[5] The population began to increase in 1878 with the stepped-up importation of immigrant labor for the sugarcane plantations. By 1900 it had reached 154,000. At that time, when employment data by industry began to be systematically recorded, Hawaii was still predominantly an agricultural society (Table 6.1).[6] Over 60 percent of the labor force in 1900 was engaged in the primary industries, of which sugarcane was by far the most important. A large portion of the nonprimary industries, such as the processing of sugar and the merchandising of farm products, was also directly related to agriculture.

In absolute numbers, the primary sector continued to maintain its employment level for several decades; its growing labor force even increased significantly in the watershed census year of 1930. But with the rapid expansion of the general economy and the subsequent Great Depression of the 1930s, employment in the primary sector steadily lost ground. Particularly in the wartime and recovery decade of 1940–1950, the sector lost its largest number of workers ever, and the precipitous decline continued during the subsequent postwar decades.

In relative terms, the primary sector's share of total employment steadily declined from an initial high of over 62 percent in 1900 to less than 8 percent in 1960. This was indeed a remarkable transformation of the Hawaiian primary sector (compare, for example, the classic case of Japan, where the decline was from 66 percent to 32 percent over the same period).[7] The six decades essentially cover Hawaii's period of territorial status. As we shall see later, the percentage fell even further, to around 3 percent, in the succeeding statehood decades.

A number of external factors such as reductions in immigrant labor, increases in federal government expenditures, expansion of the visitor industry, and stiffer international competition in the sugar and pineapple markets contributed to this dramatic decline of the Hawaiian primary sector.

During the early expansion period of sugarcane, the increasing requirements for plantation labor were met by successive importations of cheap immigrant labor, mostly but not exclusively from highly populated Asian countries.[8] This seemingly unlimited source of immigrant labor was an important factor in keeping agricultural wages at a low level.

Data on different types of agricultural wages over different periods are available in scattered sources. From 1900 to 1915 the average daily cash earnings of sugar plantation fieldworkers increased only $.005, from $.735 to $.740.[9] In addition, a system of work incentives including bonuses was designed to increase labor productivity. But even with these bonuses, another source covering a later period shows a relative decline in the average daily earnings of plantation laborers from 1924 to 1934 (Table 6.2).

This early expansion phase of Hawaiian agriculture can be explained by the Lewis model[10] of economic growth under an unlimited supply of labor. Figure 6.1 depicts the supply of and demand for labor in Hawaiian sugarcane plantations on the horizontal axis and the wage rate and marginal product of labor on the vertical axis. As noted, Figure 6.1 is based on data and formulas given in Table 6.3. During the period of high numbers of immigrant laborers working for the prevailing low wages, a highly elastic supply curve for labor kept these low rates from rising. This was prior to the 1920s when immigration laws were relatively liberal and labor unions were not yet formally organized to confront management. Production and employment in the sugar industry steadily expanded as management reinvested its surplus profits and shifted the marginal product of labor curves upward, thereby entering the capital-accumulation spiral of more profits and reinvestments. The upward shifts in the marginal product of labor curves reflect technological innovations that in turn led to increased labor productivities.

In essence, during the early expansion phase of agriculture, the highly elastic supply curve for labor enabled the capitalist sector to absorb the entire gains of labor productivity, which became the main financial source for reinvestments in agriculture and also for new investments in the nonagricultural sectors. The depicted expansion path could continue at the low-wage level as long as labor was available at the existing wage rates and favorable market conditions prevailed for sugar. But as Figure 6.1 shows, this was not the case; real wages took a strong turn upward sometime before the 1930s. The process of agricultural expansion in Hawaii became bogged down by several external factors, as mentioned earlier.

The reduction in immigrant labor was an important factor. In the Lewis model, the source of unlimited supply of labor is found in the domestic agrarian sector, which harbors a large reservoir of "disguised unemployment" or "concealed savings"[11] that could be tapped for industrial development. Japan's successful transformation from a traditional agrarian society to a highly industrialized economy is considered to be a typical case of the Lewis model.[12] In the case of Hawaii, however, the main source of labor supply was foreign immigrants whose availability was highly vulnerable to the international and domestic political conditions affecting U.S. immigration laws. This was clearly evident in the 1924 U.S. Immigration Act. This act, which barred further immigration from Japan, was an important factor in the reduced growth rate of the labor force. The average annual growth rate of the total labor force declined from 2.37 percent during the early 1900–1930 expansion period to 1.81 percent in the later 1940–1960 period.

The reduced growth rate of the labor supply, coupled with increased rates of federal defense and visitor expenditures, inevitably led to pushing up the general wage rates for all workers and thereby created relative labor shortages for agriculture. Figure 6.2 shows that over the period 1939–1951 the average annual earnings of civilian employees (excluding federal government workers) tripled while the numbers employed remained fairly constant. Furthermore, the active unionization of agricultural workers under the 1945 Hawaii Employment Relations Act became an important factor in increasing wage rates.[13]

Another important factor was the increased external demand for local productive resources in the form of federal defense and, later, visitor expenditures. Total defense expenditures for 1936 to 1960 amounted to $4.677 billion, which exceeded the total value of combined sales from both the sugar and pineapple industries over the same period.[14] Tourism, which attained the same status as the sugar industry in 1960 in terms of income earnings, was also responsible for the early transformation of the Hawaiian agricultural sector.

These external factors also contributed toward qualitative changes in Hawaiian agriculture. The rising wage rates and increases in federal and visitor expenditures meant higher incomes through diversification of the economy and the multiplier effects of interindustry transactions, which further induced consumer spending. Expected incomes from the increasing urban competition for land were capitalized into higher land values, which also meant higher opportunity costs of agricultural lands. These cost influences, compounded by increasing international competition in the product markets for sugar and pineapple, contributed greatly to the modernization of plantation agriculture in Hawaii into highly capital-intensive production systems. This can be seen in the sugar industry, where the average annual growth rate of real capital per worker increased from 1.1 percent in the 1900–1930 period to 5.3 percent in the 1930–1961 period (Table 6.4).[15] A similar change was experienced by the pineapple industry.

Also, the diverse job and educational opportunities created by these external sources of income accelerated the upward pressure to provide white-collar jobs and jobs requiring technical skills for second- and third-generation workers of immigrant parents. This trend was already evident in the early part of the twentieth century.[16]

An updated and more detailed picture of Hawaii's employment trend by industry for the 1940–1980 period is presented in Table 6.5. As noted, although the pre- and post-1970 data are not directly comparable, we can still trace the relative importance of agricultural employment in the economy. The number of agricultural workers and their relative share of total employment in the economy was roughly halved in each succeeding decade from 1940 to 1970. The relative share of the manufacturing sector also declined steadily after 1950, indicating its close relationship with the agricultural sector. Employment in trade, services, and government all increased sharply during the period.

An indication of the dynamic pattern of employment creation can be obtained from Figure 6.3, which gives changes in employment by industrial sectors from 1940 to 1980. Three sectors—government, trade, and services—were the major sources of new jobs; agriculture steadily lost its employment strength. It should be noted, however, that the rate of decrease in agricultural employment diminished over time. In the 1980s, agricultural employment decreased by only 1,000 as compared with larger decreases in the manufacturing (3,000) and construction (2,000) sectors. If this trend continues, agriculture may well turn into a net-employment-creating sector.

Table 6.6 presents a more-detailed picture of agricultural employment over this period from 1940 to 1982. Although the numbers of sugar and pineapple fieldworkers steadily declined, the rates of decline slowed down in later years. But most significant, in the most recent 1980–1982 period, an increase in jobs in diversified agriculture more than offset the combined decrease in jobs in the sugar and pineapple plantations.

If we view agriculture as an "agro-food industry," including food processing with local agricultural inputs, the industry's role and perspective as an important source of employment as well as a food-supplying sector becomes even more positive. The addition of a food-processing subsector to the farm subsector more than doubles the employment figures (Table 6.7).

The present overall situation of employment in Hawaiian agriculture is that the long-term decline in the number of agricultural workers seems to be finally stabilizing and the prospects for a positive turning point led by growth in diversified agricultural activities appear to be brighter than at any other time in postwar history.

Income

Statistics on wage and salary earnings can be found as early as 1825, and time-series data on family income go back to 1900.[17] Statistics on aggregate income by sectors are available in two publications. One is *Income of Hawaii;* Charles Schwartz[18] estimates aggregate income in two-year intervals over the period 1940–1952 for the Office of Business Economics of the U.S. Department of Commerce. This series has been updated by the same agency. The other is *Hawaii's Income and Expenditure Accounts:1958–1980,* compiled by the Hawaii Department of Planning and Economic Development (DPED).[19] Unfortunately, neither publication breaks down gross state product or personal income by industrial origin. They do, however, give wage and salary incomes by

industry origin, and so I shall use these figures to evaluate the relative importance of agriculture in the total income stream.

The Schwartz data, presented in Table 6.8, show the same tendency toward
relative decline, as in the case of employment. The share of agricultural wage
and salary incomes in total income nearly halved from 1940 to 1952. Although
in absolute terms agricultural income doubled in the decade after the onset of
World War II, the incomes from other sources, particularly government, far
overshadowed the relative importance of the industry.

In terms of income per worker, the trends reflect changes in both aggregate
income and employment. From 1940 to 1952, the agricultural per worker income grew by 284 percent, the highest increase of all the industries in Hawaii.
The nonagricultural sectors recorded significantly lower growth rates.[20] In effect, the relative productivity of labor in agriculture, in terms of nominal income, greatly increased because of the reduced number of workers in the sector
and because of the introduction of new labor-saving production technology, as
mentioned earlier. As a result, despite the continuous relative decline of agriculture in the Hawaiian economy, the relative per worker income of the industry
improved significantly, from 70 percent of the average per worker income of all
industries in 1939 to 83 percent in 1952.

To continue our analysis, we must skip over six years to the period covered
by the DPED study, 1958–1980. Table 6.9 shows the sources of personal income
estimated by the DPED for this later period. Farm income in this study includes
wages, salaries, and proprietors' incomes. Although this aggregate more than
tripled from 1958 to 1980, its relative importance in the total personal income
stream steadily declined from 5.5 percent in the statehood year of 1959 to only
2.2 percent in 1980. This is nearly the same position as the sector's employment
and much smaller than all other sources of income except personal rental income. Also, more than 70 percent of total personal income was generated
through nonfarm income sources, and incomes from interest, dividends,
and particularly transfer payments increased substantially over this 1958–1980
period.

Table 6.10 shows that the overall growth rate of agricultural income during
1960–1980 was less than half of that for the nonagricultural sector. However,
due mainly to the steady decrease in agricultural employment coupled with the
substantial increase in agricultural productivity, the per capita income of agricultural workers increased at about the same rate as that of nonagricultural
workers. Thus, the relative income per agricultural worker remained fairly constant during the period.

We can express this relationship in the following simple equation.

$$(Ya/Na) = alpha(Yn/Nn), \tag{1}$$

where Y   = income
       N   = employment
       a   = agriculture
       n   = nonagriculture
       alpha = parameter (about 0.85)

From equation (1), agricultural employment can be derived as follows.

$$Na = (Ya/Yn) \times (Nn/alpha) \tag{2}$$

Thus, in order to increase or sustain agricultural employment, at least one of the following must happen: (1) the relative income of agriculture (Ya/Yn) must be improved through productive investments or (2) there must be an increase in the supply of nonagricultural employment (Nn), which will lessen the relative income per worker of the nonagricultural sector given Ya/Yn.

The per capita wage and salary incomes of the trade and services sectors, which have been the most dynamic sectors, were about 9.4 percent lower than that of agriculture in 1980. These sectors have expanded in response to the boom in the visitor industry. Although the competition for labor between tourism and agriculture has been heavily in favor of tourism, this competition has apparently been more than offset by complementarities that have operated through both the secondary and tertiary sectors of the state economy.

Product Cycles

In early Hawaii, native planters cultivated a variety of crops such as taro, sweet potatoes, breadfruit, yams, coconuts, gourds, arrowroot, bananas, and sugarcane. Livestock included pigs, short-legged dogs, and chickens. Fish, seaweed, and other products from the sea were regularly harvested for community use. The various needs of the differently endowed communities were met through well-developed markets where the primary means of exchange was bartering.[21]

In time, subsistence agriculture and bartering gradually gave way to such cash crops as silk, cotton, coffee, rice, sugar, kukui oil, tobacco, bananas, honey, and pulu (a mossy filler for mattresses and pillows). But it was the introduction of the first sugarcane plantation in 1835 that served as the "entering wedge" for "the making of plantation Hawaii," the so-called sugar kingdom.[22] In the process of greater integration into the export market, a number of subsistence as well as early cash crops disappeared from the Hawaiian agricultural scene. Later, new export crops such as pineapples, macadamia nuts, papayas, and floral crops emerged.

These historical observations of changing crops suggest the existence of product cycles, first investigated by Kuznets and later elaborated on by Raymond Vernon and S. Hirsch.[23] Variations of product cycles involve specialty crops for export only, crops initially grown for domestic consumption and later for export, and the transfer of the underlying technology and the product cycle itself to foreign countries. We need not go too far into the technical details of the analytical approach to illustrate the essential aspects of product cycles.

Kuznets found that for each of thirty-five industrial products investigated, the growth pattern of sales over time typically conformed to the curve depicted in Figure 6.4. When successful new products are introduced into the market, sales rise, but the total volume remains relatively modest. This is the early (new) phase. The growth rate increases sharply in the beginning of the main growth phase and then slows down in the latter part. In the mature phase, the sales curve levels off and may either continue on a plateau or decline, depending on whether the product is replaced or continues to be bought. The characteristics of each phase in terms of technology, capital intensity, industry structure, critical human inputs, and demand structure are summarized by Hirsch at the bottom of Figure 6.4.[24]

Although product cycles have been mainly tested for manufactured products elsewhere, their applicability to the major categories of Hawaiian agricultural products is evidenced in the patterns shown in Figure 6.5. The rice industry, which went through its early- and high-growth phases in the 1800s, was already in its final mature phase at the turn of the century. After reaching its peak around 1910, it rapidly gave way to the sugarcane industry.

Sugarcane's cycle, which still continues, has now lasted about 150 years. Its early phase began with the systematic introduction of plantations after 1835 and included a number of minor booms. This first phase is not shown in Figure 6.5. By the turn of the century, sugar was already in its main growth phase. This second phase probably began around the time of the Reciprocity Treaty of 1875, which provided for duty-free sugar imports into the United States from the kingdom of Hawaii. Figure 6.5 shows the rapid increase in production over the first seven decades of this century, with periodic interruptions for such events as strikes and World War II. The postwar modernization of the industry was necessary to continue the increase in yields as the industry approached its present mature phase.

All three phases of the pineapple crop can be seen in the twentieth century. The plantation crop was introduced in the early part of the century, and after a relatively short early phase, it expanded in its growth phase at a faster rate than sugarcane. It also recovered more strongly than sugarcane after the World War II interruption. Similar resource and market conditions affected these two plantation-style industries and forced them into postwar modernizations and their present mature phases.

Prominent crops of diversified agriculture today are flowers and nursery products, macadamia nuts, and papayas. After going through relatively long early phases, these crops emerged as promising industries after the war. Their growth momentums picked up in the 1960s after statehood and the boom in the visitor industry. These crops still continue in their growth phase.

Table 6.11 presents the postwar record of the major agricultural products in terms of quantities marketed. In contrast to the mature-stage crops—sugarcane, pineapple, coffee, and taro—such crops as vegetables, fruits (excluding pineapples), and macadamia nuts grew rapidly. The development of livestock products presents a mixed picture. Milk, eggs, and broilers and chickens for other uses grew steadily; beef and pork showed considerable fluctuations. Honey recovered in 1970–1980 after two decades of slump but still remains relatively minor in the overall picture.

Although these product cycles require more careful study to detail their characteristics and phase boundaries, we can still derive some general implications from the previous observations. Product cycles emerge and develop in a constantly changing world where the economics of time is of paramount importance. This means that we cannot abstract from the difficulties presented by the uncertainties of change, particularly changes in external economic forces that are beyond the control of agricultural interests in the state. In an open and vulnerable economy such as Hawaii, the maintenance of a broad and diverse agricultural base is a rational strategy that contributes to both stability and flexibility, two important criteria for economic survival. Stability is desirable to secure investment, and flexibility is necessary to adapt to changes in technology, preferences, and institutions.

The emergence and demise of product cycles are directly related to such unpredictable changes, and the readiness for quick and positive adjustments requires reallocation of resources to foster new products with potentially high growth rates and early payoffs. Since the gestation periods for new product cycles are typically long and measured in decades, a range of new product alternatives is necessary for timely substitution of products in their late leveling off or declining stages. This means that an active and forward-looking program of research and development must be continually supported through the combined initiatives of the public and private sectors in order to develop new products, production techniques, and marketing strategies.[25] This is essential for a continuous and diverse flow of product cycles over time.

External Trade

Historical Perspective

Hawaii's history of foreign trade began in the 1780s, when trading ships first visited Hawaii and Kamehameha I was rising to power.[26] Among the earliest traded goods were such products as skins, wool, and sandalwood. Sandalwood, which was exported to China from 1815 to 1830, was the most important source of income for the Hawaiian kingdom, which held a royal monopoly on the product.

After the exhaustion of the sandalwood forests, the first sugar mill was set up in 1837,[27] and sugar in time became the dominant, nearly the all-important, export commodity. Published customs records on individual commodities trade are not available until the year 1885, when sugar was already accounting for 93 percent of total exports. Sugar production and export were accelerated through the land reform of 1848 and the Reciprocity Treaty of 1876, which permitted U.S. and Hawaiian products to be exchanged free of duty.[28] Along with sugar, sheepskins and wool products were listed as Hawaii's principal export items in 1885.[29]

As can be seen from Table 6.12, pineapple was also emerging as an important export commodity around the beginning of this century. Its export sales grew rapidly to account for 44 percent of Hawaii's total exports by 1940. Sugar and pineapple accounted for almost 95 percent of export sales in 1950 but declined to less than 88 percent by 1970. Although the export shares of the two commodities have declined in recent years, they still remain the two most important agricultural crops in Hawaii. They have had to face stiff international competition in recent years, but their relative decline is also in part due to a sharp increase in the volume of petroleum products, which are largely in the nature of re-exports. Also, exports of diversified agricultural crops such as flowers and nursery products, macadamia nuts, and papayas have grown rapidly in recent years.

Balance of Payments

The commodity trade balances presented in the last column of Table 6.12 are in large part a reflection of Hawaii's economic activities since 1875. Prior to that, from 1843 to 1868, when whaling in the Pacific was at its peak, Hawaii's commodity trade balance was continuously in deficit.[30] The exports of services, including labor for whaling vessels, paid for the growing deficits.

The commodity trade balance turned favorable in 1869 and continued with surpluses, except for a few minor deficit years, until 1936. Persistent deficits returned after that. In view of the growing commodity trade deficits of the postwar years, it is difficult to appreciate the fact that the Hawaiian economy enjoyed favorable trade balances for two-thirds of a century. Sugar and pineapple exports were the main contributing factors to trade prosperity.

The trade surpluses were accumulated and used to expand the export sector and to diversify the economic base. The succeeding development of the tourist industry was largely made possible through the early capital funds generated from agricultural exports. The early Matson Navigation hotels, which formed the base of the tourism industry up to the 1960s, were controlled by interlocking directorships from the so-called Big Five corporations (American Factors,

Castle & Cooke, Alexander and Baldwin, C. Brewer, and Theo H. Davis), which capitalized on agricultural development in the islands.

Table 6.13 shows the external transactions of the Hawaiian economy from 1958 to 1980. Although foreign and mainland investments have become increasingly important components of Hawaii's external transactions, the data on these capital accounts are not readily available. A striking characteristic of Hawaii's balance of payments is its growing deficits in merchandise trade, which have been offset by tourism and military expenditures, the latter included in transfer payments. In 1958, 55 percent of imports were offset by merchandise exports, but this proportion fell dramatically to a mere 23 percent in 1980.

External sources of income such as commodity exports and receipts from tourism and national defense increased sharply, from 29.6 percent of the gross state product in 1959 to 40.1 percent in 1980. This increase in external dependency has long been a matter of policy concern in Hawaii because of its insular geographic position and limited natural resources to ensure a safe minimum level of food security and self-sufficiency in times of emergency. The vagaries of external changes, which have affected the product cycles outlined in Figure 6.6, including tourism, subject the Hawaiian economy to increasing uncertainties. Income from tourism, for example, has shown a tendency of slowing down after nearly thirty years of vigorous growth. If tourism follows the same cyclical pattern as the previous external sources of income, Hawaii has to prepare for alternative sources of income from its primary sector.

Thus, strategies to make allowances for these increasing uncertainties are critically important for the revitalization of agriculture, including its related processing and purchasing sectors. Traditionally, such strategies have involved discounting costs and revenues in project planning, diversifying of investment portfolios, spreading the risks of crop losses through insurance schemes, and shifting the risks of price fluctuations to professional speculators in commodity markets. The essential principles of these and other strategies can be adapted to the needs and specific conditions of Hawaiian agriculture.

A new perspective is needed to look at modern agriculture as a promising source of income and employment. Schultz[31] once pointed out that agriculture should be looked at as a potential growth sector, not as a doomed declining industry, as has often been implied by some growth theorists. This is true for Hawaiian agriculture as well as for agriculture in developing economies.

Sectoral Balance and Self-Sufficiency

Table 6.14 shows the available data on both exports and imports of agricultural products in Hawaii from 1970 to 1980. Although sugar and pineapple still dominate on the export side, other products such as canned tuna, flowers, papayas, and macadamia nuts increased significantly during the period. At the same time, food imports, which presently account for about 15 percent to 16 percent of total imports, increased more rapidly than food exports. In particular, importations of processed foods and feeds increased threefold over the first eight years of record. As a result, the difference between exports and imports became negative in 1976. From a sectoral perspective, Hawaii's agricultural sector cannot now cover the costs of agricultural imports. In a basic sense, what this suggests is that the imputed value of Hawaii's agricultural resources is not sufficient to meet the demands for agricultural products in the state. We need to examine the situation closer.

From the data in Table 6.14, we can compute a sectoral self-sufficiency rate for Hawaii based on the following concept.

$$Y = \text{total agricultural production}$$
$$M = \text{total agricultural imports}$$
$$C = \text{total agricultural consumption}$$
$$X = \text{total agricultural exports}$$

If we assume zero inventory, sectoral balance is achieved when total supply is equal to total demand,

$$Y + M = C + X, \tag{3}$$

from which a sectoral self-sufficiency rate can be defined and derived as follows.

$$Y/C = 1 - (M - X)/C \tag{4}$$

If agricultural trade is in balance ($M = X$), the self-sufficiency rate is equal to 1.0.

Since the data for Y are not available, I use the right-hand side of equation (4) to compute the self-sufficiency rate. If one is interested in knowing Y, this can be obtained indirectly from equation (3), $Y = C - M + X$, where the quantity $(C - M)$, as it turns out, is the domestically produced and consumed agricultural products.

The interpretation of this concept of sectoral self-sufficiency is in terms of the economic capacity of the agricultural resource base to satisfy the total demands of the domestic population, whether through direct production for domestic consumption or through imports whose costs are offset by revenues from agricultural exports. In other words, from a sectoral standpoint, Hawaii's comparative advantage for exports should offset the cost of imports, for which the comparative advantage lies elsewhere.

From *Hawaii's Income and Expenditure Accounts: 1958–1980,*[32] the sectoral self-sufficiency rates are computed and presented at the bottom of Table 6.14. These computed rates, which correspond to the excess domestic supply, peaked in 1974 at 138 percent and then declined to about 90 percent in more recent years. In 1978, the Hawaii State Constitutional Convention addressed the problem and called on the state to conserve and protect agricultural lands, promote diversified agriculture, increase agricultural self-sufficiency, and ensure the availability of agriculturally suitable lands.[33] As a result, one of the primary objectives in the Hawaii State Plan is the continued growth and development of diversified agriculture throughout the state. Also, the governor's message in *Statistics of Hawaiian Agriculture, 1982*[34] reiterated the policy of promoting diversified agriculture with a view toward increasing self-sufficiency in producing food and in developing a wider variety of export crops. Unless the programs adopted under this policy can offset the underlying trends, we will probably continue to see declining self-sufficiency rates. This is particularly true because food imports are expected to increase with growth in population and income and with uncertainty in agricultural exports, as can be seen in the wide annual fluctuations in Table 6.14.

This concept of sectoral self-sufficiency might be challenged from two fronts. One is the neoclassical macroeconomic standpoint, which argues that as long as the food-import bill is being met through revenues from other advantageous economic activities such as tourism, sales of services to military bases, and even through foreign investments, we need not be overly concerned with sectoral balance. The rapid structural transformation of the Hawaiian economy from primary agriculture to tertiary service-oriented industries suggests that policymakers have not rejected this line of reasoning.

The major flaw of this argument is the total disregard for the potentially irreversible nature of agricultural resources and food security. Figure 6.7 shows that agriculture's relative share of resources, measured in terms of employment, declined sharply, from 62.1 percent in 1900 to 2.5 percent in 1980, in response to the preferential changes for the resources from D_1 to D_2.

The share of other resources such as land, water, and capital together with institutional arrangements have also shifted in the same direction, although not to the same extent as labor. This predominantly one-way reallocation of natural resources from agriculture to nonagricultural uses presents a problem for the neoclassical assumption of "malleability" (i.e., the smooth reallocation in all directions of highly divisible resources).

Reverse malleability, that is, resource shifts from nonagriculture to agriculture, is not easily accomplished. Because of alterations in natural resources and the particular requirements of agriculture, reverse malleability seldom occurs, and when it does, it occurs only after long and costly delays, during which time many of the initial economic advantages are lost.

Another criticism of the self-sufficiency concept presented here might come from those who tend to think of it in terms of individual food products. They may argue that the sectoral concept of self-sufficiency is tantamount to saying that in the extreme case, sugarcane cultivation alone will be good enough as long as its export earnings are sufficient to pay for the economy's food imports. But this is not the intent here. In Hawaii, because of its relative geographic isolation, limited resources, and distance from external markets, self-sufficiency in the context of food security is a real concern. Although complete self-sufficiency in all or most of the important food products is an impractical and unrealistic goal, the possibility of restoring and maintaining sectoral balance through diversification of the agricultural base is not only highly practical but also well within reach.

This sectoral-balance concept provides a more rational and realistic approach to the agricultural problems of Hawaii. Depending largely upon the state's agricultural policies, the concept can lead to more competitive diversification in agricultural products instead of monocultural specialization.

Utilization of Natural Resources

This empirical overview has thus far focused on the changing patterns of agricultural employment, income product cycles, and external trade in the context of the overall development and growth of the Hawaiian economy. The results suggest an important turning point in the structure of Hawaiian agriculture sometime around the World War II years and thereafter, when traditional labor-intensive plantation agriculture began its rapid transformation toward more capital-intensive modern agriculture. Around that time agriculture's share of the total labor force fell below its corresponding share of the gross state product. Increased purchases from and sales to the nonagricultural sectors significantly contributed to the diversification and further growth of the general economy. Not only the large sugar and pineapple plantations but also diversified agriculture have continued to modernize into more capital-intensive operating systems. Thus, in spite of the relative decline in agriculture's contribution to the growth of the general economy, agriculture has continued to grow and compete for the scarce natural resources of the state.

The natural resource base for agriculture consists mainly of renewable soil, water, and energy resources, which sustain production over time. The flow of primary energy from the sun is, for all practical purposes, nondepletable and therefore not subject to concerns regarding the scarcity of soil and water resources. The renewability of soil and water resources, however, is affected by human use, and not only are these resources depletable, but if their depletion is allowed to continue unchecked, important portions of their potentially permanent flow can be irreversibly lost from the natural resource base of the state.

Irrigated agriculture most reflects the combined use of soil and water for agricultural production. Therefore, a convenient and relevant way to gain historical perspective of the use and sustainability of these two interrelated renewable resources for agriculture is to analytically review the empirical record of irrigated agriculture in the state. There have been significant changes in this subsector over time, but little has been done thus far to systematically study these changes from an economic standpoint.

Reliable long-term records on irrigated acreages in Hawaii are available only for sugarcane, which is estimated to utilize 70–75 percent of the total irrigated croplands. Periodic estimates of total irrigated acreages are reported in the U.S. Department of Agriculture's *National Resources Inventory, Conservation Needs Inventory: Hawaii,* and *Hawaii Soil and Conservation Needs Inventory.*[35] There is, however, considerable variation in estimates between these two sources because of differences in definitions and methods. In spite of these differences, however, we can still extract an overall perspective of the situation.

A crude estimate based on data from the 1978 *Census of Agriculture* indicates that about 63 percent of the total value of agricultural products in the state was from irrigated agriculture. Unfortunately, this is the only year for which data to compute such a proportion were reported. However, since the percentage is in terms of total value of agricultural product, the estimate must be regarded as conservative if we are concerned with cropland production only.

To gain a better perspective, we need to look at acreage figures. Estimates of irrigated cropland acreages in Hawaii are reported in the three inventories cited previously. Although these are rough estimates and are intended to be aggregated with similar estimates from other states for national policy purposes, the patterns and trends for Hawaii as shown in Figure 6.8 are quite revealing. There has been a substantial increase in the proportion of croplands irrigated in the state from about 42 percent in 1958 to 65 percent in 1982, and this increase occurred during a period when agriculture's shares of state gross product and of employment were both on a general decline.

Also, there is strong empirical evidence that more quality land came under irrigation during the twenty-five-year period and that the limited supply of high-quality land resulted in the extension of irrigation onto lower-quality land over the 1967–1982 period. This can be clearly seen in Figure 6.8 by the differential shifts over time in the distributions of irrigated crop acreages in favor of land capable of higher productivity. In the earlier 1958–1967 period, irrigation moved strongly into the highest-quality Class I land and to a lesser extent into Class II land. Evidently, the increased irrigation of this higher-quality land substituted for irrigation of the lower-quality land. However, in the later 1967–1982 period, as the availability of Class I and II land became increasingly scarce, the conversion rates of lower-quality land to irrigation increased. There is little Class I land left to be converted, and the availability of Class II land is also diminishing rapidly.

Underlying these shifts is a recent trend toward drip irrigation, which is of great significance in terms of the productive capacity of the natural land and water resources of the state and in sustaining growth in the agricultural sector. The initial efforts to adopt the practice of drip irrigation began in the mid-1960s with experimental tests on sugarcane culture.[36] The subsequent proliferation of this highly efficient method extended not only into croplands for sugarcane but also into those for pineapple, macadamia nuts, papaya, protea, and a variety of other diversified greenhouse and nursery crops.

Drip irrigation leads to capital-intensive cultural practices that favor the increased use of complementary inputs such as chemical fertilizers, pesticides, and equipment that are particularly adaptable to high-yielding crop varieties. Management and labor skills must also be adjusted to operate this more modern capital-intensive system.

The expected impacts on the land and water resources of agriculture are as follows. With respect to land, capital-intensive inputs substitute for land and shift cultivation practices toward soils with higher productivity potentials. This intensifies the agricultural demand for prime irrigable lands. The increased productivity of these prime irrigable lands also raises the economic value of irrigation water and increases its use beyond any initial water savings due to the improved technical efficiency of the drip-irrigation method. In other words, the initial water savings due to increased technical efficiency is more than offset by the expanded derived demand due to higher economic efficiency.[37]

The increasing competition for scarce land and water resources for agriculture places greater emphasis on the need to better appreciate the significance of irrigation for the continued viability of agriculture and its role in the general economic growth of Hawaii.

Conclusions

Some of the highlights of agricultural development in Hawaii have been reviewed in order to gain insights into the role of agriculture in the dynamic process of economic growth of the islands. In keeping with the current literature on economic development and growth, the review has focused on the long-term structural changes in employment, income, product cycles, external trade, and the use of natural resources.

Over the past 200 years, the early subsistence agricultural economy of Hawaii transformed into a modern mixed-market economy through a succession of structural changes that were spurred by such activities as trading sandalwood and whaling in the early nineteenth century; exporting sugar and pineapple in the long interval overlapping the nineteenth and twentieth centuries; and selling and purchasing services in the defense and visitor-related industries in the more recent period since World War II and into the present statehood years.

The mode of agricultural expansion is most vividly explained by the Lewis model of unlimited supply of labor with data for the 1900 to 1930 period. The agricultural surplus made possible with successive importations of immigrant labor was the primary source of capital savings for financing reinvestments into expanding agriculture and also new investments for the purpose of diversifying the economic base. With the broadening of the economic base and the reallocation of labor to nonagricultural sectors, agriculture's growth in absolute terms was eventually accompanied by a long-term relative decline in its share of total employment and output in the economy. In effect, this long-term relative decline in employment and output reflected agriculture's capacity to provide the necessary capital and labor resources to support the economic growth of the islands.

This capacity of agriculture to support the economic growth of the islands was temporarily constrained by the U.S. Immigration Act of 1924, which restricted the growth of the immigrant labor supply from selected Asian countries. But the adoption of new labor-saving technology in response to the pressures of rising real wages gave early impetus to the eventual transformation of traditional labor-intensive plantation agriculture to more capital-intensive modern agriculture.

This new technology, in effect, also increased the capacity of agriculture to further support the economic growth of the islands. This is evidenced by the fact that agriculture's relative shares of employment and output continued to decline. Particularly sharp declines were experienced during the 1940s and 1950s when the reallocation of labor for the war effort was followed by further technological changes in the face of the emerging power of labor unions. Agriculture's dominant role in the economy began to give way to increased federal defense expenditures and a rising visitor industry.

The combined effects of institutional changes and technological advances in air transportation and communication after statehood in 1959 gave important new impetus to the economic growth of Hawaii. Further increases in federal government expenditures and expansion of the visitor industry on an international scale not only raised incomes but also forced significantly new structural changes in the economy. Agriculture's relative shares of both employment and output fell to below 5 percent. The squeeze on agriculture came from increased competition in both the factor and product markets. The increased competition in the factor markets raised the real costs of agriculture's land, labor, and capital inputs, and this, in conjunction with the increased international competition in export markets, particularly for sugar and pineapple, have combined to reduce the comparative advantage of Hawaiian agriculture.

What is the continued role of agriculture in the economic growth of Hawaii? On the surface, its capacity to support economic growth in the traditional mode appears to be limited, but in a modern and more innovative mode there are definite prospects for further positive contributions.

Despite the long-term relative decline of agriculture in the Hawaiian economy, the per capita income of workers in this sector relative to that of the nonagricultural sectors remained fairly constant, at about 80 percent, over the 1970–1990 period. This has been due mainly to a steady decrease in overall agricultural employment and an increase in productivity. It is important to note here that the growth of diversified agriculture in recent years has more than offset the decrease in employment in the sugar and pineapple plantations. New products are important to the revitalization of the agricultural sector and its continued role of making positive contributions to the economy.

It has been shown that the product-cycle approach of Kuznets, Hirsch, and Vernon can be usefully applied to illustrate the long-term cyclical changes in Hawaii's agricultural products. The importance of research and development of new product lines in an intensely competitive market situation cannot be overstressed. The economic survival of agricultural activities in the modern economy has come to depend increasingly on scientific and technological advances in such fields as biotechnology, communications, and transportation. The successful introduction of new agricultural products requires gestation periods measured in terms of decades, and a wide range of alternatives must be on hand for the timely substitution of declining products in the final third stage of the product cycle.

It has also been shown by means of the concept of "sectoral self-sufficiency" that Hawaii's agricultural sector has since the mid-1970s lost its ability to cover the costs of agricultural imports. With some further refinements, the concept offers the potential of developing a more rational and realistic approach to Hawaiian agriculture's adjustment problems. In recent years food security has been a matter of serious concern because of the islands' relative isolation, limited resources, and increasing external dependence.

Finally, we have seen how the use of land and water resources as reflected in irrigated agriculture has shifted toward the prime irrigable lands in the state. Underlying this shift has been an important recent trend toward drip irrigation, which has moved modern Hawaiian agriculture further toward capital-intensive practices. These technological innovations and efficiencies have not necessarily reduced the competition for scarce natural resources. The long-term sustainability of agricultural growth in the Hawaiian economy depends upon maintaining a high potential for expanding irrigated agriculture onto the remaining arable land. This in turn depends upon adjustments in the institutional system that can, at the minimum, safeguard such land and water resources to support economically viable farm-operating systems.

TABLE 6.1   Changes in the Industrial Distribution of the Labor Force, Hawaii, 1900–1960 (in thousands)

	1900	1910	1920	1930	1940	1950	1960
Primary[a]	56.0	55.5	56.2	63.6	54.6	31.8	16.0
	(62.1)	(54.8)	(50.3)	(41.2)	(35.5)	(19.0)	(7.6)
Industries[b]	12.9	20.9	26.1	32.8	35.0	43.8	70.8
	(14.4)	(20.6)	(23.4)	(21.2)	(22.8)	(26.2)	(33.8)
Commerce	6.1	5.6	7.3	10.6	23.9	35.4	46.9
	(6.8)	(5.6)	(6.6)	(6.8)	(15.6)	(21.2)	(22.4)
Services[c]	14.9	14.6	17.1	42.8	38.8	52.6	70.2
	(16.6)	(14.5)	(15.3)	(27.8)	(25.2)	(31.4)	(33.5)
Not allocable[d]	0.2	4.6	5.1	4.5	1.5	3.9	5.5
	(0.2)	(4.5)	(4.5)	(2.9)	(0.9)	(2.4)	(2.6)
Total	90.2	101.2	111.9	154.3	153.8	167.6	209.4
	(100.0)	(100.0)	(100.0)	(100.0)	(100.0)	(100.0)	(100.0)

Note: Figures do not necessarily add to totals due to rounding. Percentages are within parentheses.

[a]Includes agriculture, forestry, and fishing.
[b]Includes mining; contract construction; manufacturing; transportation; communication; electricity, gas, and sanitary services.
[c]Includes various personal services, government workers, and armed forces.
[d]Includes employed persons not classified elsewhere.
SOURCE: Harry T. Oshima and Mitsuo Ono, *Hawaii's Income and Expenditures, 1958, 1959, and 1960,* vol. 1 (Honolulu: Economic Research Center, University of Hawaii, January 1965), pp. 1–5.

TABLE 6.2   Average Daily Earnings with and Without Bonus of Unskilled Male Employees in Hawaii Sugar Plantations, 1924–1938 (dollars)

Year	Short-term Contractors		Day Workers		Long-term Contractors		All Unskilled Male Employees	
	Including Bonus[a]	Without Bonus	Including Bonus	Without Bonus	Including Bonus	Without Bonus	Including Bonus	Without Bonus
1924	2.038	1.652	1.662	1.347	2.110	1.876	1.841	1.517
1925	1.840	1.702	1.472	1.361	2.194	2.113	1.705	1.590
1926	1.837	1.698	1.486	1.373	2.332	2.250	1.737	1.621
1927	1.859	1.711	1.634	1.504	2.268	2.182	1.816	1.687
1928	1.864	1.724	1.499	1.386	2.286	2.205	1.756	1.640
1929	1.842	1.705	1.500	1.388	2.104	2.024	1.716	1.602
1930	1.832	1.697	1.507	1.596	2.146	2.067	1.725	1.612
1931	1.862	1.721	1.519	1.404	2.202	2.120	1.754	1.637
1932	1.626	1.569	1.416	1.367	2.093	2.057	1.603	1.553
1933	1.866	1.323	1.396	1.364	1.909	1.886	1.634	1.600
1934	1.722	1.600	1.514	1.406	1.816	1.740	1.629	1.522
1935	1.790	1.648	1.553	1.430	2.073	1.987	1.699	1.573
1936	2.019	1.766	1.703	1.490	2.233	2.090	1.884	1.663
1937	2.300	2.053	1.822	1.630	2.424	2.247	2.074	1.865
1938	2.400	2.256	1.886	1.772	2.436	2.339	2.134	2.011

[a]The bonus system ended effective September 30, 1938.
SOURCE: James H. Shoemaker, *Labor: In the Territory of Hawaii, 1939* U.S. Department of Labor, Bureau of Labor Statistics, bulletin no. 687 (Washington, D.C., June 1939).

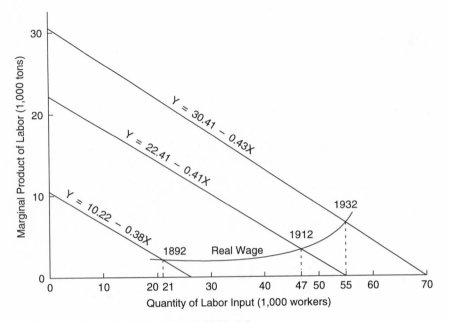

Note: Based on data and formulas given in Table 6.3.

FIGURE 6.1 Expansion of the Hawaiian Sugarcane Industry in Terms of Marginal Products of Labor and Real Wages, 1892–1932
SOURCES: James H. Shoemaker, *Labor: In the Territory of Hawaii, 1939,* U.S. Department of Labor, Bureau of Labor Statistics, bulletin no. 687 (Washington, D.C., June 1939), pp. 12, 33; Robert C. Schmitt, *Historical Statistics of Hawaii* (Honolulu: University of Hawaii Press, 1977), pp. 359–360, 418–419.

TABLE 6.3   Data and Formulas for Computing Real Wages and Marginal Products of Labor in the Hawaii Sugarcane Industry, 1892–1932

Data	1892	1912	1932
Q_t: total raw sugar output (1,000 tons)	131	595	1025
P_t: average price per pound of raw sugar in the New York market in year t ($/lb)	.0332	.0416	.0292
L_t: total labor inputs (1,000 workers)	21	47	52
w_t: average daily earnings of workers in year t ($/day)	.60	.97[a]	1.603
W_t: annual real wage in year t (tons/yr)	2.26	2.91	6.86

Computational formulas:

1. Annual real wages (assuming 250 workdays/year): $W_t = \dfrac{w_t \times 250}{P_t \times 2000}$

2. Marginal product of labor (MPL) lines are computed from the simultaneous solution of the following two equations:

$$W_t = a + bx$$

$$Q_t = \int_0^L t\,(a + bx)\,dx = ax + \frac{b}{2}x^2$$

[a]1915 datum.

DATA SOURCES: For Q and L, James L. Shoemaker, *Labor: In the Territory of Hawaii, 1939,* U.S. Department of Labor, Bureau of Labor Statistics, bulletin no. 687 (Washington, D.C., June 1939), pp. 12, 13, respectively; for P and w, Robert C. Schmitt, *Historical Statistics of Hawaii* (Honolulu: University of Hawaii Press, 1977), pp. 418–419, 359–360, respectively.

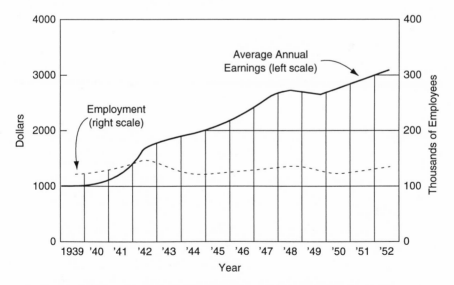

FIGURE 6.2   Trends of Average Annual Earnings and Employment in Hawaii, 1939–1951
SOURCE: Charles F. Schwartz *Income of Hawaii,* a supplement to *Survey of Current Business* (Washington, D.C.: U.S. Department of Commerce, 1953), p.10.

TABLE 6.4   Growth in Output per Worker and in Capital, Hawaii Sugarcane Industry, 1870–1961

| | Levels in Selected Years | | | Growth During Selected Periods | | | |
| | Quantity (1910–14 dollars) | | | Percentage Increase | | Percent Annual Growth | |
Year	Real Capital per Worker	Net Output per Worker	Period	Real Capital per Worker	Net Output per Worker	Real Capital per Worker	Net Output per Worker
1870	535	139	1870–1961	1,244	2,317	2.9	3.5
1900	1,055	341	1870–1900	97	145	2.3	3.0
1930	1,460	612	1900–1930	38	79	1.1	2.0
1940	1,951	857	1930–1961	392	449	5.3	5.7
1950	3,481	1,742	1940–1961	269	292	6.4	6.7
1961	7,190	3,359	1950–1961	107	93	6.9	6.2

SOURCE: J. A. Mollett, "Technological Change in Hawaiian Sugar Production and Its Relationship to Productivity," *Journal of Farm Economics,* 16, no. 1 (June 1964): 93.

TABLE 6.5 Hawaii's Employment Trend by Industry, 1940–1980

	Number (1,000)					Composition (%)				
	1940	1950	1960	1970	1980	1940	1950	1960	1970	1980
Total employment	156	170	228	331	444	100.0	100.0	100.0	100.0	100.0
Agriculture	52	27	14	12	11	33.3	15.9	6.1	3.6	2.5
Nonagriculture	104	143	214	319	433	66.7	84.1	93.9	96.4	97.5
Contract construction	8	9	18	26	24	5.1	5.3	7.9	7.9	5.4
Manufacturing	21	25	26	26	23	13.5	14.7	11.4	7.9	5.2
Transportation, communication, and utilities	7	11	15	24	31	4.5	6.5	6.6	7.3	7.0
Finance, insurance, and real estate	2	3	9	18	33	1.3	1.8	3.9	5.4	7.4
Trade (wholesale & retail merchandising)	18	27	43	69	84	11.5	15.9	18.9	20.8	18.9
Services and miscellaneous	6	15	29	57	98	3.8	8.8	12.7	17.2	22.1
Government	18	33	50	74	89	11.5	19.4	21.9	22.4	20.0
Self-employed and unpaid family workers	24	19	25	25	29	15.4	11.2	11.0	7.6	6.5

Note: Based on job rather than persons. Data for 1970 and later years are not directly comparable to data for earlier years in which workers holding more than one job were counted more than once.

SOURCES: Robert C. Schmitt, *Historical Statistics of Hawaii* (Honolulu: University of Hawaii Press, 1977); Hawaii Department of Planning and Economic Development (DPED), *Hawaii's Income and Expenditure Accounts: 1958–1980* (Honolulu, 1982).

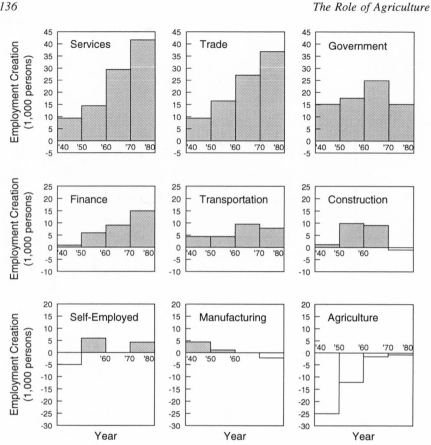

FIGURE 6.3   Net Employment Creation in Hawaii by Industry Sectors, 1940–1980

TABLE 6.6   Employment of Agricultural Fieldworkers by Major Crop Types, 1940–1982

| | *Persons* | | | | | | |
	1940	*1950*	*1960*	*1970*	*1975*	*1980*	*1982*
Total	52,391	27,235	13,790	12,180	11,050	10,650	11,300
Sugar	34,442	14,080	8,240	5,900	5,200	4,950	4,700
Pineapple	7,159	4,637	4,160	3,600	2,300	2,500	2,450
Diversified	10,790	8,518	1,390	2,680	3,550	3,200	4,150
	Percent						
Total	100.0	100.0	100.0	100.0	100.0	100.0	100.0
Sugar	65.7	51.7	59.6	48.5	47.1	49.3	41.6
Pineapple	13.7	17.0	30.2	29.6	20.8	24.9	21.7
Diversified	20.6	31.3	10.1	22.0	32.1	31.8	36.7

SOURCES: Robert C. Schmitt, *Historical Statistics of Hawaii* (Honolulu: University of Hawaii Press, 1977); Hawaii Department of Planning and Economic Development (DPED), *Hawaii's Income and Expenditure Accounts: 1958–1980* (Honolulu, 1982).

TABLE 6.7   Employment in the Agro-Food Industry Including Field- and Food-Processing Workers, 1940–1982

| | *Persons* | | | | | | |
	1940	*1950*	*1960*	*1970*	*1975*	*1980*	*1982*
Total	NA	NA	34,138	25,660	22,300	21,800	22,500
Sugar	44,605	22,893	14,542	10,930	9,650	8,850	8,550
Pineapple	15,723	12,167	11,876	8,390	5,100	5,400	5,200
Diversified	NA	NA	7,720	6,340	7,550	7,550	8,750
	Percent						
Total	100.0	100.0	100.0	100.0	100.0	100.0	100.0
Sugar	NA	NA	42.6	42.6	43.3	40.6	38.0
Pineapple	NA	NA	34.8	32.7	22.9	24.8	23.1
Diversified	NA	NA	22.6	24.7	33.9	34.6	38.9

SOURCES: Robert C. Schmitt, *Historical Statistics of Hawaii* (Honolulu: University of Hawaii Press, 1977); Hawaii Department of Planning and Economic Development (DPED), *Hawaii's Income and Expenditure Accounts: 1958–1980* (Honolulu, 1982).

TABLE 6.8   Wage and Salary Incomes by Industry in Hawaii, 1940–1952

	Millions of Dollars							Percent Composition						
	1940	1942	1944	1946	1948	1950	1952	1940	1942	1944	1946	1948	1950	1952
All Industries	179.4	492.8	895.4	559.3	550.5	510.4	654.7	100.0	100.0	100.0	100.0	100.0	100.0	100.0
Agriculture[a]	96.8	37.4	48.0	53.3	70.1	65.9	73.4	20.5	7.6	5.4	9.5	12.7	12.9	11.2
Contract construction	11.0	89.6	17.0	24.8	31.2	24.7	34.0	6.1	18.2	1.9	4.4	5.7	4.8	5.2
Manufacturing[b]	17.6	28.0	39.9	46.5	56.0	54.0	62.1	9.8	5.7	4.5	8.3	10.2	10.6	9.5
Trade[c]	23.5	33.9	49.2	59.4	76.8	74.1	85.9	13.1	6.9	5.5	10.6	14.0	14.5	13.1
Finance[d]	3.9	4.5	6.1	8.4	12.1	11.3	12.8	2.2	1.0	0.7	1.5	2.2	2.2	2.0
Transportation	7.9	16.3	24.0	20.6	25.3	24.7	29.4	4.4	3.3	2.7	3.7	4.6	4.8	4.5
Communications	4.7	6.9	7.4	9.6	11.9	12.5	14.8	2.6	1.4	0.8	1.7	2.2	2.5	2.3
Services	13.3	19.0	28.3	32.7	38.9	39.7	46.8	7.4	3.9	3.2	5.9	7.1	7.8	7.2
Government	60.6	256.7	675.3	304.1	228.1	203.4	295.4	33.8	52.1	75.4	54.4	41.4	39.9	39.6
Federal	43.6	236.8	646.4	267.6	181.9	150.5	238.3	24.3	48.1	72.2	47.9	33.0	29.5	36.4
Local	17.0	19.9	28.9	36.4	46.2	52.9	57.1	9.5	4.0	3.2	6.5	8.4	10.4	8.7

Note: Figures do not necessarily add to totals due to rounding.

aIncludes forestry and fisheries.

bIncludes mining.

cIncludes wholesale and retail merchandising.

dIncludes insurance and real estate.

SOURCE: Charles F. Schwartz, *Income of Hawaii*, a supplement to *Survey of Current Business* (Washington, D.C.: U.S. Department of Commerce, 1953).

TABLE 6.9   Sources of Personal Income in Hawaii, 1958–1980 ($ million)

	1958	1959	1963	1968	1973	1978	1980
Total personal income[a]	1,146	1,283	1,723	2,717	4,650	7,727	9,775
	(100.0)	(100.0)	(100.0)	(100.0)	(100.0)	(100.0)	(100.0)
Farm income	63	70	83	94	125	188	213
	(5.5)	(5.5)	(4.8)	(3.5)	(2.7)	(2.4)	(2.2)
Nonfarm income	890	998	1,340	2,113	3,481	5,587	6,880
	(77.8)	(77.8)	(77.8)	(77.8)	(74.9)	(72.3)	(70.4)
Other labor income[b]	27	30	36	77	171	354	474
	(2.4)	(2.3)	(2.1)	(2.8)	(3.7)	(4.6)	(4.8)
Personal rental income[c]	45	63	72	98	96	113	125
	(3.9)	(4.9)	(4.2)	(3.6)	(2.1)	(1.5)	(1.3)
Interest and dividends[d]	95	95	156	267	532	900	1,322
	(8.3)	(7.4)	(9.1)	(9.8)	(11.4)	(11.6)	(13.5)
Transfer income[e]	25	28	37	68	245	583	761
	(2.2)	(2.2)	(2.1)	(2.5)	(5.3)	(7.5)	(7.8)

Note: Figures do not necessarily add to totals due to rounding. Percentages are within parentheses.

[a] Includes wages, salaries, and proprietors' incomes.

[b] Includes employers' contributions to private pension, health and welfare funds.

[c] Includes estimate of royalties from patents, monetary interest earned, and imputed net interest of owner-occupants of nonfarm dwellings.

[d] Includes cash payments by all corporations to stockholders, and monetary and imputed interest.

[e] Includes all private and public transfer incomes for which no good or service is provided in exchange.

SOURCE: Hawaii Department of Planning and Economic Development, *Hawaii's Income and Expenditure Accounts: 1958–1980* (Honolulu, 1982).

TABLE 6.10   Per Capita Income of Agricultural Workers Compared to Nonagricultural Workers, 1960–1980

Total Income and Employment	1960	1965	1970	1975	1980	Percentage Change			
						1960–65	1965–70	1970–75	1975–80
Na Agriculture workers (1,000)	13.8	12.6	12.2	11.0	10.7	-8.7	-3.2	-9.8	-2.7
Ya Agriculture income ($ million)	58.3	72.6	89.5	107.3	143.8	24.5	23.3	19.9	34.0
Nn Nonagriculture workers (1,000)	188.9	219.4	293.7	339.1	404.1	16.1	33.9	15.5	19.2
Yn Nonagriculture income ($ million)	1,009.0	1,442.8	2,554.3	3,902.3	6,428.8	43.0	77.0	52.8	64.7
Income per worker									
$\frac{Ya}{Na}$ Agriculture ($)	4,225.0	5,762.0	7,336.0	9,754.0	13,439.0	36.4	27.3	33.0	37.8
$\frac{Yn}{Nn}$ Nonagriculture ($)	5,341.0	6,576.0	8,697.0	11,508.0	15,909.0	23.1	32.2	32.3	38.2
$\alpha = \frac{Ya/Na}{Yn/Nn}$ Agriculture/nonagriculture	79.1	87.6	84.4	84.8	84.5	—	—	—	—

SOURCE: Hawaii Department of Planning and Economic Development (DPED), *Hawaii's Income and Expenditure Accounts: 1958–1980* (Honolulu, 1982).

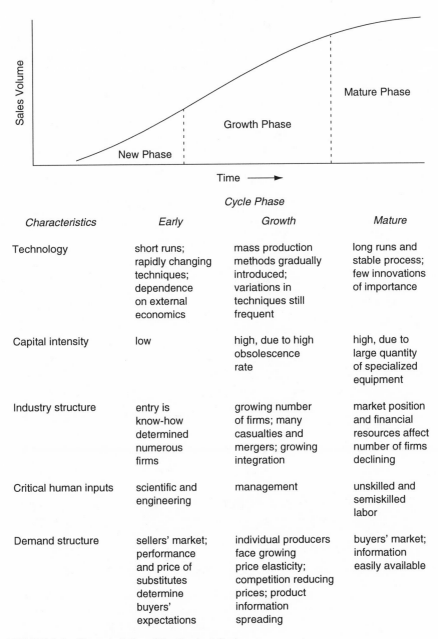

FIGURE 6.4 Characteristics of the Product Cycle
SOURCE: S. Hirsch, Location of Industry and International Competitiveness (Oxford, Clarendon Press, 1967), pp. 17, 23.

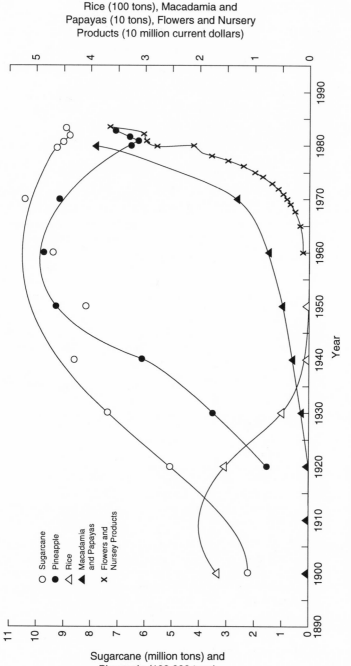

FIGURE 6.5 Product Cycles in Hawaiian Agriculture, 1890–1980
SOURCES: Hawaii Department of Planning and Economic Development (DPED), *Hawaii's Income and Expenditure Accounts: 1958–1980* (Honolulu, 1982); DPED, *The State of Hawaii Data Book, 1983: A Statistical Abstract* (Honolulu, 1983); and George Ariyoshi, "Governor's Message," in *Statistics of Hawaiian Agriculture 1982* (Honolulu: Hawaii Agricultural Reporting Service, July 1983).

TABLE 6.11 Volume of Agricultural Product Marketings, 1946–1980

| | Crops[a] | | | | | | | Livestock and Products[b] | | | | | |
	Sugar (unprocessed cane)	Pineapples (fresh equivalent)	Vegetables and Melons	Fruits (excluding pineapples)	Coffee (parchment)	Macadamia Nuts (in shell)	Taro	Beef	Pork	Milk	Eggs	Broilers and Chickens	Honey
1946	6,002	—	55,658	17,528	8,625	630	11,480	19,295	9,410	65.2	29	777	761
1950	8,175	924	45,659	13,755	9,375	755	11,740	17,672	6,710	76.6	44	1,296	890
1960	8,613	953	50,265	22,805	13,272	2,579	9,675	25,001	8,831	120.0	138	4,746	280
1970	10,457	954	54,798	36,241	4,300	13,216	8,555	32,210	7,903	135.3	196	5,688	215
1980	9,214	657	70,710	67,800	1,440	33,390	6,400	28,809	8,012	149.4	221	7,890	861
						Percentage Change							
1946–50	36.2	—	−18.0	−21.5	8.7	19.8	2.3	−8.4	−28.7	−17.5	51.7	66.8	17.0
1950–60	5.4	3.1	10.0	65.8	41.6	241.6	−17.6	41.5	31.6	56.7	213.6	266.2	−68.5
1960–70	21.4	0.1	9.1	58.9	−67.6	412.4	−11.6	28.8	−10.5	12.8	42.0	19.8	−23.2
1970–80	−11.9	−31.1	29.0	87.1	−66.5	152.6	−25.2	−10.6	1.4	10.4	12.8	38.7	300.5

[a]Sugar and pineapple in 1,000 tons; other crops in 1,000 lb.
[b]Eggs in millions; other livestock and products in 1,000 lb.
SOURCES: Robert C. Schmitt, *Historical Statistics of Hawaii* (Honolulu: University of Hawaii Press, 1977); George Ariyoshi, "Governor's Message," in *Statistics of Hawaiian Agriculture 1982* (Honolulu: Hawaii Agricultural Reporting Service, July 1983).

TABLE 6.12   Sugarcane and Pineapple Products in Hawaii's Trade, 1875–1980
(in thousands of current dollars)

	Exports				
Year	Total Exports (A)[a]	Sugar[b]	Pineapple[b]	Total Imports (B)[a]	Balance of Trade (A − B)
1875	2,018	1,229		1,682	336
1880	4,876	4,352		3,673	1,203
1885	9,069	8,363		3,831	5,238
1890	13,143	12,167		6,962	6,181
1895	8,474	7,978		5,714	2,760
1900	14,114	13,919		10,684	3,430
1905	36,172	35,113	193	14,768	21,404
1910	46,490	42,631	1,775	25,166	21,324
1915	62,465	53,145	6,189	30,721	31,744
1920	195,821	159,378	29,453	86,337	109,484
1925	104,625	64,227	33,562	83,754	20,871
1930	100,916	56,566	37,728	91,126	9,790
1935	100,034	59,820	33,886	84,553	15,481
1940	103,068	48,876	45,673	135,447	−32,379
1945	88,047	53,520	26,935	267,046	−178,999
1950	229,600	119,399	97,400	363,000	−133,400
1956	287,000	143,000	117,000	429,600	−142,600
1960	263,800	122,900	113,000	566,100	−302,300
1965	331,600	167,138	122,000	1,174,700	−843,100
1970	358,600	188,293	125,700	1,396,600	−1,038,000
1975	875,300	365,785	134,200	2,824,100	−1,948,800
1980	1,258,700	559,000	167,058	5,381,300	−4,122,600

SOURCES: [a]For 1875–1956: Robert C. Schmitt, *Historical Statistics of Hawaii* (Honolulu: University of Hawaii Press, 1977), pp. 540–545; for 1960–1980: Hawaii Department of Planning and Economic Development, *Hawaii's Income and Expenditure Accounts: 1958–1980* (Honolulu, 1982), pp. 172–173; for 1875–1945: Kathleen Pierson, "Development of Trade in Hawaii: A Statistical Analysis of Basic Trends," unpublished M.A. thesis submitted to the University of Hawaii (June 1948), pp. 56–70; and Bank of Hawaii, *Hawaii Potentials and Programs for Island Growth* (Honolulu 1957). [b]For 1875–1945: Kathleen Pierson, "Development of Trade in Hawaii: A Statistical Analysis of Basic Trends" (Unpublished M.A. thesis submitted to the University of Hawaii, June 1948), pp. 56–70; Bank of Hawaii, *Hawaii Potentials and Programs for Island Growth* (Honolulu, 1957).

TABLE 6.13 External Trade Balance of Hawaii, 1958–1980 (in millions of current dollars)

		1958	1959	1960	1962	1964	1966	1968	1970	1972	1974	1976	1978	1980
A	Merchandise exports	253	276	264	294	322	351	378	359	374	1,038	677	828	1,259
	Food products	NA	NA	NA	NA	NA	NA	NA	330	340	825	381	477	820
	Sugar and molasses	118	129	123	154	161	179	190	188	185	676	236	267	559
	Pineapple	109	119	113	109	120	123	122	126	133	125	112	146	167
B	Merchandise imports	460	521	566	547	650	965	1,053	1,397	1,426	2,473	3,201	3,861	5,381
C = A − B	Trade balance	−207	−245	−302	−253	−328	−614	−675	−1,038	−1,052	−1,435	−2,524	−3,033	−4,122
D	Tourism (net)	39	63	74	87	125	182	321	397	625	1,001	1,361	1,829	2,469
E	Other services (net)[a]	−30	−35	−31	−56	−83	−73	−73	−113	−172	−293	−280	−337	−405
F = D + E	Invisible trade balance	9	28	43	31	42	109	248	284	453	708	1,081	1,492	2,064
G	Transfer payment (net)	246	270	305	313	342	449	521	545	736	917	1,276	1,480	1,530
H = C + F + G	Current-account balance	48	53	46	91	56	−56	94	−209	137	190	−167	−61	−528

Note: Data on capital accounts are not available; NA = not available.

[a]Includes services and income from investments.

SOURCE: Hawaii Department of Planning and Economic Development (DPED), *Hawaii's Income and Expenditure Accounts: 1958–1980* (Honolulu, 1982).

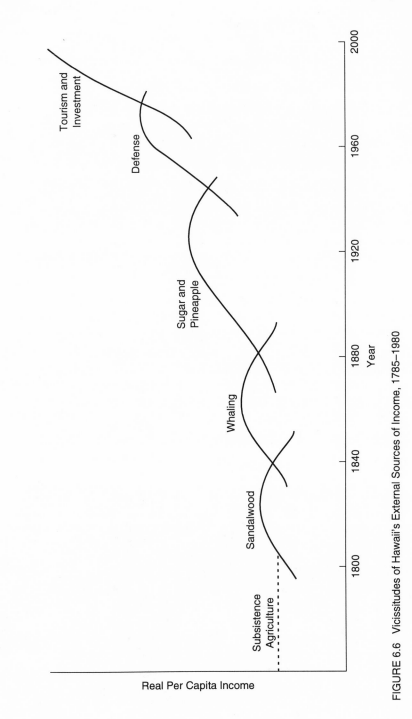

FIGURE 6.6 Vicissitudes of Hawaii's External Sources of Income, 1785–1980

TABLE 6.14 Balance of Agricultural Trade and Self-Sufficiency Rate of Hawaii, 1970–1980 (in millions of current dollars)

		1970	1971	1972	1973	1974	1975	1976	1977	1978	1979	1980
X	Exports	330	402	340	453	825	526	381	364	477	570	820
	Sugar and molasses	188	204	185	223	676	366	236	195	267	323	559
	Pineapple	126	177	133	204	125	134	112	124	146	177	167
	Canned tuna	9	11	13	14	12	12	16	24	29	29	41
	Flowers	2	3	3	4	4	5	6	7	10	12	14
	Papayas	2	2	2	3	4	4	5	6	6	7	6
	Macadamia nuts	1	2	2	2	2	2	4	5	8	10	20
	Coffee	1	1	1	1	1	1	–	–	2	2	1
	Other agriculture[a]	1	2	1	1	1	2	2	3	9	10	12
M	Imports	206	200	232	321	390	405	437	531	598	NA	NA
	Farm products	23	25	29	41	53	36	29	39	32	NA	NA
	Processed foods and feeds	183	175	203	280	337	369	408	492	566	NA	NA
X – M	Difference	124	202	108	132	435	121	–56	–167	–121	NA	NA
S	Total domestic supply	798	965	945	1,100	1,567	1,400	1,381	1,429	1,696	NA	NA
C	Total consumption	674	763	837	968	1,132	1,279	1,437	1,596	1,817	1,979	2,404
S/C	Self-sufficiency rate	1.18	1.26	1.13	1.13	1.37	1.09	0.962	0.898	0.935	NA	NA

Notes: – = negligible; NA = not available.
[a]Includes ginger root, meat, live animals, and seed corn.
SOURCE: Hawaii Department of Planning and Economic Development, *Hawaii's Income and Expenditure Accounts: 1958–1980 (Honolulu, 1982).*

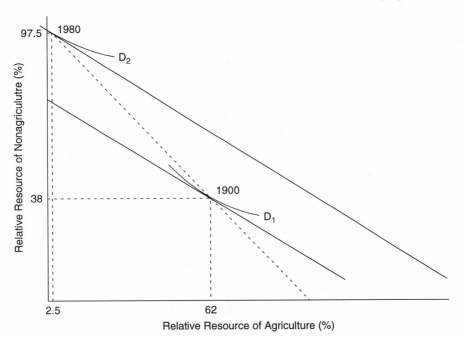

FIGURE 6.7   Relative Shares of Employment in Agriculture and Nonagriculture in Hawaii, 1900 and 1980

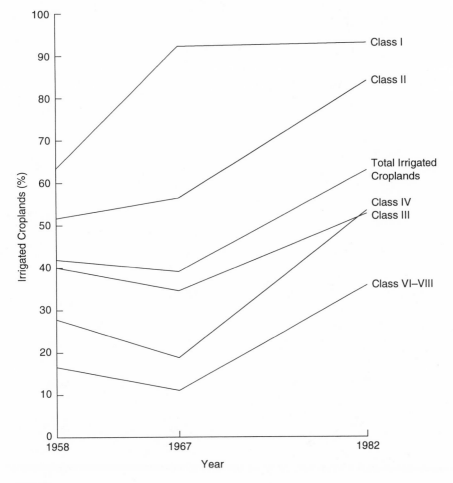

Definitions:

Inventory acres include land areas of main islands—Kauai, Oahu, Molokai, Lanai, Maui, and Hawaii—excluding federal noncrop areas, urbanized and built-up areas, and inland water areas.

Classes I to III are suitable for regular or continuous cultivation and a wide range of other uses.

Class IV is marginal for common cultivated crops but is suitable for other uses. There are no Class V lands in Hawaii.

Classes VI to VIII are not suitable for ordinary cultivation and generally be kept in vegetation.

FIGURE 6.8 Distribution of Irrigated Croplands in Hawaii, 1958, 1967, 1982
sources: U.S. Department of Agriculture, *National Resources Inventory* (Ames: Iowa State University, 1982); *Conservation Needs Inventory: Hawaii* (Washington D.C.: Soil Conservation Service, 1972; and *Hawaii Soil and Conservation Needs Inventory* (Honolulu: Hawaii Conservation Needs Committee, 1961).

7

The Boomerang Economy and
Future Prospects in the Ryukyu Islands

The Ryukyu Islands[1] consist of more than 100 islands (of which 40 are inhabited), and most of these islands are located more than 500 kilometers from the main island of Okinawa, which is 1,000 kilometers from mainland Japan. Although the Ryukyus' human and nonhuman resource endowments and location are more favorable to self-reliant economic development than are those of other Pacific island economies, including Hawaii, the Ryukyuan economy possesses many important characteristics common to these small island economies.

The Okinawa prefectural government (OPG) and the Okinawa Development Agency of the Japanese government (ODAJ) jointly drafted the First Okinawa Promotion and Development Plan (1972–1981) and the Second Development Plan (1982–1991). The plans list two important goals: (1) to reduce the various socioeconomic gaps existing between Okinawa and mainland Japan and (2) to establish a basis for achieving self-reliant economic development. In particular, the level of per capita income was targeted to reach up to 80 percent of the Japanese level. The second plan was completed at the end of the 1991 Japanese fiscal year, namely March 1992. The Third Five-Year Development Plan is now being implemented.

In this chapter, I focus on the development issues and problems of the Ryukyuan economy since the islands' reversion to Japan in 1972.[2]

Economic Performance of the Ryukyus After the 1972 Reversion

Before the future course of the Okinawan economy can be charted, the economic performance of Okinawa during 1972–1991, the period covered under the development plans, must be evaluated. Data are available up to 1988; Table 7.1 summarizes the important performance indicators of the economy from 1972 to 1988. Despite enormous uncertainties brought about by internal reversion issues, which were immediately followed by the external oil shock, Okinawa's macroeconomic performance was quite impressive. Every forecasting model predicted that the population would decline substantially owing mainly to the reduction of U.S. military expenditures, which accounted for 28 percent of the islands' national income and directly supported about 10 percent of the Ryukyuan total labor force in 1971. Quite the contrary, the population increased by 3 percent the year immediately following the reversion owing to the unexpected "reversion boom" coupled with the less-than-expected shock from the military force reduction. The population continued to increase from 970,000 in 1972 to 1.2 million in 1988, a 25 percent increase, which was far beyond what the plans envisaged. The sizable increase in population has itself been considered an indication of successful "development." The growth in population was accompanied by an impressive real growth rate in the gross prefectural product (GPP), which was recorded at 7.4 percent annually during the first plan period (1972–1982) and 5.1 percent thereafter (1982–1988). As a matter of fact, the growth rates were higher than those of Japan proper, whose economic performance was rated the highest among the industrialized countries. As a result, the per capita income of the Ryukyus increased by about four times, from a mere ¥450,000 ($1,490) in 1972 to ¥1.7 million ($13,281) in 1988. The level of per capita income was almost comparable to that of France.

Although the per capita income gap between the Ryukyus and Japan was substantially reduced from 62 percent of Japan's level in 1972 to 73 percent in 1988, the plan's target (80 percent) was not realized. Actually the per capita income gap has been widening in recent years. There has been, however, an increasing perception among the people that the targeted income gap should be dropped from the goals of economic development.

The consumer price index (CPI) doubled during the first plan period due mainly to oil shocks and excessive domestic demand created by a massive inflow of public funds. CPI, however, was remarkably stabilized thereafter as the economy was gradually integrated into the supply-oriented Japanese system. Despite a relatively buoyant economic performance, unemployment has been the most-discussed critical issue since reversion took place. As a matter of fact, the plans attempted to slow down population growth while unrealistically emphasizing the promotion of manufacturing industries in order to absorb the unemployed labor force. The plans failed on this important point. The unemployment rate rose from 3 percent of the labor force in 1972 to 4.9 percent (2.4% for Japan) in 1982 and remained there. It is puzzling that the unemployment rate has remained so high in recent years despite the extremely tight labor market in Japan proper. One possible reason is that the labor force under the age of twenty-four, which accounts for nearly two-thirds of the unemployed, is not willing to move to mainland Japan for cultural reasons. But it should be emphasized here that during 1972–1988, 139,000 jobs were created in the Ryukyuan labor market.

We have also witnessed a rapid change in the Okinawan production structure during the two plan periods. Despite a heavy emphasis on agriculture in the plans, the GPP share of this primary industry followed an established empirical law, declining from 7 percent in 1972 to a mere 3 percent in 1988; tertiary industries, particularly the private service sector, jumped from 67 percent to 78 percent during the same period. One important distortional exception to the empirical law is the secondary industry, which remained almost constant in its GPP share. A "structurist" would be delighted to point out that the GPP share of construction (14% in 1988) was much larger than the share of manufacturing (6 percent in 1988). It is very rare to find such a twisted industrial structure even at a regional level. The major reason for this "great twist" can be found in the unique financial sources of economic activities, which will be discussed in the following section.

As we have already seen in the preceding chapters, a small island economy is characteristically distinguished from other large economies in its forms of external transactions. The trade deficit of the Ryukyus, including the commodity and service trades, almost quintupled during the first plan (1972–1982). Although the trade deficit–GPP ratio declined from 25 percent in 1982 to 15 percent in 1988, the relative burden of the deficit is still considered to be very high, as is discussed in the following section. The most important source of financing the deficit has been fiscal transfers from the Japanese government, which accounted for 32 percent of GPP at the end of the first plan. Net transfer incomes more than covered trade deficits (Table 7.1). Transfer incomes have played roles similar to that of Japan's ODA to small island nations.

The most noteworthy development after the reversion was a rapid expansion of the tourism industry, which increased to 10 percent of GPP in 1988 from a mere 4 percent in 1971. Although tourism has many problems to resolve, the industry has no doubt become a mainstay of the Ryukyuan economy. Another important aspect of the postreversion economy is the diminishing role of U.S. military base incomes as a source of foreign exchange earnings. Base incomes accounted for only 5 percent of the Ryukyus' GPP compared to 16 percent in 1972 and about 30 percent just before reversion.

The bases, however, still generate ¥131 billion and directly employ nearly 8,000 local people. It should also be noted that all military land rentals and wages of local base workers are now paid by the Japanese government. Furthermore, the Japanese government has been covering various so-called base maintenance expenditures, including various subsidies to areas surrounding the bases. These expenditures amounted to ¥59 billion in 1986.

The other important socioeconomic indicators are also shown in Table 7.1. Along with macroeconomic expansion, monthly average wages increased by 2.6 times during 1972–1988, but net household savings (total household savings − total household borrowings) turned into a negative in 1988 due mainly to high living expenses. The ratio of owner-occupied homes also deteriorated from 68 percent in 1972 to 60 percent in 1982, when the latest survey data were available. Social indicators also show a mixed performance. Infrastructure facilities such as roads, sewage and water systems, harbors, schools, and hospitals improved remarkably during the plan periods. At the same time, however, social problems such as criminal offenses, traffic accidents, and yakuza-related crimes have risen sharply since the reversion. In particular, recent so-called Okinawa yakuza conflicts have caught nationwide attention through intensive coverage by Japan's mass media and have sent a shiver of fear through the island's growing, peaceful tourism industry, whose main customers are security-conscious Japanese mainlanders.

The Ryukyu Islands are among the most highly concentrated islands in the Pacific region in terms of population and economic activities (Table 7.2). Although the land size of the Ryukyus accounts for only 8.2 percent of the Solomon Islands, their gross island product (GIP) is more than 100 times higher than that of the Solomons. It should be noted here that the Ryukyus' per capita income exceeded $20,000 in 1992. This figure is almost comparable to that for Hawaii, which Ryukuans once called the paradise of the Pacific.

A New Economic Relationship Between the Ryukyus and Japan

The purpose of this section is to see in more detail the economic relationship between the Ryukyu Islands and Japan, focusing on the postreversion period. The structure of economic transactions between the Ryukyus and Japan prior to the reversion was a very simple one. The Ryukyuan economy was called a fragile base economy because of its heavy dependency on precarious military base incomes. As we have already seen, about 30 to 40 percent of the Ryukyuan gross domestic product in the 1960s was directly generated through selling goods and services to military bases. I once calculated the multiplier effect of the base incomes using an input-output table originally constructed for the economy.[3] The military base incomes and the U.S. direct aid to the Ryukyus were dominant sources of foreign exchange earnings, which accounted for nearly 70 percent of the islands' total imports in the 1960s. Increasing inflows of base incomes under the positive open-door trade policies of the U.S. Civil Administration of the Ryukyu Islands (USCAR) coupled with the economy's poor productive capacities accelerated the dependency on imports, which were mostly supplied by Japan. When military base expenditures exploded during the Korean War and the Vietnam War during the early 1950s and the late 1960s, the imports increased more than proportionally. The country benefiting most from these boom periods was Japan, which badly needed hard currencies for its rapid economic development. Almost 90 percent of the base demand was siphoned off by Japanese imports. It is interesting to note that the Ryukyus' import dependency on Japan was much higher (89%) in 1960 than in 1988 (83%), indicating that the Ryukyus were economically (but not politically) more integrated into the Japanese system in earlier years. It is ironic that the United States financed Ryukyuan economic development through a military buildup that in turn contributed to the declining economic power of the United States while accelerating Japan's economic emergence.

After the reversion, the economic as well as sociopolitical integration of Okinawa into the Japanese systems accelerated. As a matter of fact, the major aim of the two development plans was to achieve a unification (*ittaika*) of various systems of the Ryukyus with those of Japan through various highly complicated soft-landing adjustment programs and measures. These programs and measures were initially designed to be dismantled within the first ten-year plan period, but some important ones were still being implemented nearly twenty years after the reversion. The unification measures were fairly straightforwardly implemented for the various public institutions such as the government of the Ryukyu Islands, the University of the Ryukyus, and monetary authorities. Despite many trade-offs, the unification measures have been a smashing success story in the modern history of socioeconomic integration due largely to the strong support of the islanders coupled with "sweet" financial support from the Japanese government.

There is, however, one important aspect missing from this unification process, namely, the self-reliance of the Ryukyuan economy. It is worthwhile to note here that the discussion on the balance of payments, a vital subject before 1972, disappeared from economic forums after the reversion because the border between the Ryukyus and Japan disappeared. My controversial 1982 article[4] was designed to bring this critical issue under intellectual scrutiny again by discussing the future state of the Ryukyuan economy. It is unfortunate that the issue has not been debated since then. Almost all Ryukyuan economists who have actively participated in discussions of the previous two development plans seem to have lost interest in the future state of the Ryukyus. It is also quite ironic that outsiders are more eager than the resident islanders to be informed about the Ryukyuan "reversion trap."

Indicators of Self-Reliant Economic Development

Although there have been numerous discussions and aspirations regarding self-reliant economic development, no serious attempt has been so far made to measure this self-reliance. We can define it as economic development based upon an island's own resources and initiative. A self-reliance indicator can be defined using the following two-gap model:

$$Y = C + I + (X - M), \qquad (1)$$

where Y = gross domestic product, C = consumption expenditure, I = investment expenditure, X = exports, and M = imports. Rearranging equation (1), we get the following domestic supply (Y) and demand ($C + I$) balance, which is identical to the trade balance ($X - M$)

$$Y - (C + I) = X - M \qquad (2)$$

From equation (2) it is obvious that whenever an island's productive capacity (Y) is greater than its domestic expenditure (C + I), the island economy can be considered as "viable" because it has more than enough capability to meet its own demand. Or it is equivalent, ex post, to say that the economy has been creating net foreign assets through net exports (X − M). However, if Y has been continuously smaller than (C + I), then the economy may not be sustainable in the long run because the widening foreign exchange gap (X − M) cannot be filled unless the island economy falls deeper into its dependency on external sources of transfer receipts.

A condition for self-reliant development or a sustainable development path is Y = C + I or X = M. Although this is the simplest expression of a macroeconomic formula, we need some innovative idea to quantify it. Exports of goods and services (X) include only those that will contribute to the idea of self-reliant development. Thus, exports (sales) to U.S. military installations or incomes from U.S. bases are conceptually excluded from X. Exports of weapons, which was an indirect cause of the Gulf War, are also excluded from X, although we need not worry about this for the Ryukyus at the moment. Imports are also adjusted accordingly.

Figure 7.1 shows the results of an estimation for the Ryukyuan economy. Although the deficit of what I call the "self-reliance balance" (X − M) jumped more than threefold during the first decade of reversion (1972–1982), it has been declining in recent years. The relative size of the deficit in terms of GPP dramatically declined, from 34 percent in 1972 to 17 percent in 1988. This suggests that expanding domestic economic activities reduced the relative importance of the trade deficit.

The histogram in Figure 7.1 also shows that the self-reliance finance ratio (X/M) also improved, from 43 percent in 1972 to 54 percent in 1988. These figures are also reflected in the dependency ratio for "non-self-reliant" external sources (receipts from U.S. bases + net transfer income from the Japanese government/GPP), which declined from 38 percent in 1972 to 25 percent in 1988. I should, however, warn that even though the self-reliancy macroindex has improved since the reversion, nearly 50 percent of the deficits are still financed by non-self-reliant external sources.

A similar self-reliancy index has also been computed for each industrial sector based upon input-output tables of Okinawa as follows:

$$Y = E + (X - M), \qquad (3)$$

where   Y = vector of actual gross domestic output of goods and services,
         E = vector of gross domestic output that will just meet gross
                domestic demand including consumption and investment,

> X = vector of gross domestic output that will just meet gross export demand, and
>
> M = vector of gross domestic output that must be subtracted due to import leakages.

The self-reliancy index is defined as

$$Sr = Y/E(\times 100) = 1 + (X - M)/E \ (\times 100) \tag{4}$$

From (4), it is obvious that whenever domestic demand (E) is equal to domestic output (Y), or export demand (X) is equal to import demand (M), the self-reliancy index is 100 percent. The actual computational results are shown in Table 7.3. Although the index improved over the 1975–1985 decade, only four industries—fisheries, petroleum products, transportation and communication, and business and personal services—were self-reliant in 1985.

The petroleum industry, which accounts for 26 percent of the gross manufacturing output, is almost entirely composed of offshore operations, that is to say, crude oil is imported from the Middle East to the refineries located on the East China Sea side of the central part of the Ryukyus and then the petroleum products are shipped to mainland Japan. The industry therefore is a typical enclave type with negligible linkages with the local economy despite its preponderant size in the Ryukyuan manufacturing sector. Transportation and services are non-exportable industries; therefore their self-reliancy indexes are expected to exceed 100 percent. The structure of the self-reliance or dependency of each industrial sector can be clearly demonstrated by following skyline charts (Figures 7.2A and 7.2B) of the Ryukyus and Japan. If the industry's skyline bar is greater than 100 percent, the industry has excess capacity (Y > E) to meet export demands and if the skyline bar is less than 100 percent, the industry cannot supply its own domestic demand. Most Japanese industries are more than self-sufficient, indicating the most powerful supply-oriented economy in the world.

The "Economic Boomerang"

Although the self-reliance of the Ryukyuan economy has improved since the islands' reversion to Japan, its structural dependency on Japan has remained unchanged. The economic relationship between the Ryukyu Islands and mainland Japan is similar to that of the relationship between island nations and their former suzerain countries. The "economic boomerang" has been used to describe such a relationship. The term implies that since most financial assistance is tied to the country that provides the assistance, benefits of the assistance are returned to the donor country through imports from the donor. The term can be referred to as the reverse of the "boomerang effect," which has been conventionally used by Japanese economists. The "economic boomerang" has been

manifested on a more grandiose scale in the Ryukyu Islands than in any other
Pacific island nations through trade, tourism development, corporate mergers
and acquisitions (M&As) and affiliations, and the Japanese government's special financial assistance tied to the maintenance of the U.S. bases.

Table 7.4 shows statistical evidence of the economic boomerang. Japan's
penetration into the Ryukyuan economy intensified after the reversion. In 1988,
92 percent of Ryukyuan exports were directed to Japan compared with 87 percent just before the reversion; 83 percent of imports were from Japan compared
to 78 percent previously; 95 percent of tourists were from Japan compared to 77
percent previously; 61 percent of base spending was financed by the Japanese
government compared to zero in 1971; and, most significant, in 1988 all public
transfers came from Japan. It is interesting to note that receipts from Japan
financed only 26 percent of Ryukyu's trade deficit in 1971, but in 1988 they
financed more than 100 percent. Moreover, net income receipts from Japan, including base income, financed 82 percent of the deficit in 1988 compared to 18
percent in 1971. The percentage is almost comparable to the deficit-finance
ratio of the U.S. military expenditure in the 1960s, a major difference being the
source of funding. The incomes transferred to the Ryukyus by the U.S. government were siphoned off by Japanese exporters in the 1950s and 1960s. Now
almost all Japanese transferred incomes are siphoned off by the same old Japanese exporters.

Another important difference is the method of financing the trade deficit.
The base income-deficit ratio declined from 57 percent in 1972 to 19 percent in
1988; the public transfers-deficit ratio increased sharply from 20 percent to 71
percent during the same period. However, both base incomes and public transfers, which I call "non-self-reliant sources of income," still finance about 80
percent of Ryukyuan trade deficits. It is critically important to realize that the
reduced base income since the reversion has been supplemented by government
fiscal transfers. More than 10 percent of these transfers involve the so-called
kichi taisaku hi (base maintenance expenditures), such as construction of public
facilities in areas surrounding bases, compensations for base-related nuisances,
and direct subsidies to municipalities where bases are located.

There is an interesting study, summarized in Figure 7.3, showing that among
exogenous expenditures, public investment has created the largest boomerang
effects, or lowest multiplier effects, on the Ryukyuan economy. One unit of public investment generated 1.0 unit of domestic demand in the initial year (1984),
1.3 units in the second year (1985), 1.4 units in the third year (1986), and 1.2
units in the fourth year (1987), in contrast to the highest multiplier effects of
tourism expenditure. Public investment generated a sizable negative multiplier
effect on the trade balance; that is, one unit of public investment induced 0.046
units of exports and 0.459 units of imports, and therefore 0.413 units of trade
deficit (0.459 − 0.046) in the initial year, and so on. This suggests that the
massive increase of public expenditure after the reversion has not contributed to

self-reliant development as defined previously. Instead, the expenditure has intensified the dependency on the Japanese economy through the boomerang effects.

The economic boomerang of the Ryukyus, at least in absolute quantitative terms, has also been intensified through rapid development of the tourism industry. As has been already discussed, the tourism industry has grown more than six times since the reversion, accounting for about 10 percent of GPP. The industry has no doubt gradually substituted for military base–related industries and contributed to the high postreversion growth rate of the economy. The tourism industry, however, has been developed mainly through package tours orchestrated by huge Japanese tourism developers including Japan Airlines and All Nippon Airway. Resort facilities are mostly constructed in enclaved beach areas that have narrow and weak linkages with local economies. Japanese investment funds are quickly boomeranged back to Japan with some spillover effects on the local economy. Furthermore, according to a 1986 survey conducted by the Okinawa Development Agency, 78 percent of administrative posts (division chief and above) of five typical resort hotels on the island of Okinawa are occupied by the Japanese; Ryukyuans occupy the rest. Here we can see the dual structure of the employment pattern: top managerial, high-paid posts are occupied by the Japanese; low-paid, sweat labor is reserved for the locals.

One survey estimated that the number of resort-type hotels would more than quadruple from fifteen (2,777 rooms) in 1988 to sixty-three (6,029 rooms) in 2000.[5] This rapid and massive "resortization" of the Ryukyus will exert significant impacts on its socioeconomic structure. This is particularly so because the tourism industry has been increasingly capital-, space-, and water-use-intensive since the enactment of the so-called Resort Law in 1987. Small local hotels may be forced from the islands by giant Japanese firms. Devoting a huge space to the construction of a resort complex with an eighteen-hole golf course, for example, will raise land prices, which will in turn push up the opportunity costs of local agricultural and manufacturing production as well as construction of housing and public facilities.

Furthermore, there will be a constant pressure on public utilities and the Ryukyus' enviable environmental amenities. In particular, the water shortage will be a serious and continuing issue.[6] Already Ryukyuans have been experiencing water rationing. According to the previously mentioned Okinawa Development Agency survey, a typical resort hotel consumes 1,192 liters of water per customer per day compared with 810 liters for a typical city hotel and 391 liters for the average household. This means that the boomerang effect is not only apparent in distributing the profits from the tourism industry but it also hits the very resource base on which the Ryukyuan livelihood and the thriving tourism industry are founded. Furthermore, according to David Lowenthal, pleasure-oriented "mass tourism" will eventually erode insular traits such as the charms of the people, their traditions and heritage, and the environmental amenities that attracted those tourists in the first place.[7] It is also ironic that the "culture tourists," people who come to the Ryukyus looking more for archaeology and other educational pursuits than for pleasure boats and golf courses, are the ones to suggest that the Ryukyuans resist the erosive degradation of mass tourism.

Conclusions—Future Directions

If my previous assessments of the Ryukyuan economy are acceptable, a question naturally boomerangs back to us. Where we should go from here? Is there any alternative? This question must be further discussed because I do not have a definite answer. I hope to at best provide some food for thought about effecting a disintegration of the economic boomerang. The key words are "diversification" and "human resource networking."

Diversification Versus Specialization

As we have already seen, all small island economies should target their development plans toward diversifying their economic activities so that the economies are less vulnerable to external forces beyond their control. Diversification, however, is very difficult to realize in such a small island economy. Economic diversification is simply defined as the shift from a simple, monocultural productive base to a more complex, interrelated type of production activity. There are two types of diversification. One is horizontal, that is, diversification from the production of a single or a few products such as sugar, pineapple, and coconuts to the production of multicommercial products such as tropical fruits, vegetables, and flowers. The other is vertical diversification, a shift in the production process from upstream activities of raw material production to downstream activities of manufacturing, thereby generating more intra- or interindustry linkages and value-added production activities. For example, sugarcane can be processed into sugar and molasses, which in turn can be processed into rum and other value-added products. In the case of the Ryukyus, horizontal diversification means structural change from service-oriented industrial activities to more agricultural and manufacturing activities. Vertical diversification means the promotion of domestic value-added activities such as processing local materials and expanding tourism-related activities.

Diversification of Ryukyuan economic activities is necessary for two important reasons. One is in order to "disintegrate" the system of economic boomerang just discussed. Diversification means deeper economic linkages or integration among the domestic economic sectors. A key phrase here is "high-value-added economic activities" supported by local research and development (R&D). There is a convincing study indicating that an increasing proportion of government and tourism expenditures will be locally absorbed if locally oriented appropriate technologies are available (technology is very important for the Ryukyus' self-reliant development, but this topic has been one of the most-neglected areas of Ryukyuan studies).[8]

The second reason for diversification is in order to acquire a socio-economic "resilience" in the face of uncertain external forces, or to establish a socio-economic safety net. This is particularly important for an island economy such as the Ryukyus where socioeconomic activities are highly vulnerable to changes in external environments.

Geographical isolation from large market centers and being subjected to occasional natural hazards such as typhoons and droughts are also important reasons to consider an island security system. We should, however, remember that diversification must be consistent with the current open economic system. That is to say, it must be promoted in open, competitive environments. If diversification is envisaged under a protective, traditional import-substituting regime, the well-known cost-escalating process will damage not only protected industries but also existing competitive industries. The international competitiveness of the world-renowned Puerto Rican rum, Bacardi, for example, has been sustained because cheap imported molasses instead of using its own more expensive molasses has been used.[9]

Economic diversification of the Ryukyus during 1978–1988 was a mixed blessing, as is shown in Table 7.5. In terms of the overall industrial sector, the economy moved more toward specialization in tertiary economic activities, which in 1988 accounted for 78 percent of all income earnings. In particular, private service activities, supported by tourism, increased sharply, and agriculture and manufacturing further reduced their relative weights in the economy.

However, if we take a look at agriculture, diversification has been proceeding steadily. Traditional agricultural products such as sugarcane, pineapple, and hogs have been gradually replaced by new export products such as vegetables, tropical fruits, and beef, and especially by flowers, which have been emerging as a star export product of the Ryukyus. Flowers are a typical example of what I call "high-value-added" products whose income elasticity is higher than one; that is to say, demand for the products increases more than the increase in income. Flowers are also a typical success story of cooperative efforts among the Okinawa prefectural government, the Ryukyu University's research team, and local agricultural cooperatives. Geographical location, warm weather, young innovative farmers, and reduced transportation costs between the Ryukyus and mainland Japan have also contributed to the success story.

Human Resource Networking

As I have already clarified, "diversification" does not mean that a "fortress" Ryukyus should be created. On the contrary, diversification must lead to a strengthening of the Ryukyus' socioeconomic resilience as well as to a rich diversity based upon its people, resources, and location. A key phrase here is "human resource networking," which means people-oriented productive activities through private-sector-based horizontal socioeconomic cooperative interactions. This will eventually lead to socioeconomic integration among people of different cultural backgrounds. Human resource networking is also an effective means to break up the system of economic boomerang, characterized by highly centralized, vertical, stratified, and enclave activities.

Human resource networking is difficult to carry out because of the sociopolitical ramifications of the concept. However, we should start where we can. Fortunately, the recent socioeconomic trend in Japan is toward more "liberalization," "globalization," and "borderlessness." As I have discussed elsewhere, the Ryukyus' socioeconomic system has been moving more inward, particularly after the reversion, than have such systems in the neighboring Kyushu prefectures. This rather anachronistic phenomenon is due largely to an intensive unification process and the resulting boomerang effects.

When "internationalization" became a catchword in Japan some time ago, it quickly spread from Tokyo (the center), where the word was created, to the rural prefectures (the peripherals). The last prefecture that became fascinated with internationalization was the Ryukyus, whose Second Development Plan (1982–1991) proudly listed it as a major objective. The word has a magical boomerang effect in siphoning off human resources, funds, and information from the peripherals into Tokyo, which is now the most internationalized metropolis in Japan.

Despite the Ryukyus' long, rich historical heritage in economic and cultural exchange with neighboring Asian countries, nobody would believe that today's Ryukyu Islands are more internationalized than Kyushu's prefectures, where even the prefectural government has started employing foreign staff and where numerous small businesses are venturing into Asian markets.

There is, however, no alternative left to the Ryukyus except to pursue true internationalization of the islands. Fortunately, many Ryukyuans are now beginning to realize the true meaning of internationalization. The Okinawa Free Trade Zone (OFTZ), which was established in 1988 as the first-free trade zone in Japan, turned out to be a complete failure because the concept was wrong from the beginning (this topic is fully discussed in Chapter 8).[10] OFTZ was created to promote commodity exports from Okinawa primarily to mainland Japan through reexporting foreign goods, which were imported into the zone duty-free. The Ryukyuans have learned a lot of lessons from OFTZ. They have realized that (1) OFTZ must be fully opened to foreign capital (only a small amount of Taiwanese capital was previously allowed); (2) exports from the zone to the mainland should also be duty-free; (3) the zone must be expanded to include military bases; (4) functions of the zone should not be limited to the commodity trade but should also include the consumption and service trade including consultants, banking, training, and education; and (5) business experts should be mobilized on a global scale through the establishment of a human resource networking system. There are numerous areas to which the Ryukyuan people can contribute and enrich themselves through a global human networking system. For example, the Ryukyus can transfer their well-developed fruit-fly-eradication program and underground dam technologies to the South Pacific islands, where they are badly needed. The Ryukyus, in turn, can be a center stage for academic and cultural exchanges with China and other neighboring countries.

The last proposal is particularly important for the future course of Ryukyuan economic development. It is obvious that in order to improve the Ryukyuans' quality of life, it is essential to upgrade their industrial structure, which in turn depends upon the quality of human resources. Although Ryukyuan planners are now realizing that the Ryukyus have a great potential comparative advantage in human resource endowment over their mainland counterparts, they do not have a coherent institutional system to nourish and make use of these most important, potentially powerful resources.

TABLE 7.1 The Ryukyu Islands: Main Economic Indicators After the Reversion to Mainland Japan, 1972, 1982, and 1988

Economic Indicators	1972	1982	1988	Growth Rate 1988÷1972
Economic fundamentals				
Population (1,000)	970	1,132	1,213	1.25
Gross pref. prod. (GPP)(¥100mil.)[a]	4,806	17,981	25,653	5.34
Per capital income (10,000)	45	134	174	3.87
Consumer price index (1972 = 100)	100.0	244.3	261.1	2.61
Unemployment rate (%)	3.0	4.9	4.9	1.63
Distribution of GPP (%)[b]				
Primary industry	7.3	5.0	3.4	0.47
	(18.1)	(13.2)	(11.9)	(0.66)
Secondary industry	27.9	21.7	21.1	0.76
	(20.9)	(20.2)	(19.9)	(0.95)
Manufacturing	10.9	7.4	6.4	0.59
	(9.1)	(6.7)	(6.0)	(0.66)
Construction	16.4	14.0	14.3	0.87
	(11.8)	(13.2)	(13.9)	(1.18)
Tertiary industry	67.3	75.6	78.2	1.16
	(61.0)	(66.4)	(68.0)	(1.11)
Services	19.8	23.9	26.8	1.35
	(24.5)	(23.1)	(26.4)	(1.08)
External transactions				
Trade balance (¥100mil.)[c]	−1,996	−7,372	−7,261	3.64
% of GPP	41.5	41.0	28.3	0.68
Fiscal transfers (net) (¥100mil.)[d]	1,326	5,704	5,593	4.22
% of GPP	27.6	31.7	21.8	0.79
Tourism income (¥100mil.)	409	1,997	2.599	6.35
% of GPP	8.5	11.1	10.1	1.19
Military base income (¥100mil.)[e]	780	1,374	1,312	1.68
% of GPP	16.2	7.6	5.1	0.31
Household economy				
Ave. monthly wage (¥10,000)[f]	11	25	29	2.64
Household savings (net) (¥10,000)[g]	n.a.	35	−196	−
Owner-occupied houses (%)[h]	68	60	n.a.	−
Social indicators				
No. of medical doc. (per 100,000)	53	95	137	2.58
Paved roads (%)[i]	32	93	98	3.06
Houses with sewage (%)	17	45	50	2.94
College enrollment (%)[j]	20.6	20.2	21.3	1.03
No. of criminal offenses (per 10,000)	119	149	137	1.15

Note: n.a. = not available; − = not applicable.

[a]At current price.

[b]Share of employed persons in parentheses.

[c]Merchandise trade balance.

[d]Fiscal receipts from the Japanese government, fiscal payments to the government.

[e]Includes wages of base workers, land rental and consumption by military personnel and their dependents.

[f]Regular employees with 30 and more.

[g]Household savings, borrowings.

[h]1983 figure, % of total housing.

[i]Prefectural roads only.

[j]As percent of high school graduates enrolled in college.

SOURCES: *Statistical Yearbook of Okinawa,* various issues.

TABLE 7.2 The Pacific Islands: Land Area, Population, GIP per Capita, and Trade
Dependencies, 1987

	Land Area (sq. km.) (1)	Population (000) (2)	GIP[a] ($ million) (3)	GIP per Capita (US$) (4)	Trade/GIP[b] (%) (5)
Ryukyu Islands	2,262	1,205	16,982	14,093	44
Hawaii	16,705	1,082	19,713	18,219	51
Fiji	18,272	726	1,061	1,463	67
Solomon Islands	27,556	292	147	503	90
Western Samoa	2,935	162	103	639	71
Vanuatu	11,880	145	124	859	69
Guam[c]	541	120	1,050	8,663	92
FSM[d]	701	98	139	1,249	n.a.
Tonga[e]	699	95	57	606	83
Kiribati	690	68	26	382	76
Marshalls[f]	181	38	46	1,284	61
American Samoa[g]	197	37	183	5,142	272
CNMI	471	31	359	11,581	63
Cook Islands[h]	240	17	34	1,959	94
Palau	494	14	32	2,342	n.a.

[a]GIP = gross island product.
[b]Trade = merchandise exports and imports.
[c]1983 data.
[d]1986 data.
[e]1985 data.
[f]1984 data.
[g]1985 data.
[h]1986 data.
SOURCES: Except the Ryukyu Islands and Hawaii, data are taken from Bob Lucus, "International Trade and Agriculture in the Pacific Islands," University of Hawaii, undated draft; *The State of Hawaii Data Book, 1989;* and *Okinawa Statistical Yearbook, 1990.*

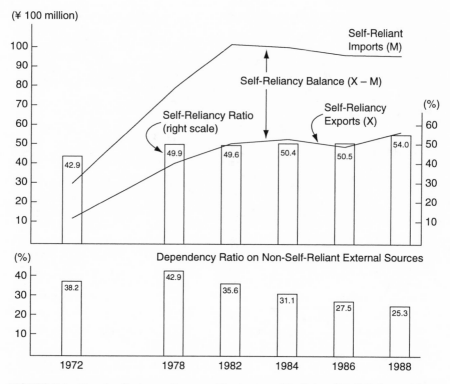

FIGURE 7.1   How the Ryukyuan Economy Has Improved Its External Self-Reliance After
the Reversion, 1972–1988
SOURCE: Constructed from *Okinawa Prefectural Income,* various issues.

TABLE 7.3   The Ryukyu Islands: Self-Reliance (sufficiency) Ratio of the Industrial Sector, 1975, 1980, and 1985 (%)

	1975	1980	1985	Percent Change 1975–1985
Agriculture & livestock	49.0	64.4	71.5	1.46
Forestry	1.9	1.4	5.8	3.00
Fisheries	109.3	126.0	152.7	1.40
Coal & iron ore	0.0	0.0	0.0	0.00
Other mining	6.5	9.9	15.9	2.45
Foods	71.8	84.3	84.0	1.17
Fiber products	11.3	12.3	10.7	0.95
Wood & furniture	48.1	51.3	30.8	0.64
Pulp & paper	9.6	10.0	10.2	1.06
Printing & publishing	38.6	39.8	53.2	1.38
Leather & fur products	0.0	0.3	1.4	–
Rubber products	1.1	0.2	0.0	0.01
Chemicals	5.6	4.2	6.5	1.16
Petroleum products	187.5	176.3	112.3	0.60
Nonmetallic mineral products	57.2	55.6	60.2	1.05
Iron & steel	7.5	11.9	12.4	1.65
Basic nonferrous metal products	7.7	10.2	4.4	0.57
Metal products	30.7	32.9	41.1	1.34
Machinery	16.4	13.3	15.9	0.97
Electrical machinery	2.8	3.7	4.3	1.54
Transport equipment	32.4	25.2	31.2	0.96
Precision instruments	1.2	2.2	4.8	4.00
Miscellaneous mfg. products	19.9	16.9	13.4	0.66
Construction	98.2	98.4	98.9	1.01
Electricity, gas, & water	72.2	77.0	80.2	1.18
Wholesale & retail	69.7	62.8	79.2	1.26
Finance, insurance, & real estate	44.8	82.3	83.5	1.10
Transportation & communication	90.2	96.7	132.3	1.47
Government services	100.0	100.1	99.9	0.99
Education & research	94.7	95.7	96.0	1.01
Business & personal services	92.2	101.4	107.3	1.16
Unclassified	79.6	107.4	88.8	1.12
Total	68.7	69.0	73.4	1.07

Note: See the text for the method of estimation.

SOURCE: Department of Planning and Coordination, Okinawa Prefectural Government, *Ken Keizai no Koozoo* (Structure of the Okinawan Economy), Input-Output Tables of Okinawa for 1985 (Okinawa, 1988).

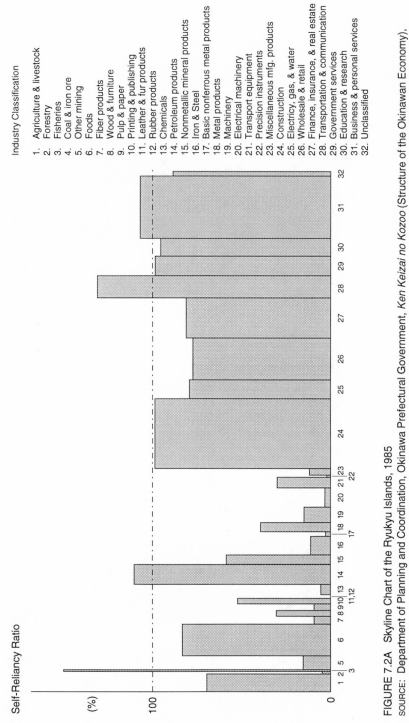

Self-Reliancy Ratio

Industry Classification

1. Agriculture & livestock
2. Forestry
3. Fisheries
4. Coal & iron ore
5. Other mining
6. Foods
7. Fiber products
8. Wood & furniture
9. Pulp & paper
10. Printing & publishing
11. Leather & fur products
12. Rubber products
13. Chemicals
14. Petroleum products
15. Nonmetallic mineral products
16. Iron & Steel
17. Basic nonferrous metal products
18. Metal products
19. Machinery
20. Electrical machinery
21. Transport equipment
22. Precision instruments
23. Miscellaneous mfg. products
24. Construction
25. Electricty, gas, & water
26. Wholesale & retail
27. Finance, insurance, & real estate
28. Transportation & communication
29. Government services
30. Education & research
31. Business & personal services
32. Unclassified

FIGURE 7.2A Skyline Chart of the Ryukyu Islands, 1985

SOURCE: Department of Planning and Coordination, Okinawa Prefectural Government, *Ken Keizai no Kozoo* (Structure of the Okinawan Economy), 1988.

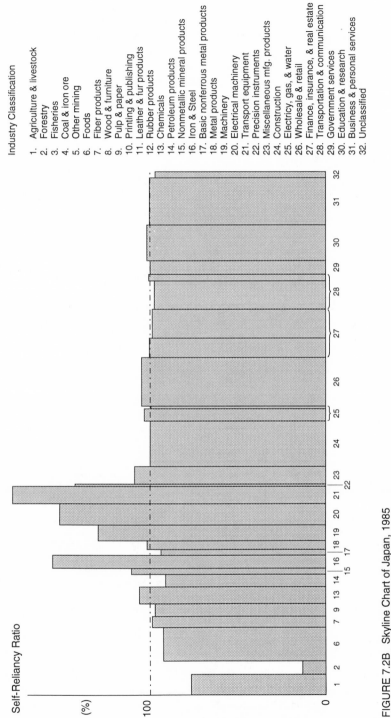

Industry Classification

1. Agriculture & livestock
2. Forestry
3. Fisheries
4. Coal & iron ore
5. Other mining
6. Foods
7. Fiber products
8. Wood & furniture
9. Pulp & paper
10. Printing & publishing
11. Leather & fur products
12. Rubber products
13. Chemicals
14. Petroleum products
15. Nonmetallic mineral products
16. Iron & Steel
17. Basic nonferrous metal products
18. Metal products
19. Machinery
20. Electrical machinery
21. Transport equipment
22. Precision instruments
23. Miscellaneous mfg. products
24. Construction
25. Electricy, gas, & water
26. Wholesale & retail
27. Finance, insurance, & real estate
28. Transportation & communication
29. Government services
30. Education & research
31. Business & personal services
32. Unclassified

Self-Reliancy Ratio

(%)

100

0

FIGURE 7.2B   Skyline Chart of Japan, 1985
SOURCE: General Administration Agency of the Japanese Government, *1985 Input-Output Tables*, 1988.

TABLE 7.4   Statistical Evidence of the Ryukyuan Boomerang Economy, 1971, 1988
(¥100 million)

	1971[a]		1988[b]	
Trade				
Exports	450		1,740	
Japan	87%		92%	
Imports	2,298		9,001	
Japan	78%		83%	
Trade balance	−1,848	(100.0)[c]	−7,261	(100.0)
Tourism income	152	(8.2)	2,643	(36.4)
Japan	77%		95%	
Military base income	1,061	(57.4)	1,352	(18.6)
Japan	0%		61%	
United States	100%		39%	
Public transfers (net)	366	(19.8)	5,149	(70.9)
Japan	90%		100%	
United States	9%		0%	

[a]The year before the Ryukyus' reversion to Japan.
[b]16 years after the reversion.
[c]Parentheses are percentage ratios of financing trade deficits.
SOURCES: Constructed from various issues of *Kenmin Shotoku Tookei* (Okinawa Prefectural Income Statistics).

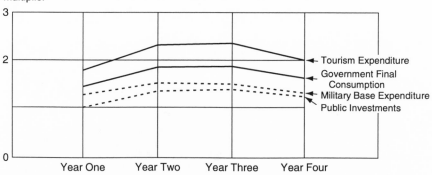

FIGURE 7.3   Multiplier Effects of Major Exogenous Variables on the Ryukyuan Economy, 1984–1987
SOURCE: S. Nozaki, "Prefectural Income," in *Okinawa Shakai Keizai Hendo Chosa Hokoku Sho* (A Report on the Changes in Socio-economic Aspects of Okinawa), ed. Okinawa Development Agency (Naha, 1990), pp. 189–195.

TABLE 7.5　How Ryukyu's Industrial Structure Has Been Diversified During 1978–1988 (percentage share of totals)

	1978	1988
All industries	100.0	100.0
Primary industry	6.7	3.4
Agriculture	5.3	2.8
Forestry	0.0	0.0
Fishery	1.4	0.7
Secondary industry	21.4	21.2
Manufacturing	6.7	6.4
Construction	14.3	14.3
Tertiary industry	71.9	78.2
Wholesale & Retail	15.6	14.9
Services	12.9	17.8
Gross agricultural product[a]	100.0	100.0
Sugarcane	36.4	30.4
Vegetables	20.3	19.9
Flowers	1.5	9.6
Fruits[b]	3.5	3.2
(Pineapple)	(2.7)	(1.9)
Tobacco	2.7	2.3
Potatoes	1.0	1.4
Rice	1.0	0.6
Hogs	18.2	16.2
Beef cattle	5.3	9.7
Poultry & eggs	6.6	4.9
Processed products	0.0	0.0

[a]Figures are for 1977.
[b]Fruits include pineapple.
SOURCE: Ministry of Agriculture, Forestry and Fishery, *Seisan Noogyo Shotoku Tookei* (Agricultural Production Income Statistics), 1990.

8

The Singapore Economy in Transition: With Reference to Okinawa and Hawaii

Unique Characteristics of Singapore

In many ways, Singapore is marvelous country. First, Singapore is 633 square kilometers, only one-third the size of of Okinawa. Despite Singapore-watchers' cautions that the statistics on the land size should be read very carefully because Singapore expands every year through reclamation, the size expanded only 17 kilometers, or 3 percent of the total land area, since Singapore's independence in 1965. In other words, the natural constraints, including land and water, have not been eased even under the charismatic leader and founder of Singapore, former prime minister Lee Kuan Yew. These harsh constraints of land resources have basically determined the very direction of Singapore as a nation-state, and these constraints will remain in the future.

Second, this small area was home to 2.7 million people in 1990. When Sir Stamford Raffles of the East India Company obtained a permanent leasing right on Singapore from the sultan of Johore in 1819, there were only 150 Malays living in the jungles[1]. With the establishment of a thriving free port in 1823, the population increased to 230,000 in 1901, and by 1970 exceeded 2 million, twice as large as Okinawa's in the same period. During 1970–1990, the population of Singapore increased by 620,000 (in contrast to 270,000 for Okinawa), which in turn intensified the population density per square kilometer (km²) from 3,369 persons (420 persons for Okinawa) to 4,250 persons (540 persons for Okinawa). Although Okinawa's population density is considered to be high by Japanese standards, Singapore's is about eight times higher than Okinawa's.

Singapore's rapid population growth casts serious doubts about the empirical law of population, that is, total population tends to stabilize when population density per km² reaches around 500 persons.[2] In prewar Okinawa, a population density of 250 persons per km² was considered to be "overpopulation," and emigration was promoted on that basis. Around the time of the Okinawan reversion to mainland Japan in 1972, there was also a debate on overpopulation when the population density reached 500 persons per km². Although Singapore has experienced overpopulation, in terms of the population-land ratio, it has been facing a serious problem of labor shortages in recent years due to robust economic activities. The experience of Singapore provides valuable lessons to many "overpopulated" small island economies.

Third, the role of government is probably the most important factor distinguishing Singapore from Okinawa, Hawaii, and other small island economies. Although Singapore was established by the People's Action Party (PAP), which came into power in 1959 with its major thrust on establishing a society based on socialism, the country has been managed according to a "state capitalism." The economy has been managed based on a blend of socialist and capitalist principles under the unique mixture of a parliamentary democracy and a paternalistic-oriented authoritarian government.[3] Socialist aspects of the Singapore economy have particularly manifested in such areas as land use, housing, development finance, and various cooperative movements. According to one source, the number of state-owned corporations was 450 at the end of 1985, and they accounted for about 40 percent of Singapore's GDP.[4] Another study,[5] however, says that GDP generated in the manufacturing sector by the state-owned corporations was about 10 percent in 1984. Although no one knows the precise weight of the public corporations in the economy, their operations are quite often indistinguishable from those of the private sector. The most prominent public finance institution, the Central Provident Fund (CPF), has been the catalyst for Singapore's unique mixture of public and private enterprise systems.[6] The state has been at least as efficient as the private sector in managing the public corporations. In the global privatization frenzy, Singapore is an exceptional country, one that could revitalize an ailing private enterprise under state management.

Furthermore, what is more significant is the fact that the Singapore economy has depended far less on government expenditures than have Okinawa and other small island economies. Although Singapore's defense expenditure was the highest among the ASEAN countries, accounting for 21 percent of its total government expenditure in 1989, the ratio of government expenditure to GNP was only 23 percent compared to its neighboring Malaysia's 30 percent.[7] For a small country like Singapore, it is a daunting task to provide an adequate national defense system as well as an adequate social infrastructure and security. Singapore, however, has shown the best performance in Asia on these accounts. I should reemphasize here that Singapore's state management system is quite unique, particularly when we think of small island states such as those in the South Pacific where even current government operating expenditures are financed by foreign economic assistance. Although it is obvious that the essence of the Singapore model lies in its state management system, no one has yet fully succeeded in analyzing the model, an analysis that would require a multidisciplinary approach including economics, politics, geopolitics, and cultural anthropology.

Fourth, Singapore's open economy has functioned under an authoritarian state control system that is sometimes referred to as the Lee Company.[8] This open cum authoritarian regime has worked well in the economic development of the Asian NIEs. China has also been adopting a similar model, although its political ideologies are quite different from those of the NIEs. According to a textbook prescription, the first step toward this open economic system is to decontrol or abolish various regulations on trade, investment, and the use of economic resources including labor, capital, and land. We all know that Singapore's economic openness is comparable to that of Hong Kong. From the standpoint of the availability of well-organized statistical information and political stability, Singapore's system of openness would be more reliable than that of Hong Kong.

One important measure of economic openness is the degree of foreign exchange liberalization, which is tightly controlled even in some developed countries. Singapore's foreign exchange regime is left almost completely to free-market forces. All major foreign currencies, regardless of whether they are in spot or forward transactions, are freely exchanged without restrictions on the period of transactions. There are no regulations on the rate of foreign capital subscription and no legally required rates for local capital subscription. Such outright liberalization of exchange and financial markets has been possible under the efficient authoritarian state, and the system cannot be imitated by Okinawa, Hawaii, and probably most other small island economies.

Prime Minister Lee's most courageous external economic policy was to move to the Article 8 status of IMF in 1968, only three years after Singapore's independence from Malaysia. The article prohibits Singapore from restricting its trade and foreign exchange transactions for balance-of-payments reasons. Once Singapore crossed the Rubicon, it had to go all way through to the road of free trade because there was no viable alternative. Singapore's success story demonstrates that Lee's open economic policy was the right direction and demonstrates how far a small economy can prosper under the harsh realities of natural resource constraints. Having overviewed the major characteristics of Singapore, I will discuss the structure of the Singapore economy with reference to the economies of Okinawa and Hawaii.

A Comparative Analysis of the Singapore Economy

Location is a controlling factor in the destiny of any small island economy. Singapore is located near the equator, about 2,400 kilometers southwest of Okinawa. Hawaii is located in the opposite direction, about 5,000 kilometers east of Okinawa. Okinawa is two hours ahead of Singapore and nineteen hours ahead of Hawaii. These three island economies have similarities as well as dissimilarities.[9]

Similarities

First, geographically they are composed of relatively small islands. Although the main island of Singapore is connected to the Johore state of Malaysia by a causeway, the country consists of one predominant island and several islets. Okinawa and Hawaii have forty and eight inhabited islands, respectively. Of the three island economies, Hawaii is endowed with the richest natural resources, followed by Okinawa and Singapore. It is no exaggeration to say that Singapore possesses only good harbors (locationwise) and human resources. This is due largely to the small size of Singapore compared to Hawaii and Okinawa, which are 26 and 3.6 times larger than Singapore, respectively (Table 8.1). Singapore's population density is sixty-four and six times higher than those of Hawaii and Okinawa, respectively.

The second similarity is that all three economies are highly specialized in the service industry. Singapore is the most service-oriented economy in Southeast Asia, as are Okinawa and Hawaii within their respective countries. This common characteristic is largely attributable to the relatively small sizes of the domestic markets, which prevent these economies from realizing scale economies in agricultural and manufacturing activities. Hawaii is the most service-dependent economy among the three; the services sector accounts for 89 percent of its total employment (86% in terms of total income), followed by Okinawa (69%, 78%, respectively) and Singapore (62%, 65%, respectively). Within the service industry, Singapore is highly specialized in financial services; Hawaii and Okinawa are oriented heavily toward tourism, trade, and public services. Singapore's service industry is highly information-oriented, having one of the most efficient finance, information, and transportation centers in the Asia-Pacific region. This is why Singapore's per capita income in the service industry is much higher than for its national average; in Hawaii, Okinawa, and other small island economies the reverse is common.

The third similarity is high trade dependency, on imports in particular, a dependency that stems from openness. Singapore has the highest trade (exports and imports) dependency in the world, accounting for 205 percent of its GNP in 1989 (Table 8.1). This high trade dependency dwarfs similar figures for Okinawa (63%) and Hawaii (53%). Singapore's high trade dependency is largely attributable to its status as an entrepôt trade of international cargos. The three economies are more import-oriented than export-oriented; therefore, trade balances have been chronically in deficit. Singapore, however, has the lowest trade deficit–GNP ratio (16%) compared to Okinawa (32%) and Hawaii (39%).

There are also some similarities in financing the trade deficits. Incomes from tourists financed 94 percent, 73 percent, and 41 percent of Hawaii's, Singapore's and Okinawa's trade deficits, respectively, in 1989. In addition to generating tourism income, Singapore has generated a huge income from foreign investments, transportation, and communication services, which have sustained the country's persistent current-account surpluses. Okinawa has also recorded a sizable current-account surplus due largely to receipts from central government expenditures, which have financed about 70 percent of the Okinawan trade deficit. This is coupled with receipts from U.S. military expenditures, which used to finance 30–40 percent of the trade deficits before reversion to Japan.

The last similarity of the three economies is that the sizes of the economies in terms of GNP are more or less the same, amounting to around $20 billion in 1988. Although the per capita income of Hawaii ($19,657) was higher than that of Okinawa ($13,593) and Singapore ($8,635) in 1988, these economies have enjoyed high standards of living among the world's small economies.

Dissimilarities

Probably the dissimilarities between the three economies are more eye-catching and important than the similarities. First, as has already been touched upon, the styles of macroeconomic management are quite different from one another. Singapore is an independent, sovereign state that can formulate its own economic policies to achieve its national objectives with its own policy tools, including the issuance of its own currency. Okinawa and Hawaii are small parts of their respective national economies, and they are not in a position to formulate independent policies like those of Singapore. Hawaii has been given relatively more autonomy as a U.S. state than Okinawa, whose prefectural status in Japan is severely limited under the national government's highly centralized bureaucracy. It has been said that a typical Japanese prefectural government possesses only 30 percent autonomy due to its heavy fiscal dependency on the central government. Okinawan autonomy, measured in terms of the fiscal dependency ratio, has been only 10–15 percent since its reversion to Japan.

Furthermore, Singapore is a city-state with virtually no rural area and thus is not subject to the severe rural-urban policy disputes that occur in Okinawa and Hawaii. For Singapore, food security has been an international trade issue. In Okinawa and Hawaii, however, food security has been the problem of domestic rural communities and farmers. The almost total lack of agriculture in Singapore is a weakness as well as a strength. Agriculture is an important source of income to fall back on when a small economy faces difficult times. However, the agricultural sector, which is usually protected and which requires supplementary income measures in any island economy, tends to prevent the economy from achieving total liberalization, forcing a second-best situation.

Labor mobility is also an important institutional difference in the three economies. Employment policy in Hawaii enjoys a certain degree of freedom because the unemployed can easily move to the U.S. mainland. In Singapore, and to a lesser extent in Okinawa, employment creation has always been a top priority because the unemployed have largely remained within the economies for national, legal, geographical, and cultural reasons. Although there is no national boundary between Okinawa and the Japanese mainland, strong cultural as well as geographical barriers have prevented a large outflow of the Okinawan unemployed into the Japanese mainland job markets. But after the Okinawan reversion to Japan in 1972, labor mobility between the two gradually increased. In this sense, the social risk and associated cost of unemployment in Singapore are much greater than in Hawaii and Okinawa, where "mainland" work is, to some extent, a cushion or safety net against social instability.

The second dissimilarity is the racial problem. Singapore is what J. S. Furnivall calls a typical plural society,[10] comprising 78 percent Chinese, 14 percent Malays, 7 percent Indians, and 1 percent other races in 1990. This racial composition has not changed for more than two decades. In spite of the fact that the Chinese are the predominant race, Singapore is a cosmopolitan society, not a Chinese society. A basic philosophy of Lee Kuan Yew has been to form a common "Singaporean" consciousness through enhancing the diversified cultural heritages of all races.[11] Toward this end, any policy with a trace of racial discrimination had to be carefully purged. A particularly cautious approach has been taken regarding the Malays, who are the poorest ethnic group in Singapore. The fact that Singapore's national language is Malay is not well-known to outsiders. Singapore may not be able to sustain itself as a nation-state without having neighboring Malaysia as an important source of income as well as water supply.

Unlike in Singapore, there is no racial issue and tension in Okinawa, which consists of historically and culturally homogeneous peoples. However, precisely because of this homogeneity, Okinawans have nurtured an easy-going, paternalistic social characteristic, which has prevented a social dynamism such as that seen in Singapore. Although Hawaii is a multiracial society like Singapore, racial tension has been successfully contained with a stable institutional system of common social values and a common language.

The differences in the social value system seem to have determined the characters of political leaders. A charismatic leader like Lee Kuan Yew was probably necessary because of Singapore's unique sociopolitical culture, that is, because of the need to encompass different value systems. Okinawa has never had a leader like Lee in its long history. This is probably due to the simple fact that the social climate has been resistant to a strong leader. In a homogeneous society like Okinawa, the social order has been maintained not by a hierarchical system, which requires a charismatic leader, but through a paternalistic community system.

Hawaii has experienced strong competition among the ethnic groups. There is no dominant ethnic group. Even within the Japanese ethnic group, which accounts for about 25 percent of Hawaii's total population, there has been keen social competition according to the subgroups' ancestral prefectures in Japan. This social competition is not explosive because it is based on common social value systems; such competition more or less corresponds to what exists among the subgroups' group-oriented Japanese counterparts. The Hawaiian example suggests that in order to revitalize a social system in an orderly fashion, a society needs to create an environment where different ethnic backgrounds can mix.

The third dissimilarity is related to geopolitics. Singapore has enjoyed the greatest geographical advantage among the three economies, being located at the crossroad of the world's busiest marine transportation route, which connects the Asia-Pacific region to as far as Europe. The sealane that passes by Singapore has been a lifeline for Japan. It is precisely this geographical advantage that has made Singapore one of world's busiest air and cargo ports. Many multinational corporations (MNCs) have established their operational headquarters (OHQ) there, being lured not only by Singapore's locational advantages but also by its political stability, well-established infrastructural facilities, and financial and information networks.

In comparison with Singapore, Okinawa is far away from the major markets of Southeast Asia, China, and mainland Japan. Okinawa is a tiny island in the western Pacific Ocean, if we look at it from the vast expanse of the Asian continent. Okinawa, for many years, has struggled to find its niche in the Asia-Pacific region because of its isolated location. A recent conspicuous pattern of Asian economic development is the spillover of economic dynamism emanating from one of the growth poles to adjacent areas.[12] In the case of Okinawa, however, the economic dynamism emanating from mainland Japan stops there, and it has failed to generate a successive wave that spreads to the neighboring regions. This lack of economic spillover effects is due largely to Okinawa's location and its small economy.

Hawaii has played a vital role as a cultural catalyst between Asia and the United States. This role will be further enhanced toward the twenty-first century because the world's two largest economies are expected to interact with each other more closely than ever before. Hawaii, the headquarters of the U.S. Seventh Pacific Fleet (CINCPAC), plays a key role in the regional security of Asia and the Pacific. This role has become ever more important with the end of the Cold War. The United States has been gradually withdrawing its military forces from the Asia-Pacific region; examples are the total pullouts from the Subic and Clark bases in the Philippines. The Hawaii-based Seventh Fleet is the only realistic option for filling a possible security vacuum created by the U.S. withdrawal from the area. At the same time, this changing security configuration in the post–Cold War era would diminish Okinawa's role as the keystone of the western Pacific's regional security, a role Okinawa has played internationally since World War II. The time is ripe for Okinawa to establish a clear vision of its new role in the post–Cold War era before the complete withdrawal of the U.S. bases from the island is implemented.

The fourth dissimilarity between Singapore and the other two countries is in their industrial structures. Singapore's manufacturing sector accounted for 28.7 percent and 30.1 percent of its total GDP and labor force, respectively, in 1988; the figures for Okinawa (and Hawaii) are only 6.4 percent (5.2%) and 5.7 percent (4.5%), respectively. Okinawa's industrial structure is similar to Hawaii's but quite different from Singapore's, which is a typical NIE type. A number of factors explain this difference. First, as has already been discussed, Singapore has struggled to promote its industrialization by introducing foreign capital through providing infrastructure and various incentive measures.

In Okinawa particularly after its reversion to Japan, the regional division of labor has been clearly envisaged in its development plans, aimed at closing the various gaps between Okinawa and the rest of Japan proper based on the island's potential comparative advantage in the national economy. Regional development based on regional comparative advantage was the right direction, considering Okinawa's economic performance after the reversion. As a result of vigorous expansion in the tourist industry, Okinawa enjoyed a higher per capita growth rate than the national average during 1972–1982, thereby closing the per capita income gap from 60 percent of the national average to 72 percent during this period.

If the Okinawan economy had been developed along the lines of the developing manufacturing industry, as was done in Singapore, it might have suffered heavily from structural adjustments, particularly after the rapid appreciation of the yen in the mid-1980s. The comparisons of unit costs in the manufacturing sector right after the Okinawan reversion to Japan clearly demonstrate that the Okinawan unit-cost index (taking Japan proper as 100) was about three and five times higher than that of Japan proper in 1973 and 1978, respectively (Figure 8.1). All other Japanese prefectures comparable to Okinawa manifested better cost performances than did Okinawa, and these performances almost entirely determined the positions of the manufacturing sectors in each economy, that is, Okinawa 8.1 percent, Kochi, 11 percent, and Japan proper 27.8 percent (see the solid line in Figure 8.1). The increasing specialization in the tourism industry, which is future-oriented and high-income elastic, has not only stimulated the Okinawan economy but has also prevented the island from environmental disruptions, which have often been caused in Japan by heavy industrialization.

The second factor is the wage differential between Singapore and Okinawa. Singapore's average monthly wage rate (equivalent to ¥120,000) is still 40 percent of Okinawa's despite its rapid increase in recent years. This indicates that Singapore can still accommodate some labor-intensive industries that are no longer viable in Okinawa. Furthermore, Singapore is better located than Okinawa for introducing low-wage laborers from neighboring countries and, at the same time, for relocating less-competitive labor-intensive industries to these areas, as we shall later see in the case of Batam Island.

Third, Singapore has taken advantage of its position as the largest oil refinery base and as a major free port of industrial raw materials in Southeast Asia. The costs of petroleum products and raw materials in Singapore are much lower than in Okinawa and Hawaii. In addition to benefiting from tax-free imports of raw materials and capital goods, Singapore industrialists have been favored by easy access to Singapore's growing capital market.

Fourth, although Singapore's population density is one of the highest in the world, it has developed forty-nine industrial parks, and their rental rates are much lower than those in Okinawa. This is not due only to the lower development costs of industrial sites in Singapore relative to those in Okinawa but, more important, to the systematic control of land use by the government, which owns practically all industrial land in Singapore.

Recent Performance of the Singapore Economy

Rebound from the Economic Crisis

ASEAN's founding motto is resilience. The Singapore economy may be the most resilient among the ASEAN economies. After an average annual real growth rate of more than 10 percent during the first half of the 1980s, the Singapore economy, for the first time in its history, plunged into negative growth rates during 1985–1986 (Figure 8.2, Table 8.2). The major contributing factor to the "economic crisis,"[13] as it was described by some Singapore-watchers, was a worldwide slump in the primary commodities markets. The fall in primary commodity prices impacted heavily on the Malaysian economy (a major exporter of primary commodities), on which Singapore's exports have heavily depended (nearly 13% of Singapore's exports went to Malaysia in 1990). Another important factor was the delay in the adjustment of the Singapore dollar after the 1985 Plaza Accord and the resulting yen appreciation. Singapore lost its competitive edge in export markets over its rival NIEs. Their currencies were tied to the U.S. dollar, which depreciated substantially against the Japanese yen.

The manufacturing and construction sectors were hit most by reduced exports and reduced domestic construction demand. Economic slowdowns in the United States, Malaysia, and Japan, which together absorbed nearly 50 percent of Singapore's exports, were major contributing factors to the severe slump. Furthermore, Singapore's high-wage policy, which had been adopted for a decade to alleviate labor shortages and at the same time to promote high-tech industries, pushed up the cost of exports. Reflecting Singapore's tightening labor shortages, real-wage costs increased more than productivity in the manufacturing sector during 1986–1987 (Figure 8.3).

The Singapore economy, however, rebounded quickly from its worst ever slump with the support of the government's export promotion policies and with drastic adjustments in the industrial structure through currency and wage-rates realignments. The manufacturing industry grew by 15 percent during 1987–1989 and was the main engine of GDP growth in the late 1980s. The growth momentum continued into the 1990s, surpassing the performances of Singapore's rival NIEs.

As a result of the rapid economic growth rate, coupled with the lowered population growth rate, Singapore's per capita GNP jumped from $4,400 in 1980 to $11,000 in 1990, a 2.5-fold increase. Singapore's per capita income level is the highest in Asia after Japan and is much higher than those of such OECD countries as Spain and Ireland.

The resiliency of the Singapore economy can also be found in its price stability. Despite its nearly overheated economy during the late 1980s, with an unemployment rate of less than 2 percent, the consumer price index increased less than 4 percent. The relative price stability was due mainly to the steady rise in wages and the small and open economic regime. A small economy such as Singapore's has a great advantage over larger ones such as the Japanese and the U.S. economies in terms of achieving price stability during a period of economic expansion. Singapore would be a perfect case for a "small country assumption" application. That is to say, the country's increased domestic demand rarely influences its import prices because the demand is a small fraction of the world's total. The size of the Singapore economy is only 1 percent that of Japan's. It is no secret that the relative smallness of the Singapore economy in conjunction with Singapore's open economic system enabled it to achieve both a high growth rate and price stability.

As we have seen, foreign trade, including the service trade, has determined the direction of the Singapore economy. For Singapore, trade is not merely the "engine of growth," as is conventionally asserted,[14] it is the core of economic survival. This is why Singapore has been the foremost advocate of an open-trade system within the ASEAN countries. It is significant to note, however, that Singapore has suffered from a chronic commodity trade deficit (Table 8.2). If we look carefully at Singapore's trade structure, we find that commodity trade reveals only one side of the coin. The other side is the service trade, which includes, among others, transportation, banking, tourism, and various consulting businesses. Imported commodities are value-added within Singapore through transborder transportation services and through financial and information services and sales to tourists. That is to say, the Singapore economy has successfully transformed itself from an entrepôt trade economy into an entrepôt-manufacturing economy, and further into a manufacturing-service-exporting economy. The net total receipts from these services have far exceeded the deficits in the commodity trade balances. For example, the current-account balance, which included both the commodity and the invisible service trades in 1990, recorded a S$4 billion surplus (Figure 8.4).

In addition to having persistent current-account surpluses, Singapore has been a large net recipient of foreign capital, which has financed its growing manufacturing and finance sectors. At the end of 1990, the total accumulated foreign direct investment (FDI) amounted to S$40 billion, of which the manufacturing and finance sectors accounted for 43 percent and 42 percent, respectively. As has been touched on, foreign capital investments, in particular MNCs, have played a dominant role in Singapore's economic development. Although official statistics are not available, these MNCs accounted for 70 percent of gross output and 81 percent of total exports in 1985 and 83 percent of total commitments for manufacturing investments in 1988.[15] Of the total manufacturing investments, Japan accounted for 42 percent, followed by the United States (36%) and the EC (20%). The Japanese MNCs, whose investments were concentrated in the export-oriented electronics industry, replaced the United States as the number one investor in 1985. This shift of investing country also reflects the shift of manufacturing investments from the petroleum industry—in which the U.S. MNCs have kept a comparative advantage—to the electronics industry, where Japan has enjoyed an enormous competitive edge over the United States.

The Growing Service Industry

As we have seen, the Singapore economy has changed from a manufacturing-oriented to a service-oriented structure in recent years. This is a natural transformation if we think of Singapore's altered position in the world economy, particularly in Asia.[16] Manufacturing bases in Asia, particularly those footloose electronics industries, have been rapidly shifting from Japan to the NIEs and from the NIEs to the ASEAN and China in recent years, spurred mainly by rising Japanese and NIE currencies and wage costs and by trade frictions with the United States and the EC. In order to avoid trade frictions, the Japanese electronics MNCs have been successively shifting their domestic operations first to the NIEs and more recently to the ASEAN countries, where they can continue to expand their exports. But this "export shell game"[17] also has become a major target of the United States and the EC. Thus the Japanese MNCs have been diversifying their production and marketing strategies from exporting to third-country trade and markets to developing their operations in host countries and to directing shipments back to Japan. This strategic change has adversely affected Singapore as a production base because it has a very small domestic market compared to that of the four other ASEAN countries and China.

Singapore, however, has acted quickly to adjust for such changes in the international environment. It has begun to provide incentive measures such as investment tax credits and to improve "soft" infrastructures—for example, communication systems, OHQ, the International Procurement Office (IPO), and Approved Oil Traders (AOT). The Asian Dollar Market (ADM) and the Singapore International Monetary Exchange (SIMEX) were created to promote trade and service-oriented industries including financial, R&D, tourism, and business-consulting services.

The MNCs have positively responded to Singapore's initiatives. The ADM, which was established in 1971, expanded sixfold, from $54 billion in 1980 to $346 billion in 1990, with 122 foreign participating banks.[18] Singapore has grown into a major financial center in Asia along with Hong Kong and Tokyo. Singapore's success in creating a financial center cannot be duplicated by Okinawa and Hawaii because their locations are far from major domestic as well as world economic centers.

Tourism is another rapidly expanding, service-oriented industry in Singapore. The number of tourists doubled from 2.6 million in 1980 to 5.3 million in 1990. Income from tourism amounted to S$7.6 billion, which accounted for 12 percent of GDP in 1990. Asian visitors accounted for 60 percent of all visitors, followed by visitors from the EC (23%), from Oceania (9%), and from North America (7%). Of the visitors from Asia, ASEAN topped the list with 40 percent, followed by Japan (31%), India (8%), and South Korea (7%). In response to the Singapore government's particular efforts to promote tourism from Japan, the number of visitors from Japan increased more than threefold, compared to a twofold increase from all regions in 1982–1992. Japanese tourists have been increasingly attracted to Singapore mainly because of its safety and cleanliness, excellent infrastructural facilities, and shopping attractions and because of its position as an ideal crossroad to the other ASEAN countries. Japanese visitors to Singapore experience only two hours' jet lag compared to nineteen hours, including the dateline change, when they travel to Hawaii. The influx of Japanese tourists invited a flood of Japanese FDI in hotels, department stores, and real estate. As in the manufacturing sector, Japanese FDI is becoming a dynamo for transforming Singapore's industrial structure.

Singapore has been intensifying its role as the hub of Asia's major transportation system. The service receipts from transportation increased 2.5-fold, from S$1.2 billion in 1980 to S$3.0 billion in 1990, making transportation the third-largest foreign exchange earner after finance and tourism. For example, the number of marine cargo transports increased 3.4-fold during the same period, making Singapore the world's largest container port in 1990, surpassing Hong Kong.[19] Singapore's role as one of Asia's transshipment hubs is further strengthened as ASEAN's robust economic growth continues and as Hong Kong, Singapore's rival in international transshipment, continues toward its 1997 scheduled reversion to mainland China.

The Singapore-Johore-Riau Growth Triangle and the Diamond Peace Trade Zone

Singapore-Johore-Riau

Encouraged by the recent trend of regional cooperation in the Asia-Pacific region, various "subregional economic zones (SREZs)" or growth triangles such as the Southern China Economic Zone (SCEZ), the Baht Economic Zone (BEZ), the Bohai Economic Zone (BEZ), the Tumen River Delta Economic Zone (Tumen Delta), the Singapore-Johore-Riau Growth Triangle (SIJORI), and the Diamond Peace Trade Zone (DPTZ) have emerged.[20] There are some common features in these growth triangles: (1) they are being formed more or less through spontaneous market forces led by mutual economic interests; (2) these triangles are mostly located within free economic and trade zones (FTZs) in order to promote economic development in selected regions; (3) they are designed to attract export-oriented foreign capital; (4) they, for the most part, lack technology and capital but possess comparative advantages in location (markets), labor, or natural resources; and (5) the development of the triangles has been pursued as a national or provincial development policy of the concerned governments.

SIJORI, which is also called the JSR Growth Triangle and which is made up of Singapore and Johore in Malaysia and Riau in Indonesia, was created by government-led initiatives (Figure 8.5).[21] SIJORI was initiated in 1989 by Prime Minister (then deputy prime minister) Goh Chok Tong of Singapore for the purpose of simultaneously relocating Singapore's labor-intensive industries and expanding and diversifying Singapore's economic and resource frontiers, which have been constrained by Singapore's small land size and labor force. Batam Island, the center of SIJORI, is only 20 kilometers away from Singapore. For Indonesia, SIJORI has the merits of (1) creating employment opportunities for its growing young labor force, (2) earning foreign exchanges, (3) accelerating technology transfers, (4) helping its economically backward region, and (5) stimulating domestic import-substituting industries. Malaysia, however, has difficulty in identifying the merit of SIJORI because the concept competes with its own free-trade zones in Johore and also conflicts with Malaysia's five-year economic plan, which envisages "the spread of growth northwards and eastwards away from Singapore."[22] The development of SIJORI is significant not only as a regional development model of the post–Cold War era but also as a booster for intra-ASEAN trade, which has stagnated in recent years despite ASEAN's robust economic growth in the late 1980s.

The Indonesian government designated all of Batam Island ($416km^2$) as a "bonded area," or duty-free zone, in order to attract export-oriented processing industries. As of 1990, more than twenty-five foreign investors from Singapore, the United States, Japan, and the United Kingdom started operations in the Batam Industrial Park (BIP), which was established jointly by the Indonesian Salim Group, Singapore Technologies, and Jurong Environmental.[23] Sumitomo Wiring Systems Batam Indonesia (SBI) was established jointly with the Salim Group in the Batam Industrial Park in 1989 as a part of the Sumitomo Group's global operations (Figure 8.6) with $5 million capital and about 600 local employees. Sumitomo Electric Automotive Products (Singapore) is responsible for the coordination and administration of SBI. According to SBI's brochure, the company "operates by uniting Japanese advanced technologies and management techniques with the abundant Indonesian human resources."[24] SBI imports about 100 different parts duty-free from its Nagoya-based Sumitomo Electric Automotive Products, then assembles them into various types of automotive wiring harnesses by making full use of Indonesian workers, mostly migrated female workers from West Java. Assembled wiring harnesses are all exported to a Nagoya-based automobile company.

This is a typical example of the new international division of labor of Japanese MNCs. Japanese MNCs have been increasingly outsourcing labor-intensive yet highly advanced parts and components from their overseas subsidiaries, particularly after the appreciation of the yen in the mid-1980s. The Toyota Motor Company is a typical example of Japanese automobile companies establishing parts and components centers in each ASEAN country to supply one another.[25] Siam Toyota in Thailand buys transmissions from Toyota Motor in the Philippines and electrical equipment from its Malaysian partners to make diesel engines that will be sourced to Toyota's Indonesian partner. Therefore, SIJORI is considered to be one of the outsourcing bases for Japanese MNCs.

SIJORI is still attractive to Japanese MNCs because of its location, low labor costs—about one-fourth of Singapore's and one-third of Malaysia's—and cheap land and shipping costs compared to Singapore. Wage costs in SIJORI, however, are 50 percent higher than in West Java and almost double those of China's Hainan Province, which has been competing with SIJORI in attracting foreign investors.

BIP has been successful, but the other seven industrial parks on Batam Island and a new one on Bintan Island are already having difficulties in attracting foreign investors. In addition to pure economic motives and interests, noneconomic factors are equally important in regional cooperation. "Singapore's role is enhancing the role of Chinese capital in areas where the ethnic division of labor remains a sensitive issue. The Chinese nature of Singapore and the economic and social impact of Singapore are perceived of as a typical case of Chinese exploitation of indigenous resources."[26]

Despite the triangular nature of SIJORI, actual operations are conducted on a bilateral basis, that is, Singapore-Indonesia, Singapore-Malaysia, and Indonesia-Malaysia instead of trilateral arrangements. In order to have full development of SIJORI and regional integration, a formal trilateral organization based on trilateral agreements is essential. SIJORI is considered to be a window to see whether the newly created ASEAN Free Trade Area (AFTA) can succeed.

The Diamond Peace Trade Zone

The Diamond Peace Trade Zone (DPTZ), comprising Taiwan, Okinawa, Kyushu (Japan), and Shanghai, was proposed by this author (Figure 8.7).[27] The major purposes of DPTZ are (1) to create trade and investment opportunities through a subregional FTZ; (2) to enhance regional economic activities through decentralization of the decisionmaking process; (3) to reduce Japan's growing trade surplus by first opening up its regional markets; and (4) to reduce politico-military tensions, which have been dangerously building up in recent years, over the territorial disputes on the Spratly Islands in the South China Sea by intensifying mutual economic interests.

As can be seen in Figure 8.7, Okinawa is much closer to Taiwan (630km) and

Shanghai (820km) than to Tokyo (1,600km), on which the Okinawan economy heavily depends. If geographical proximity is a key factor for a successful regional economic integration—since it implies lower transaction costs such as for travel, transportation, and communication—then it would be natural for Okinawa to have closer economic ties with Taiwan and Shanghai than with Tokyo.[28] The reality, however, is the other way around. A very strange practice has been pursued for many years whereby Taiwan products are first shipped to Yokohama or Kobe and then to Okinawa. This practice has been rationalized on the basis that there has been only one tanker trip per week between Okinawa and Taiwan, mainly because of the lack of cargo to and from Okinawa. If economic activities expand through DPTZ, more frequent trips among the participating regions will become economically feasible.

The first free-trade zone (FTZ) in Japan was created in Okinawa in 1988 for the purpose of promoting trade and investment among Okinawa, neighboring Asia, and mainland Japan. After five years of operations, however, the FTZ has proven to be a complete failure owing to the small size of operations—which serve a small and isolated domestic market—flawed institutional factors such as cumbersome regulations and a lack of incentives, and the lack of entrepreneurship and infrastructure both hard and soft. The FTZ concept was ambiguous and ill-conceived from the beginning. The FTZ was to be an import-oriented type, that is, raw materials or semiprocessed products would be imported into the FTZ (Figure 8.8) and then exported to mainland Japan after storing or further processing within the zone. There was, however, no plan to open up the FTZ to foreign and mainland investors, as was vigorously promoted in Singapore. A small Taiwanese trading company was the only visible foreign-owned venture, but it pulled out from the zone after a few years' operations. Almost all ventures in the FTZ were aimed at the mainland market despite the fact that the FTZ system seemed to work more effectively for export-oriented activities. Although import duties were applied only to raw materials when they were processed within the zone into higher-value-added products and then exported to the mainland, the advantage was very small because the average Japanese tariff rates, on raw materials in particular, were already the lowest among the OECD countries.

The idea behind DPTZ is similar to that for the special economic zones adopted in Shenzhen, Xiamen, and Batam (Figure 8.8). Like Batam Island, the whole area of Okinawa can be designated as an FTZ that allows not only duty-free processing but also duty-free consumption of imported goods and other deregulated economic activities such as offshore finance, R&D, and technology transfers. In order to have such an open economic system within a relatively closed Japanese territory, current politico-administrative systems must be completely dismantled. This would be, without doubt, a revolution within the market system. This may not be a realistic option for Okinawa, but it seems to be the only way for the island to break away from the time-honored center (Tokyo)–periphery (Okinawa) dependency configuration.

Conclusions

According to a famous dictum by Adam Smith "As it is the power of exchanging that gives occasion to the division of labour, so the extent of this division must always be limited by the extent of that power, or, in other words, by the extent of the market."[29] As we have seen, small island economies suffer from limited domestic markets. Singapore, in its formation years, embarked on an import-substituting type of industrialization with great expectations for expanding its domestic market through an economic union with Malaya. But the formation of Malaysia in 1963 resulted in the Indonesian "confrontation,"[30] which deprived Singapore of its most important trading partner at that time. Because of mounting political differences between Malaya and Singapore, the latter had to be separated from Malaysia in 1965. Moreover, the British government announced in 1968 that it would withdraw its military forces from Singapore by 1971, which meant that Singapore would lose military expenditures of S$550 million in 1966, or 16.3 percent of its GDP.[31] Faced with such a harsh reality, Singapore chose to pursue an open economic policy to crack its domestic market constraints.

The shift in Singapore's industrialization policy from import substitution to export promotion was the result of political developments brought about by "opportune historical conditions."[32] Singapore's economic success story stems more from the creation of the People's Action Party (PAP) state, or the so-called Lee Company, which controlled all spheres of social, political, and economic activities, rather than from the triumph of neoclassical comparative advantages based on free-market forces. Because of the strong leadership of the Lee Company, the Singapore economy could rebound from economic crises such as the negative growth episode of 1985–1986. In the process, Singapore has most successfully revitalized free-market forces to maximize its state objectives.

The future course of the Singapore economy depends on the sustainability of strong political leadership under the PAP. The recent exodus of professionals and skilled personnel from Singapore may reflect what some perceive to be impending political instability due to the change in political leadership in 1990. Singapore cannot sustain development by replacing these professionals with unskilled "guest workers."[33] As in other small economies, including Okinawa and Hawaii, policies to develop human resources are of utmost importance. If Singapore succeeds in maintaining a strong and stable leadership together with high-quality human resources, its comparative advantage for MNCs should not diminish.

TABLE 8.1   Comparisons of the Main Economic Indicators: Singapore, Okinawa, and Hawaii, 1989

	Unit	Singapore	Okinawa	Hawaii
Land area	km²	633	2,264	16,705
Population	000	2,685	1,222	1,112
Population density	persons/km²	4,287	693	67
Employed persons by industry				
All industries	%	100.0	100.0	100.0
Primary industries	%	1.6	10.9	2.1
Secondary industries	%	36.7	20.2	9.2
Manufacturing	%	30.1	5.7	4.5
Tertiary industries	%	61.7	68.7	88.7
Trade	%	21.2	29	26.3
Services	%	20.6	27.3	27.1
Government services	%	6.1		20.3
Unemployment rate	%	2.2	4.4	3.2
GNP or GPP at market prices	US$ mil.	28,888	20,018	21,587
Per capita GNP or GPP	US$	8,635	13,593	19,657
GDP or GPP by industry				
All industries	%	100.0	100.0	100.0
Primary industries	%	0.4	3.4	2.0
Secondary industries	%	34.3	21.1	11.3
Manufacturing	%	28.7	6.4	5.2
Tertiary industries	%	65.3	78.2	86.4
Trade	%	17.6	14.9	15.5
Services	%	10.4	26.8	19.8
Government services	%		9.7	23.6
Merchandise exports	US$ mil.	39,318	3,048	1,503
% of GNP or GPP	%	136.0	37.0	7.0
Merchandise imports	US$ mil.	43,869	9,532	9,908
% of GNP or GPP	%	152.0	37.0	46.0
Trade balance	US$ mil.	−4,551	−6,484	−8,405
% of GNP or GPP	%	15.8	32.4	38.9
Tourist arrivals	000	4,830	2,671	6,142
Tourist income	US$ mil.	3,307	2,122	7,904
% of GNP or GPP	%	11.1	10.7	36.8

Notes: Okinawan figures for GPP (gross prefectural product), exports, imports, and tourist incomes are on the basis of fiscal year (April-March); figures for employed persons by industry, GNP or GPP, and exports and imports are in 1988; exchange rates for 1988 and 1989 are $1 = ¥128.15 and $1 = ¥137.96, respectively.

SOURCES: *Yearbook of Statistics, Singapore, 1990; The State of Hawaii Data Book, 1989;* and *Okinawa Economic Outlook, 1991.*

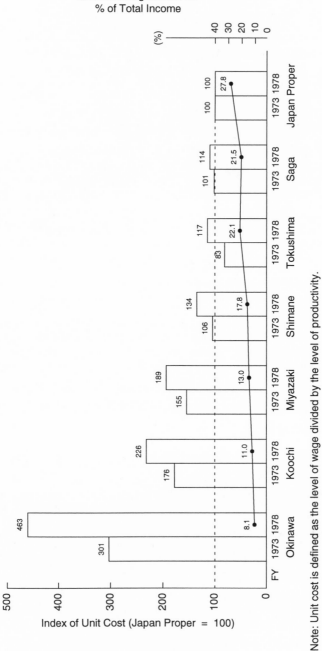

FIGURE 8.1 Comparisons of the Unit Cost of the Manufacturing Sector: Okinawa and Other Selected Prefectures, FY1973 and FY1978

SOURCE: Computed from *Annual Report on Prefectural Income Accounts, FY 1980.*

Note: Unit cost is defined as the level of wage divided by the level of productivity.

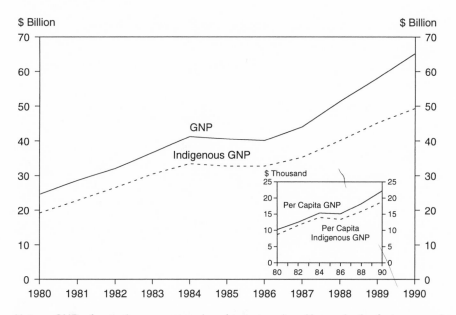

Notes: GNP refers to the aggregate value of output produced by productive factors owned by Singapore residents irrespective of whether they are located within Singapore's domestic territory or abroad; indigenous GNP refers to the aggregate value of output produced within the domestic territory of Singapore. Indigenous GNP is much smaller than GNP because it excludes incomes accruing to foreign workers and foreign enterprises that are incorporated— in Singapore, therefore, residents of Singapore.

FIGURE 8.2   GNP, GDP, and per Capita GNP: Singapore, 1980–1990
SOURCE: Department of Statistics, Singapore, *Yearbook of Statistics: Singapore, 1990.*

TABLE 8.2 Main Economic Indicators: Singapore, 1980–1991

	Unit	1980	1981	1982	1983	1984	1985	1986	1987	1988	1989	1990	1991	Avg. Annual Growth Rate 1980–85	Avg. Annual Growth Rate 1985–91
Population	.000	228	232	237	241	244	248	252	255	260	265	271	276	1.7	3.2
Unemployment rate	%	3.5	2.9	2.6	3.2	2.7	4.1	6.5	4.7	3.3	2.2	2	1.9	3.2	−9.7
Gross domestic product	US$Mn	13,466	14,959	15,781	17,291	18,552	17,691	18,206	20,602	23,962	27,010	31,489	35,249		
Gross domestic product	S$Mn	28,833	31,603	33,772	36,537	39,573	38,924	39,641	43,387	48,222	52,678	57,073	60,896	6.2	13.3
Manufacturing	S$Mn	8,500	9,291	8,965	9,216	9,908	9,184	9,956	11,673	13,773	15,122	16,558	17,431	1.6	12.7
Construction	S$Mn	2,056	2,418	3,299	4,267	4,927	4,168	3,234	2,917	2,804	2,845	3,050	3,691	15.2	10.2
Services	S$Mn	9,252	10,390	11,404	12,543	13,813	15,229	15,338	17,739	18,830	21,541	24,249	26,068	10.5	18.8
Per capita GNP	US$	5,781	6,291	6,421	7,090	7,793	7,391	7,647	7,910	9,181	10,271	11,711	12,948	5.0	14.4
Gross domestic investment	% of GDP	50.0	46.3	47.9	47.9	48.5	42.5	38.5	39.0	36.5	34.5	38.7	38.2	46.3	38.4
Gross domestic saving	% of GDP	40.4	41.7	42.3	45.0	45.3	40.0	39.3	40.0	42.1	44.1	44.9	45.6	40.2	42.5
Resource gap	% of GDP	−9.6	−4.6	−5.6	−2.9	−3.2	−2.5	0.8	1.0	5.6	9.6	6.2	7.4	−6.0	4.1
Inflation rate	% change in CPI	8.3	15.5	6.5	3.9	3.9	4.0	−1.4	0.5	1.5	2.4	3.5	3.4	6.2	1.0
Exports	US$Mn	19,376	20,967	20,787	21,833	24,070	22,812	22,495	28,687	39,360	44,665	52,752	59,663	6.2	20.6
Imports	US$Mn	24,007	27,572	28,167	28,158	28,667	26,285	25,511	32,559	43,863	49,667	60,899	115,939	3.3	30.0
Trade balance	US$Mn	−4,631	−6,605	−7,380	−6,325	−4,597	−3,473	−3,016	−3,872	−4,503	−5,002	−8,147	−56,276	1.8	
International reserves	US$Mn	6,567	7,459	8,480	9,264	10,416	12,847	12,939	15,227	17,073	20,345	27,749	34,128	14.4	31.6
Exchange rates	per US$, average	2.1412	2.1127	2.14	2.1131	2.1331	2.2002	2.1774	2.106	2.0124	1.9503	1.8125	1.7276	0.5	−3.5

Note: GDP figures are in 1985 constant prices.
SOURCES: *Yearbook of Statistics, Singapore, 1990;* and ADB. *Key Indicators of Developing Asian and Pacific Countries, 1992.*

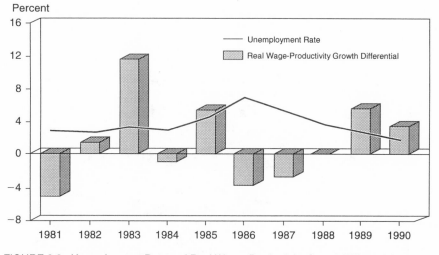

FIGURE 8.3   Unemployment Rate and Real Wage–Productivity Growth Differential:
Singapore, 1981–1990
SOURCE: Department of Statistics, Singapore, *Yearbook of Statistics: Singapore, 1990.*

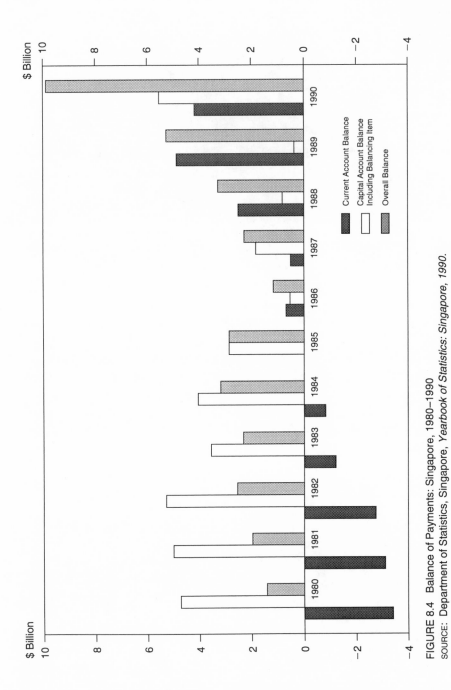

FIGURE 8.4 Balance of Payments: Singapore, 1980–1990
SOURCE: Department of Statistics, Singapore, *Yearbook of Statistics: Singapore, 1990.*

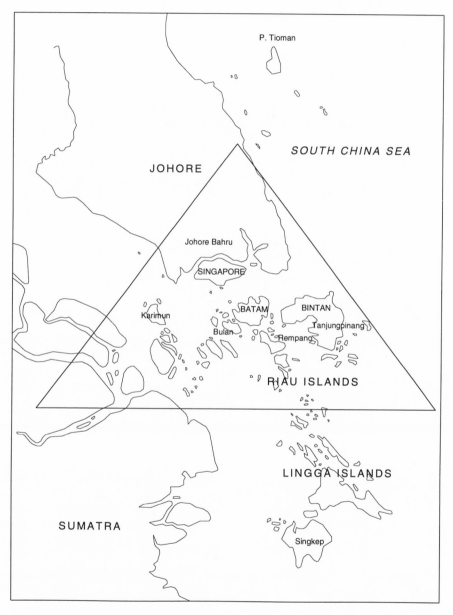

FIGURE 8.5   The SIJORI Growth Triangle
SOURCE: Lee Tsao Yuan, ed., *Growth Triangle: The Johore-Singapore-Riau Experience*
(Singapore: Institute of Southeast Asian Studies, 1991).

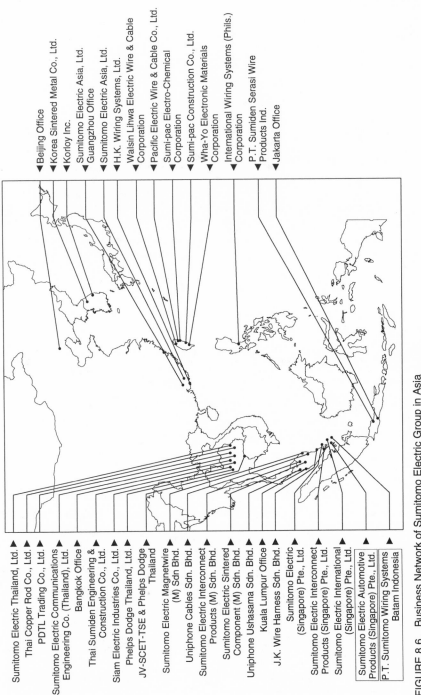

FIGURE 8.6   Business Network of Sumitomo Electric Group in Asia

SOURCE: SBI, *SEI & SWS Business Network in Asia* (company brochure, not dated).

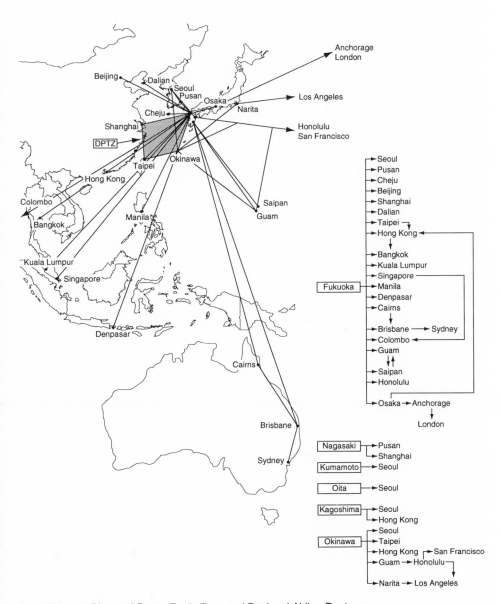

FIGURE 8.7   Diamond Peace Trade Zone and Regional Airline Routes
SOURCE: Japan Travel Bureau, September 1992.

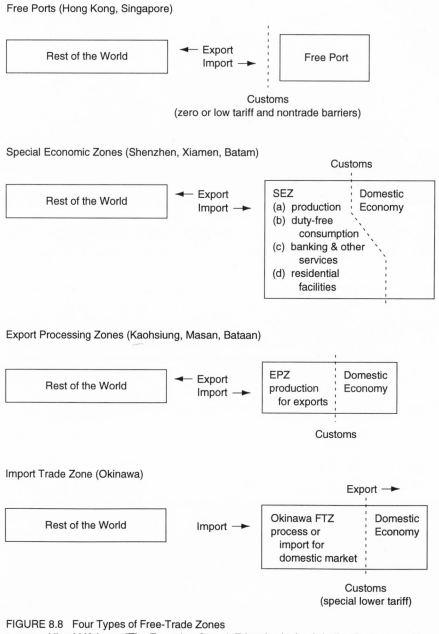

FIGURE 8.8 Four Types of Free-Trade Zones
SOURCE: Hiroshi Kakazu, "The Emerging Growth Triangles in the Asia-Pacific Region with Particular Emphasis on the Tumen River Delta" (Paper presented to the ADB-IUJ Joint Workshop on Growth Triangles in Asia (Manila: Asian Development Bank, February 1993).

Acknowledgments

Many of the chapters in this book are based on previously published papers or reports. Although all papers are revised and updated, I would like to gratefully acknowledge various publishers for allowing me to use the original papers.

Chapter 1: *Trade and Development of Small Island Economies with Particular Emphasis on the South Pacific,* United Nations Center for Regional Development, Working Paper no. 85-4 (Nagoya, June 1986).

Chapter 2: "Trade and Diversification in Small Island Economies with Particular Emphasis on the South Pacific," *Singapore Economic Review,* 30, no. 2 (October 1985): pp. 18–35.

Chapter 3: *International Resource Transfers and Development of Pacific Island Economies* (with Hiroshi Yamauchi), College of Tropical Agriculture and Human Resources, University of Hawaii, Research Series 065, Honolulu, October 1990, pp. 1–24.

Chapter 4: "Economy of the Commonwealth of the Northern Mariana Islands: Its Structure, Absorptive Capacity and Diversification," *Bulletin of the Sohei Nakayama IUJ Asia Development Research Programme,* 3 (March 1991): pp. 1–35.

Chapter 5: "Long Term Strategy for Water Resources Management in Small Island Economies: The Case of Saipan," (with Hiroshi Yamauchi and Nobuya Miwa), *Insula, International Journal of Island Affairs,* no. 2 (Spring 1993): pp. 39–47. Originally appeared as *Water Supply and Demand Problems in Rapidly Growing Small Islands,* Nobuya Miwa, Water Resources Research Center, University of Hawaii at Manoa, Project Report PR-94-03, September 1993.

Chapter 6: *Agriculture: Its Long-Term Role in Hawaii's Economy* (with Hiroshi Yamauchi), College of Tropical Agriculture and Human Resources, University of Hawaii, Research Series 038, Honolulu, July 1985, pp. 1–42.

Chapter 7: "The Boomerang Economy and Future Prospects: The Case of the Ryukyu Islands," a paper presented to the International Society for Ryukyuan Studies, Okinawa Convention Center (August 8–9, 1991).

Chapter 8: "The Singapore Economy in Transition: With Reference to Okinawa and Hawaii," *RIAD Bulletin,* 2 (March 1992): pp. 219–256.

Notes

Chapter 1

1. See Pacific Commission, *The Proceedings of the South Pacific Commission,* First and Second Sessions, Sydney, Australia (1948).

2. E.A.G. Robinson, ed., *Economic Consequences of the Size of Nations* (London: Macmillan, 1960).

3. B. Benedict, ed., *Problems of Smaller Territories* (London: Athone Press, 1967).

4. R. T. Shand, "Island Smallness: Some Definitions and Implications" (Paper presented to the Development Studies Centre Conference of the Australian National University, May 1979), p. 4.

5. William G. Demas, *The Economic Development in Small Countries with Special References to the Caribbean* (Montreal: McGill University Press, 1965).

6. Peter J. Lloyd, *International Trade Problems of Small Nations* (Durham, N.C.: Duke University Press, 1968).

7. E. K. Fisk, *The Political Economy of Independent Fiji* (Canberra: Australian National University Press, 1968).

8. R. F. Watter, *Koro: Economic Development and Social Change in Fiji* (Oxford: Clarendon Press, 1969).

9. A. S. Stanley, *Microstates and Micronesia: Problems of American Pacific Islands and Other Minute Territories* (New York: New York University Press, 1970).

10. B. Lockwood, *Samoan Village Economy* (Melbourne: Oxford University Press, 1971).

11. David Vital, *The Survival of Small States* (London: Oxford University Press, 1971).

12. H. C. Brookfield and D. Hart, *Melanesia: A Geographical Interpretation of an Island World* (London: Methuen, 1971).

13. H. C. Brookfield, *Colonialism, Development, and Independence: The Case of the Melanesian Islands in the South Pacific* (Cambridge: Cambridge University Press, 1972); and H. C. Brookfield, ed., *The Pacific in Transition: Geographical Perspectives on Adaptations and Change* (London: Edward Arnold, 1973).

14. I. J. Fairbairn, *The National Income of Western Samoa* (Melbourne: Oxford University Press, 1973).

15. B. R. Finney, *Big-Men and Business: Entrepreneurship and Economic Growth in the New Guinea Highlands* (Honolulu: University of Hawaii Press, 1973).

16. V. A. Lewis, ed., *Size, Self-Determination and International Relations* (Kingston: Caribbean Institute of Social and Economic Research, 1976).

17. S. Schiavo-Campo, ed., *Monetary Policy in a Small Developing Country* (Suva: University of the South Pacific, 1978).

18. F. R. Fosberg, ed., *Man's Place in the Island Ecosystem* (Honolulu: University of Hawaii Press, 1978).

19. F. M. Smith, ed., *Micronesian Realities: Political and Economic* (Santa Cruz: Center for South Pacific Studies, University of California, 1972).

20. B. Farrell, ed., *Views on Economic Development in the Pacific* (Santa Cruz: Center for South Pacific Studies, University of California, 1975).

21. J. B. Hardaker, ed., *The Subsistence Sector in the South Pacific* (Suva: University of the South Pacific, 1975).

22. J. N. Hurd, ed., *The Emerging Pacific Island States: The Proceedings of the Fourth Annual Pacific Islands Studies Conference* (Honolulu: Pacific Islands Studies Center, University of Hawaii, 1979).

23. Conference of the Development Studies Center, Australia National University, *The Island States of the Pacific and Indian Ocean: Anatomy of Development* (Canberra, April 1979).

24. J. Rappaport, E. Muteba, and J. J. Therattil, *Small States and Territories: Status and Problems* (New York: Arno Press for the United Nations Institute of Training and Research [UNITAR], 1971).

25. United Nations Conference on Trade and Development (UNCTAD), *Proceedings of the United Nations Conference on Trade and Development*, Third Session, Santiago, Chile, April 13–May 21, 1972, vol. 1 (New York, 1973), p. 74.

26. United Nations Conference on Trade and Development (UNCTAD), *Developing Island Countries: Report of the Panel of Experts* (New York, 1974).

27. United Nations Economic and Social Council (UNECOSOC), *Special Economic Problems and Development Needs of Geographically More Disadvantaged Developing Island Countries: Note by the Secretary-General* (New York, 1975).

28. International Bank for Reconstruction and Development (IBRD), *The Economic Development of Territories of Papua New Guinea* (Baltimore: John Hopkins University Press, 1965); and *The Economy of the British Solomon Islands Protectorate* (Washington, D.C., 1969).

29. Commonwealth Secretariat, *Meeting on Problems of External Finance for Small Islands* (Western Samoa, April 1979), and with the South Pacific Bureau for Economic Cooperation (SPEC), *Industrial Development and Trade Relations in the South Pacific: A Report by a Team of Experts* (London, May 1978).

30. R. G. Ward and A. Proctor, eds., *South Pacific Agriculture: Choices and Constraints* (Manila: Asian Development Bank in association with Australian National University Press, 1980).

31. C.G.F. Simkin, "The South Pacific Islands: Patterns and Strategies of Economic Development, 1975–1990," *Economic Bulletin for Asia and the Pacific,* 31 (December 1980): pp. 77–113.

32. Economic and Social Commission for Asia and the Pacific (ESCAP), *Domestic Stabilization of International Trade Instability in the South Pacific* (Unpublished conference papers, DP/DSITI/3, June 1982); and *Problems and Prospects of Foreign Trade of South Pacific Island Developing Countries in the Context of Multilateral Trade Negotiations—A Regional Select Study,* prepared for ESCAP by Sadagopa Raghavan (Tonga, 1983).

33. United Nations Industrial Development Organization (UNIDO), *Study of Harmonization of Industrial Incentives in the South Pacific Region* (DP/SPOF/80/002, Vienna, 1983).

34. UNECOSOC, *op. cit.,* p. 13.

35. *Ibid.,* p. 3.

36. C. L. Taylor, "Statistical Typology of Micro-States and Territories: Towards a Definition of a Micro-State," in Rappaport et al., *Small States and Territories,* pp.183–202.

37. S. Kuznets, "Economic Growth of Small Nations," in Robinson, ed., *Economic Consequences of the Size of Nations,* pp. 14–32.

38. Lloyd, *op. cit.,* p. 11.

39. Shand, *op. cit.*

40. C. P. Kindleberger, *International Economics* (Homewood, Illinois: Richard D. Irwin, 1968), p. 82.

41. A. Marshall, *Industry and Trade* (London: Macmillan, 1927), p. 25; and G. M. Meier, *International Economics of Development* (New York: Harper and Row, 1968).

42. See G. F. Erb and S. Schiavo-Campo, "Export Instability, Level of Development, and Economic Size of Less Developed Countries," *Bulletin of Oxford University Institute of Economics and Statistics* (November 1969): pp. 263–283; and R. Garnaut, *Economic Instability in Small Nations: Macro-Economic Responses* (Paper presented to the Development Studies Centre of Australian National University, July 1979). The Secretariat of the South Pacific Conference, however, believes that these vulnerability and dependency arguments exaggerate the state of Pacific economies where a relatively strong subsistence agriculture sector exists. See South Pacific Commission, *Special Problems of Small Island Countries* (Paper presented by the Secretariat at the Eighteenth South Pacific Conference, Noumea, New Caledonia, October 7–13, 1978).

43. See E. M. Salato, "South Pacific Regionalism-Unity in Diversity," *South Pacific Bulletin,* 20, no. 4, (1976): pp. 30–35; South Pacific Bureau for Economic Cooperation (SPEC), *Problems of Trade Affecting the Smaller Pacific Island Countries* (Suva, November 1980), pp. 1–32; and R. A. Herr, *Institutional Sources of Stress in Pacific Regionalism* (working paper) (Honolulu: Pacific Island Studies Program of the University of Hawaii, 1980), pp. 1–19.

44. See S. M. Mark and Mitsuo Ono, "Growth Analysis of a Subnational Economy: The Hawaiian Experience, 1900–76" (draft paper, 1978).

45. H. Kakazu, "Okinawa Keizai Jiritsu e no Michi" (A Direction Toward Self-Reliant Economic Development in Okinawa), *Shin Okinawa Bungaku,* 56 (1983): pp. 2–53.

46. UNECOSOC, *op. cit.*

47. H. C. Brookfield, *The Transport Factor in Island Development* (Paper presented at the Development Studies Center Conference of the Australian National University, "The Island States of the Pacific and Indian Oceans: Anatomy of Development" April 1979).

48. A. Proctor, "Transport and Agricultural Development," in Ward and Proctor, eds., *South Pacific Agriculture,* pp. 156–180.

49. UNECOSOC, *op. cit.,* p. 23.

50. UNCTAD, *Developing Island Countries,* p. 13.

51. See ESCAP, *Domestic Stabilization of International Trade Instability in the South Pacific,* and R. Shuster, *Urbanization in the Pacific: A Tentative Survey*

(Honolulu: Pacific Islands Center, University of Hawaii, 1979); and Jim Crisafull, *A Spatial Analysis of Problems and Prospects for Agricultural Growth Centers in Rural Fiji* (Seminar report, Polsc 780/Politics of Regions, Professors George Kent and Macu Salato, Spring 1981), p. 5.

52. South Pacific Commission, *South Pacific Economies: Statistical Summary* (Noumea, August 1982).

53. UNCTAD, *Developing Island Countries,* p. 11.

54. See Josée Penot-Demetry, *Transnational Corporations in the Insular Pacific: A Bibliography* (Honolulu: Pacific Islands Development Program, East-West Center, 1983).

55. UNCTAD, *Proceedings,* Third Session, April 13–May 21, 1972, p. 3.

56. See R. A. Sowelem, *Towards Financial Independence in a Developing Economy* (London: George Allen and Unwin, 1967); and H. Myint, "The Classical Theory of International Trade and the Underdeveloped Countries," *Economic Journal,* 63 (June 1958): pp. 313–337.

57. Demas, *op. cit.,* p. 91.

58. D. H. Robertson, "The Future of International Trade," Reprinted in American Economic Association, *Readings in the Theory of International Trade* (New York: Blasiton, 1949), pp. 501–502.

59. A. Smith, *The Wealth of Nations,* 4th ed. (London: Methuen, 1925).

60. J. S. Mill, *Principles of Political Economy,* ed. W. J. Ashley (London: Longmans, Green, 1909).

61. F. D. Graham, *The Theory of International Values* (Princeton: Princeton University Press, 1948).

62. Lloyd, *op. cit.,* p. 89.

63. See G. Haberler, *International Trade and Economic Development* (Cairo: National Bank of Egypt, 1959).

64. See Kindleberger, *International Economics;* and R. W. Jones, *International Trade: Essays in Theory* (Amsterdam: North-Holland, 1979).

65. P. S. Bellowod, "The Peopling of the Pacific," *Scientific American,* 243, no. 5 (1980): pp. 174–185.

66. A. Couper, "Islanders at Sea, Change and the Maritime Economies of the Pacific," in Brookfield, ed., *The Pacific in Transition,* pp. 229–248, p. 231.

67. *Ibid.,* p. 231.

68. B. H. Quain, *Fijian Village* (Chicago: University of Chicago Press, 1948), p. 231.

69. A. M. Hocart, *The Northern States of Fiji* (Royal Anthropological Institute of Great Britain and Ireland, Occasional Publications no. 11) (London: Alcain Press, 1952), p. 290.

70. See S. Amin, *Accumulation on a World Scale: A Critique of the Theory of Underdevelopment,* trans. Brain Peace (New York: Monthly Review Press, 1974); G. Myrdal, *Economic Theory and Underdeveloped Regions* (London: Duckworth, 1957); and A. G. Frank, *Capitalism and Underdevelopment in Latin America* (New York: Monthly Review Press, 1967).

71. Fisk, *op. cit.,* p. 31.

72. J. C. Furnas, *Anatomy of Paradise: Hawaii and the Islands of the South Seas* (New York: William Sloane Associates, 1937), p. 7.

73. E. C. Hald, "Development Policy and the Subsistence Sector," in Hardaker, ed., *Subsistence Sector in the South Pacific,* p. 4.

74. I. J. Fairbairn, "The Subsistence Sector and National Income in Western Samoa," in Hardaker, ed., *Subsistence Sector in the South Pacific,* p. 192.

75. S. Inder, "The Pacific Islanders: Too Late to Go Back to the Village," *Pacific Islands Monthly* (August 1980): pp. 5–15.

76. S. M. Mark, *Agricultural Development of Small, Isolated Tropical Economies: The American-Affiliated Pacific Islands* (Honolulu: Hawaii Institute of Tropical Agriculture and Human Resources, University of Hawaii, April 1979), p. 7.

77. H. Myint, "The Classical Theory of International Trade and the Underdeveloped Countries," p. 33.

78. R. G. Ward, *Agricultural Options for the Pacific Islands* (Paper presented at the Conference of the Development Studies Centre, Australian National University, April 1979), p. 7.

79. Hald, *op. cit.,* p. 6.

80. D. E. Yen, "Pacific Production Systems," in Ward and Proctor, eds., *South Pacific Agriculture,* pp. 72–106.

81. H. Myint, *The Economics of the Developing Countries* (London: Hutchinson University Library, 1967), p. 32. Apparently, however, imported goods have stimulated too much consumption beyond the ability of most South Pacific countries to pay for them. The "want development" that is described by economists as a natural part of the maturing process of a developing country has outrun the industrialization that it was meant to pursue." See S. J. Hezel, *Reflections on Micronesia* (Collected papers of Father Francis) (Honolulu: Pacific Islands Studies Program, University of Hawaii, 1982), p. 6.

82. R. R. Thaman, "Deterioration of Traditional Food Systems, Increasing Malnutrition, and Food Dependency in the Pacific Islands," *Journal of Food and Nutrition,* 39, no. 3 (1982): pp. 109–120.

83. Myint, "Classical Theory of International Trade and the Underdeveloped Countries," p. 34.

84. M. Moynagh, *Brown or White? A History of the Fiji Sugar Industry, 1873–1973* (Pacific Research Monograph, no. 5) (Canberra: Australian National University, 1981).

85. See K. Buckley, "The Role of Staple Industries in Canada's Economic Development," *Journal of Economic History* (December 1958): pp. 439–450; and M. H. Watkins, "A Staple Theory of Economic Growth," *Canadian Journal of Economics and Political Science,* 29 (May 1963): pp. 143–158.

86. I. J. Fairbairn, "The Subsistence Sector and National Income in Western Samoa," p. 179.

87. R. Nurkse, *Problems of Capital Formation in Underdeveloped Countries* (Oxford: Basil Blackwell, 1953).

88. R. Prebisch, "Commercial Policy in Underdeveloped Countries," American Economic Review, Papers and Proceedings, 49 (May 1959): pp. 261–264.

89. H. W. Singer, *International Development: Growth and Change* (New York: McGraw-Hill, 1964).

90. Myrdal, *op. cit.*

91. J. Bhagwati, "Immiserizing Growth: A Geometrical Note," *Review of Economic Studies,* 25 (June 1958): pp. 201–205.

92. H. Myint, "Economic Development Strategies of the South East Asian Nations and an Assessment of their Future Prospects" (Conference paper for the Project on the United States, Japan, and South East Asia: The Issues of Interdependence, sponsored by the East Asian Institute and the International Economic Research Center, Columbia University, Maui, December 1983), pp. 1–52.

93. Ian M. Little, T. Scitovsky, and M. Scott, *Industry and Trade in Some Developing Countries* (London: Oxford University Press, 1970).

94. The terms of trade for Fiji, for example, improved more than 50 percent during 1970–1980; see International Labour Office, *Year-book of Labour Statistics, 1982.*

95. Fisk, *op. cit.*, p. 31.

96. R. Bedford, "A Transition in Circular Mobility: Population Movement in the New Hebrides, 1800–1970," in Brookfield, ed., *The Pacific in Transition*, pp. 187–227.

97. See S. Tupouniua, R. Crocombe, and C. Slatter, eds., *The Pacific Way: Social Issues in National Development* (Suva: South Pacific Social Sciences Association, 1975); I. J. Fairbairn, *South Pacific Economies: Some Observations* (Background paper, Pacific Islands Area Seminar, East-West Center, Pacific Islands Development Program, Honolulu, January 1983), pp. 1–16; H. M. Gunasekera, "Trends in Regional Planning in the South Pacific," pp. 49-64, both in Benjamin Higgins, ed., *Regional Development in Small Island Nations, Regional Development Dialogue* (Special issue of the Nagoya, Japan, 1982).

98. Barry Shaw, "Smallness, Islandness, Remoteness, and Resources: An Analytical Framework," in Higgins, ed., *Regional Development in Small Island Nations*, p. 100.

99. See Neil D. Karunaratne, "Development in the Pacific," in Benjamin Higgins, ed., *Regional Development in Small Island Nations* (Nagoya: United Nations Center for Regional Development, 1982).

100. R. G. Ward and E. Hau'ofa, "The Demographic and Dietary Contexts," in Asian Development Bank, *South Pacific Agricultural Survey, 1979* (Manila, 1979), p. 44.

101. E. K. Fisk, "Subsistence Affluence and Development Policy," in Higgins, ed., *Regional Development in Small Island Nations*, pp. 1–12.

Chapter 2

1. I. J. Fairbairn, "The Subsistence Sector and National Income in Western Samoa," in J.B. Hardeker, ed., *Subsistence Sector in the South Pacific* (Suva: University of the South Pacific, 1975, p. 193; and E. K. Fisk, "Subsistence Affluence and Development Policy," in Benjamin Higgins, ed., *Regional Development in Small Island Nations*, Regional Development Dialogue (Special issue of the United Nations Centre for Regional Development, Nagoya, Japan, 1982).

2. See Fisk, *op. cit.*, F. Doumenge, *Viability of Small Island States: A Descriptive Study* (United Nations Conference on Regional Trade and Development, TD/B/950, July 1983); and I. J. Fairbairn and C. Tisdell, "Subsistence Economies and Unsustainable Development and Trade: Some Simple Theory," *Journal of Development Studies*, 20, no. 2 (January 1984): pp. 227–241.

3. I. J. Fairbairn and C. Tisdell, *Economic Growth Among Small Pacific Countries: Can It be Sustained?* (United Nations Centre for Regional Development, Working paper no. 83-5, Nagoya, Japan, 1983), p. 3.

4. See C. P. Kindleberger, *International Economics* (Homewood, Illinois: Richard D. Irwin, 1968).

5. See T. G. McGee, *Food Dependency in the Pacific: A Preliminary Statement* (Working paper no. 2, Research School of Pacific Studies of the Australian National University, 1975)

6. I. J. Fairbairn and C. Tisdell, *op. cit.*

7. I. J. Fairbairn and C. Tisdell, *op. cit.,* p. 14.

8. B. Higgins and J. D. Higgins, *Economic Development of a Small Planet* (New York: W. W. Norton, 1979), p. 122.

9. See H. Myint, *The Economics of the Developing Countries* (London: Hutchinson University Library, 1967).

10. E. C. Hald, "Development Policy and the Subsistence Sector," in Hardaker, ed., *Subsistence Sector in the South Pacific.*

11. See F. D. Graham, *The Theory of International Values* (Princeton: Princeton University Press, 1948); and P. J. Lloyd, *International Trade Problems of Small Nations* (Durham, N.C.: Duke University Press, 1968).

12. I. J. Fairbairn, *Island Economies: Studies from the South Pacific* (Suva: University of the South Pacific, 1985), pp. 87–89.

13. J. Bounmemaison, "The Impact of Population Patterns and Cash Cropping on Urban Migration in the New Hebrides," *Pacific Viewpoint,* 18, no. 2 (September 1977): p. 340.

14. See Government of Western Samoa, Department of Economic Development, *Western Samoa's Fifth Development Plan 1985–1987* (Apia, 1985).

15. J. Penot-Demetry, *The Role of Financial Centres in Economic Development in the Pacific* (Honolulu: East-West Center, 1983), p. 24.

16. See Myint, *op. cit.;* and I. Little, T. Scitovsky, and M. Scott, *Industry and Trade in Some Developing Countries* (London: Oxford University Press, 1970).

17. See S. V. Ciriacy-Wantrup, *Resource Conservation Economics and Policies* (Berkeley: University of California Press, 1952).

18. See Hiroshi Yamauchi and H. Onoe, "Analytical Concepts and Framework for Environmental Conservation," *International Review of Economics and Business,* 30, no. 8 (August 1983): pp. 759–778.

19. *Ibid.,* p. 771.

20. Hiroshi Yamauchi, "U.S.-Japan Agricultural Adjustment Problem" (April 1984), pp. 4–5, mimeo.

21. R. Taylor, G. Koteka, and K. Mokoputua, *Prevention and Control of Non-Communicable Diseases: Present Situation in the Cook Islands* (Noumea: South Pacific Commission, 1983), p. 19.

22. Asian Development Bank, *Economic Survey of Western Samoa* (Manila, 1984), p. 111.

23. N. D. Karunaratne, "Development in the South Pacific," in Higgins, ed., *Regional Development in Small Island Nations,* pp. 49–50.

24. See Little, Scitovsky, and Scott, *op. cit.,* and R. R. Thaman, "Deterioration of Traditional Food Systems, Increasing Malnutrition and Food Dependency in the Pacific Islands," *Journal of Food and Nutrition,* 39, no. 3 (1982): pp. 109–121.

25. I. J. Fairbairn, "Rural Development and Employment in the South Pacific," in Higgins, ed., *Regional Development in Small Island Nations,* pp. 26–27.

26. A. C. Walsh, "Subsistence Agriculture and the Communication of Innovations: Some Niuean Examples," in Hardaker, ed., *Subsistence Sector in the South Pacific,* p. 119.

27. N. V. Lam, "Population and Economic Activity," in *Population of Papua New Guinea,* Country Monograph Series no. 72 (Bangkok: South Pacific Commission, 1982), p. 146.

28. Government of Western Samoa, Department of Economic Development, *Western Samoa's Fourth Five-Year Development Plan 1980–1984* (Apia, 1980), p. 230.

29. Government of Tuvalu, Planning Office, *Second Development Plan 1980–1983* (New Zealand: Stredder Pint, 1980), p. 25.

30. Fisk, *op. cit.,* pp. 1–12.

31. See W. G. Demas, "Economic Independence," in P. Selwyn, ed., *Development Policy in Small Countries* (Institute of Development Studies of Sussex, 1975).

32. T. G. McGee, *op. cit.,* p. 5.

33. Myint, *op. cit.;* and Little, Scitovsky, and Scott, *op. cit.*

34. G. T. Harris, "Food Imports and Macroeconomic Policy in the South Pacific" (Unpublished paper, Economics Department of the University of New England, Australia, 1982), p. 5.

35. See South Pacific Commission, *South Pacific Economies: Statistical Summary* (Noumea, 1978).

36. R. E. Ward, *Agricultural Options for the Pacific Islands* (Paper presented for the 1979 Development Studies Centre Conference of the Australian National University, April 1979), p. 16.

37. See A. B. Desai, "Commercialization of Subsistence Agriculture," and B. A. Pointer, "Rural Migration in the South Pacific," both in Hardaker, ed., *Subsistence Sector in the South Pacific.*

38. S. G. Britton, "The Political Economy of Tourism in the Third World," *Annals of Tourism Research,* 9 (1982): p. 119.

39. See S. M. Mark, "Agricultural Development of Small, Isolated Tropical Economies: The American-Affiliated Pacific Islands " (Unpublished manuscript, Hawaii Institute of Tropical Agriculture and Human Resources, Honolulu, 1983).

40. See E. K. Fisk, *The Island of Niue: Development or Dependence for a Very Small Nation* (Occasional Paper no. 9, Development Studies Centre, Australian National University, Canberra, 1978).

Chapter 3

1. See, for example, E. K. Fisk, *The Island of Niue: Development or Dependence for a Very Small Nation* (Occasional Paper no. 9, Development Studies Center, Australian National University, Canberra, 1978); and B. Knapman "Aid and the Dependent Development of the South Pacific Island States," *Journal of Pacific History,* 21, no. 3–4 (July 1986): pp. 139–152.

2. Ann O. Krueger, "The Political Economy of the Rent-Seeking Society," *American Economic Review,* 3, no. 3 (1971): pp. 291–303; and G. Bertram, "Development, Dependence and Viability " (June 1984), mimeo.

3. See J. Bhagwati, "Directly-Unproductive Profit-Seeking (DUP) Activities," *Journal of Political Economy,* 90 (October 1982): pp. 988–1002; J. Bhagwati, "DUP Activities and Rent Seeking," *Kyklos,* no. 36 (1983): pp. 634–637.

4. J. Bhagwati, R. Breacher, and T. Hatta, "The Generalized Theory of Transfers and Welfare: Exogenous (Policy-Imposed) and Endogenous (Transfer-Induced) Distortions," *Quarterly Journal of Economics,* 100, no. 3 (1985): pp. 697–714.

5. See David Ricardo, *Principles of Political Economy and Taxation* (London: J. Murray, 1817).

6. See T. N. Srinivasan, "The Costs and Benefits of Being a Small, Remote, Island, Landlocked, or Ministate Economy," *World Bank Research Observer,* no. 2 (July 1986): pp. 205–218.

7. See Table 2 in G. Bertram, "Development, Dependence and Viability " (Unpublished mimeograph, Victoria University, Wellington, New Zealand, 1984).

8. See I. M. Little, T. Scitovsky, and M. Scott, *Industry and Trade in Some Developing Countries* (London: Oxford University Press, 1970).

9. See Toshio Watanabe, *Economics and Contemporary Asia* (Tokyo: Nihon Hyoron Sha, 1986); and Ann O. Krueger, *The Developmental Role of the Foreign Sector and Aid* (Cambridge, Mass.: Harvard University Press, 1974).

10. See, for example, R. G. Crocombe, "Productive Potentials of the Pacific Islands," *Journal of the Pacific Society* (April 1987): pp. 21–132.

11. See S. M. Mark, *Agricultural Development of Small Isolated Tropical Economies: The American-Affiliated Pacific Islands* (Honolulu: Hawaii Institute of Tropical Agriculture and Human Resources, University of Hawaii, 1983).

12. A more-detailed analysis is given in H. Kakazu and Te'o Fairbairn, "Trade and Diversification in Small Island Economies with Particular Emphasis on the South Pacific," *Singapore Economic Review,* 30, no. 2 (October 1985): pp. 17–35.

13. Bertram, *op. cit.,* p.12.

14. Crocombe, *op. cit.,* p.128.

15. See Y. Matsui, "Kokusaiteki Sekinin e Enjo Rinen no Kakuritsu o" (Establishing Aid Principles to Meet International Responsibility), *Economisuto* (April 13, 1987): pp. 74–75; and I. J. Fairbairn, *Island Economies: Studies from the South Pacific* (Suva: Institute of Pacific Studies, University of the South Pacific, 1985).

16. Crocombe, *op. cit.,* p.129.

Chapter 4

1. S. William, *Business Reference & Investment Guide to the Commonwealth of the Northern Mariana Islands* (Saipan: Economic Service Counsel, 1988), p. 3.

2. See data in Kiyoko Nitz, "The Data for Agricultural Policy Decision Making" (Honolulu: Department of Political Science, University of Hawaii, 1990), mimeo.

3. For the model of unlimited labor supply, see A. Lewis, "Economic Development with Unlimited Supplies of Labour," *Manchester School of Economics and Social Studies,* 22 (May 1954): pp. 139–191.

4. CNMI, *Overall Economic Development Strategy* (Saipan, 1989), p. 37.

5. See N. Miwa, "The Problems of Water Supply and Demand in Rapidly Growing Small Islands" (Okinawa: University of the Ryukyus, 1990), mimeo.

6. For BOP concepts, see IMF, *Balance of Payments Manual,* 4th ed. (Washington D.C., 1977).

7. See S. William, *op. cit.*

8. See School of Travel Industry Management, the University of Hawaii, *The Impact of Tourism on the Commonwealth of the Northern Mariana Islands* (Honolulu, 1989).

9. CNMI, "Overall Development Strategy: A Prospectus for Guiding Growth" (Saipan, undated draft), p. 3.

10. The capital-output ratio tends to be higher for a smaller island economy due mainly to the indivisibility of investment and weak productive capacity. See Christopher Browne, *Economic Development in Seven Pacific Island Countries* (Washington, D.C.: IMF, 1989).

11. See H. Kakazu, "Industrial Technology Capabilities and Policies in Selected Asian Developing Countries," *Asian Development Review,* 8, no. 2 (1990): pp. 46–76.

12. H. Kakazu and Te'o I. J. Fairbairn, "Trade and Diversification in Small Island Economies with Particular Emphasis on the South Pacific," *Singapore Economic Review,* 30, no. 2 (October 1985): pp. 46–76.

13. See Browne, *op. cit.*

Chapter 5

1. On March 31, 1988, the Special Joint Legislative Committee on Water Resources was formed from selected committees in the Senate and House of the CNMI government to conduct a comprehensive study of the water crisis in Saipan and report in sixty days with recommendations on how to correct the problem. A more graphic description of the problem than that given in the committee's report is hard to imagine (see the appendix to this chapter).

2. Miyako, however, is pioneering in subsurface dam technology, which promises to greatly improve its potential to capture and use more natural flow.

3. See Nobuya Miwa, Hiroshi Yamauchi, and Dai Morita, *Water and Survival in an Island Environment—Challenge of Okinawa* (Honolulu: Water Resources Research Center, University of Hawaii, 1988); and Nobuya Miwa, "Water Resources Conservation of Saipan, CNMI" (in Japanese, Saipan ni okeru mizu shigen hozen), *Journal of the Society of Tropical Resources Technologists,* 7, no. 1 (1991): pp. 7–13.

4. Capturing and reusing rainwater is becoming more popular in many places. The Ryogoku Kokugikan sumo arena in Tokyo is one of the leading facilities in Japan. Rainfall is collected from its 8,400 square meter roof and stored in a 1,000 cubic meter underground tank for use in the stadium's flush toilets and air-conditioning system. Following this example, nearly 100 public facilities in Tokyo have recently introduced rainwater utilization systems. In the private sector, structures such as the Tokyo Dome—a gigantic multipurpose hall that hosts professional baseball games, concerts, and other activities—use rainwater for flush toilets and air-conditioning. Neighborhood rainwater catchment systems are also being reintroduced in places like Sumida Ward, where the rainwater collected from neighboring houses and stored in tanks is used by local residents for various outdoor watering purposes. See M. Murase, "Rainwater Is Becoming a Valuable Reusable Resource," *Japan Times,* Friday, November 1, 1991.

5. The basic principle for the safe minimum standard of conservation is to minimize the maximum possible losses associated with the use of critical-zone-flow resources such as groundwater. The concept was originally rationalized by Ciracy-Wantrup. See Hiroshi Yamauchi and Hisao Onoe, "Analytical Institutional Economics of Water and Environmental Conservation," *Water International* (The Netherlands: Elsevier Sequoia, 1983.

6. Capital projects in 1990 and 1991 were primarily for water-system maintenance and upgrade and for the exploration and development of new water sources.

7. We must differentiate between water use at different levels—final demands at consumers' levels and intermediate demands at producers' levels. Water use at the final-demand level is mainly for human consumption, whereas at the intermediate level water is used mainly for production of goods and services. Various subcategories are possible at each of these levels, for example, drinking, cooking, bathing, and other human consumption purposes can be grouped into private households, offices, and public institutions and can be meaningfully expressed in terms of per capita consumption of water. At the intermediate demand level, water use is primarily for production purposes such as irrigated agriculture, processing, manufacturing, construction, and commercial services including resorts and hotels and can be more meaningfully expressed in terms of productivity ratios such as input-output ratios. See Hiroshi Yamauchi and Wen-yuan Huang, "Organization and Statistical Analysis of Water Consumption Data at the Local Level," *American Waterworks Association Journal,* 69, no. 1 (January 1977): pp. 35–38.

Chapter 6

1. See James H. Shoemaker, *Labor: In the Territory of Hawaii, 1939,* U.S. Department of Labor, Bureau of Labor Statistics, Bulletin no. 687 (Washington, D.C., June 1939); Theodore Morgan, *Hawaii, A Century of Change, 1778–1876* (Cambridge, Mass.: Harvard University Press, 1948); Perry F. Philipp, *Diversified Agriculture of Hawaii* (Honolulu: University of Hawaii Press, 1953); and Shelley M. Mark and Robert L. Lucas, *Development of the Agricultural Sector in Hawaii* (Honolulu: Hawaii Institute of Tropical Agriculture and Human Resources, University of Hawaii, July 1982).

2. See Simon Kuznets, *Economic Change: Selected Essays in Business Cycles, National Income, and Economic Growth* (New York: W. W. Norton, 1953).

3. See Arthur W. Lewis, "Economic Development with Unlimited Supplies of Labour," *Manchester School of Economics and Social Studies,* 22 (May 1954): pp. 139–191. Reprinted in A. N. Agawala and S. P. Singh, eds., *The Economics of Underdevelopment* (London: Oxford University Press, 1958).

4. See Theodore W. Schultz, *Transforming Traditional Agriculture* (New Haven: Yale University Press, 1964).

5. See Robert C. Schmitt, *Historical Statistics of Hawaii* (Honolulu: University of Hawaii Press, 1977).

6. See Harry T. Oshima and Mitsuo Ono, *Hawaii's Income and Expenditures, 1958, 1959, and 1960,* vol. 1 (Honolulu: Economic Research Center, University of Hawaii, January 1965); Oshima and Ono, "Statistics on Income in Hawaii, 1825–1966," *Hawaii Historical Review: Selected Readings* (Honolulu: Hawaiian Historical Society, 1969), pp. 174–284; and Oshima and Ono, *The Economy of Hawaii in 1947, with Special*

Reference to Wages, Working Conditions, and Industrial Relations, U.S. Bureau of Labor Statistics Bulletin 926 (Washington D.C., 1948).

7. See Yujiro Hayami, *A Century of Agricultural Growth in Japan* (Tokyo: University of Tokyo Press, 1975).

8. See Ronald Takaki, *Pau Hana: Plantation Life and Labor in Hawaii, 1835–1920* (Honolulu: University of Hawaii Press, 1983).

9. Schmitt, *op. cit.,* p.134.

10. See Lewis, *op. cit.*

11. See Hla Myint, *The Economics of the Developing Countries,* 4th rev. ed. (London: Hutchinson University Library, 1973).

12. Hayami, *op. cit.,* p. 6.

13. Herbert K. Marutani, *Labor-Management Relations in Agriculture: A Study of the Hawaiian Sugar Industry* (Ph.D. dissertation submitted to the Graduate Division of the University of Hawaii, College of Tropical Agriculture, 1970), pp. 90–115.

14. Schmitt, *op. cit.,* p. 668.

15. J. A. Mollett, "Technological Change in Hawaiian Sugar Production and Its Relationship to Productivity," *Journal of Farm Economics,* 15, no. 1 (June 1964): 88–97.

16. See Shoemaker, *op. cit.*

17. See Schmitt, *op. cit.*

18. See Charles F. Schwartz, *Income of Hawaii,* a supplement to *Survey of Current Business* (Washington, D.C.: U.S. Department of Commerce, 1953).

19. See Hawaii Department of Planning and Economic Development (DPED), *Hawaii's Income and Expenditure Accounts: 1958–1980* (Honolulu, 1982).

20. See Schwartz, *op. cit.,* p. 16.

21. See Craighill E. S. Handy, *The Hawaiian Planter: His Plants, Methods and Areas of Cultivation,* Bernice P. Bishop Museum, *Bulletin* 161 (Honolulu, 1940).

22. See Takaki, *op. cit.,* p. 37.

23. See Kuznets, *op. cit.:* Raymond Vernon, "International Investment and International Trade in the Product Cycle," *Quarterly Journal of Economics,* 80, no. 2 (May 1966): pp. 190–207; and S. Hirsch, *Location of Industry and International Competitiveness* (Oxford: Clarendon Press, 1967).

24. See Hawaii Department of Planning and Economic Development (DPED), *The State of Hawaii Data Book, 1983: A Statistical Abstract* (Honolulu, 1983).

25. See Mark and Lucas, *op. cit.*

26. See Kathleen Pierson, "Development of Trade in Hawaii: A Statistical Analysis of Basic Trends " (Unpublished M.A. thesis submitted to the University of Hawaii, June 1948).

27. Ralph Kuykendall and A. Grove Day, *Hawaii: A History from Polynesian Kingdom to American Commonwealth* (New York: Prentice Hall, 1948), p. 92.

28. *Ibid.,* pp. 70–71.

29. Schmitt, *op. cit.,* p. 555.

30. *Ibid.,* p. 541.

31. Schultz, *op. cit.,* p. 5.

32. See DPED, *Hawaii's Income and Expenditure Accounts.*

33. See Hawaii Revised Statutes as amended, 1984, Hawaii State Plan, Chapter 226, Section 7.

34. See George Ariyoshi, "Governor's Message," in *Statistics of Hawaiian Agriculture 1982* (Honolulu: Hawaii Agricultural Reporting Service, July 1983).

35. See U.S. Department of Agriculture, *National Resources Inventory* (Ames: Iowa State University, 1982); *Conservation Needs Inventory: Hawaii* (Washington, D.C.: *Soil Conservation Service*, 1972); and *Hawaii Soil and Conservation Needs Inventory* (Honolulu: Hawaii Conservation Needs Committee, 1961).

36. See Warren Gibson, "Drip Irrigation of Sugarcane in the Hawaiian Story," *International Sugar Journal*, 80 (1978): pp. 362–373.

37. See Hiroshi Yamauchi, "Impact of Drip Irrigation on Groundwater Resources," *Water Resources Bulletin* (August 1984): pp. 557–563.

Chapter 7

1. Since an 1879 decree replaced the kingdom of the Ryukyus with the Okinawa prefecture under the Meiji government, "Okinawa" has been interchangeably used with "the Ryukyu Islands" in official documents. In this study, I try to use the latter unless inappropriate.

2. The following studies are useful to identify and resolve the Ryukyuan development issues: Hirotaka Makino, *Okinawa Keizai o Kangaeru* (A Reflection on the Okinawan Economy) (Naha: Ryukyu Shimmp-sha, 1978); Okinawa Labor and Economic Research Institute, *Fukki 10 nenme no Kaihatsu Kadai to Temboo:Futatabi "Okinawa no Kokoro" o Motomete* (Issues and Prospects After a Decade of the Reversion: Re-seeking the "Heart of Okinawa") (Naha: Okinawa Labor and Economic Research Institute, 1981); and the Okinawa Development Agency, *Okinawa no mirai o Kangaeru* (Searching for the Future of Okinawa), a symposium report commemorating the tenth anniversary after the reversion (Tokyo: Okinawa Development Agency, 1983).

3. Those who are interested in the topic, see Hiroshi Kakazu, *A System of Input-Output Accounts for Okinawa* (Lincoln: University of Nebraska, 1971).

4. See Hiroshi Kakazu, "Okinawa Keizai Jiritsu e no Michi" (A Path Towards Self-Reliant Development of the Okinawan Economy), *Shin Okinawa Bungaku,* 56 (1983): pp. 2–53.

5. For a comprehensive study on the concept of "resort islands of Okinawa," see Okinawa Keizai Keikaku Kenkyusho, *Rezooto Kaihatsu ni tomonau Keizai Hakyu Kooka Sokutei Choosa* (A Study on Economic Impacts of Resort Development) (Okinawa, 1990).

6. For an excellent account of Ryukyuan water problems, see N. Miwa, H. Yamauchi, and D. Morita, *Water and Survival in an Island Environment: Challenge of Okinawa* (Honolulu: University of Hawaii Press, 1988).

7. See David Lowenthal, "Island Self-Reliance or Expert Delusion?" (Draft paper presented at the Second World Conference on Island Economies, Tasmania, 1988). This also gives an interesting account of the islanders' life-style.

8. See Miwa, Yamauchi, and Morita, *op. cit.*

9. See Hiroshi Kakazu, "The Economy of the Commonwealth of the Northern Mariana Islands," *Bulletin of the Sohei Nakayama IUJ,* no. 3 (March 1991): pp. 1–35.

10. See Hiroshi Kakazu, *Okinawa no Jiyu Boeki Chiiki* (Okinawa Free Trade Zone), Monograph no. 62 (Tokyo: Okinawa Association, September 1981).

Chapter 8

1. See an interesting account on the early days of the British colonial empire in Singapore by Nobuo Seisaburo, *Sir Stamford Raffles* (in Japanese) (Tokyo: Heibonsha, 1943).

2. See Simon Kuznets, *Growth, Population and Income Distribution: Selected Essays* (New York: W. W. Norton, 1980); and Harry T. Oshima, *Economic Growth in Monsoon Asia: A Comparative Survey* (Tokyo: University of Tokyo Press, 1987), chap. 6, pp. 177–198.

3. Shee Poon-Kim, "Singapore in 1977: Stability and Growth," *Asian Survey,* 18, no. 2 (February 1978): p. 194.

4. *Far Eastern Economic Review* (January 8, 1987): p. 69.

5. Lawrence B. Krause, Koh Ai Tee, and Lee Yuan, eds., *The Singapore Economy Reconsidered* (Singapore: Institute of Southeast Asian Studies, 1987), p. 118.

6. Singapore is often described as a high-saving, high-investment society. During the economic boom, a significant part of its higher incomes was channeled into savings, both private and public, making it the country with the highest national saving rate in the world (40% of GDP during 1988–1990). Institutionalized or "forced" savings, particularly the contributions to the CPF and customary budgetary surpluses, accounted for much of the savings. Although the combined employer and employee CPF rate has been reduced from the peak of 50 percent to 39.5 percent (employers and employees contributed 17.5% and 22%, respectively) in 1991, total CPF savings nevertheless continued to increase owing to the expansion in employment. For the operational mechanism of CPF, see Lim Chong Yah et al., *Policy Option for the Singapore Economy* (Singapore: McGraw-Hill, 1988).

7. Data are from *Economic Survey of Singapore* and ADB, *Key Indicators of Developing Asian and Pacific Countries,* various issues.

8. Teruhiko, Toh, "The City-State: Singapore" (in Japanese), in Kunio Yoshihara, ed., *The Southeast Asian Economy* (in Japanese) (Tokyo: Koobundo, 1991), pp. 275–309.

9. Hiroshi Kakazu,"Comparative Development: Singapore and Okinawa," *Ryukyu University Economic Study,* no. 24 (September 1982): pp. 47–90, gives an earlier account on the subject. See also Hiroshi Kakazu and Hiroshi Yamauchi, *Agriculture: Its Long-Term Role in Hawaii's Economy,* Research Series 038 (Honolulu: University of Hawaii, July 1985).

10. J. S. Furnivall, *Colonial Policy and Practice: A Comparative Study of Burma and Netherlands India* (New York: New York University Press, 1956), p. 17.

11. See Goh Keng Swee, *The Economics of Modernization and Other Essays* (Singapore: Asia Pacific Press, 1972). See also John A. MacDougall, "Birth of a Nation: National Identification in Singapore," *Asian Survey,* 16, no. 6 (June 1976): pp. 510–524.

12. See Hiroshi Kakazu, "Five Economic Trends in the Asia-Pacific Region: Emerging Issues and Japan's Role," *RIAD Bulletin,* 1 (March 1992): pp. 101–138.

13. See Lim Chong Yah and Ow Chwee Huay, "The Economic Development of Singapore in the Sixties and Beyond," in You Poh Seng and Lim Chang Yah, eds., *The Singapore Economy* (Singapore: Eastern University Press, 1971).

14. Toh, *op. cit.,* pp. 287–289.

15. For the latest discussions on the subject, see Hiroshi Kakazu, "Five Economic

Trends in the Asia-Pacific Region: Emerging Issues and Japan's Role, *RIAD Bulletin,* 1 (March 1992): pp. 101–138.

16. For an in-depth comparative study of the service sectors between Singapore and Hong Kong, see Harry T. Ohima, *op. cit.,* chap. 6.

17. Many U.S. economists believe that a recent surge of exports from the ASEAN countries is attributable to Japanese investments in these countries. For more details, see Hiroshi Kakazu, "Five Economic Trends in the Asia-Pacific Region: Japan's Role," *RIAD Bulletin,* 1 (March 1992): pp. 101–138.

18. For the latest data, see Singapore International Chamber of Commerce, *Investor's Guide: To the Economic Climate of Singapore* (Singapore, 1992).

19. *Japan Economic Journal,* March 2, 1992, p. 9.

20. See Hiroshi Kakazu, "The Emerging Growth Triangles in the Asia-Pacific Region with Particular Emphasis on the Tumen River Delta" (Paper presented to the ADB-IUJ Joint Workshop on Growth Triangles in Asia, Manila, Asian Development Bank, February 1993).

21. See Lee Tsao Yuan, ed., *Growth Triangle: The Johore-Singapore-Riau Experience* (Singapore: Institute of Southeast Asian Studies, 1991).

22. *Far Eastern Economic Review* January 7, 1993, p. 54.

23. Data are from the Batam Industrial Development Authority (BIDA).

24. SBI, *SEI & SWS Business Network in Asia* (Company brochure, not dated).

25. See Hiroshi Kakazu, "Intra-Industry Trade Between Japan and ASEAN: Comparison Between Electric and Automobile Industries" (Paper presented to the Fifty-First Annual Convention of the Japan Society of International Economics, Fukushima, October 1992), and in *World Economic Review* (Sekai Keizai Hyoron) (May 1993): pp. 21–32.

26. *Far Eastern Economic Review* January 7, 1993, p. 54.

27. See Hiroshi Kakazu, "From Locational Tragedy to Advantage: After the Twenty-Year's Reversion of Okinawa," *Sekai* (June 1992): pp. 217–225.

28. See R. M. Townsend, "Intermediation with Costly Bilateral Exchange," *Review of Economic Studies,* 45 (1987): pp. 417–425, and Edward K.Y. Chen, "Southern China Growth Triangle: An Overview" (Paper presented to the ADB-IUJ Joint Workshop on Growth Triangles in Asia, Manila, Asian Development Bank, February 1993) for a transaction-cost approach to regional economic integration.

29. Adam Smith, *The Wealth of Nations,* 4th ed. (London: Methuen, 1925), p. 17.

30. The formation of the Malaysian Federation, which included peninsular Malaya, East Malaysia (Sabah and Sarawak), and Singapore brought about the Indonesian military "confrontation" with Malaysia over the territorial disputes of East Malaysia, which lasted from 1963 to 1966.

31. Yah and Huay, *op. cit.,* p. 29.

32. Garry Rodan, *The Political Economy of Singapore's Industrialization: National State and International Capital* (Kuala Lumpur: Forum, 1989), p. 208.

33. To ease the labor shortages, the government allowed the importation of foreign labor. The number of foreign workers is not known precisely, but it is estimated to be as high as 400,000 for the latest year (see Asian Development Bank, *Asian Development Outlook, 1992,* p. 89). The Singapore government adopted an elaborate two-tier labor levy in 1991. The manufacturing sector charges S$300 per worker up to 35 percent of the

work force. If more than 30 percent of a work force are foreigners, a higher levy of S$450 is charged. But not more than 45 percent of a work force can be of foreign origin (ADB, *ibid.,* p. 87). Employers of five or more illegal workers are liable to three cane strokes across the back and fines of as much as $14,000 for each violation (See *Time,* April 5, 1993, p. 36).

About the Book and Author

Focusing especially on Pacific Islands such as Fiji, Tonga, Western Samoa, Hawaii, Saipan, and the Ryukyu Islands, this book examines the self-reliant, sustainable development of small island economies. Hiroshi Kakazu also considers Singapore's unique success story. Insular and small, most island economies face enormous problems such as diseconomies of scale, overdependence on external trade and official economic assistance, extremely limited resource bases, the high cost of transportation and other infrastructures, extensive out-migration, and vulnerability to natural disasters and environmental disruptions. Despite painful trial and error, most island economies are far from achieving self-reliance. Based on original small island development models as well as on solid empirical studies, this study offers a range of policy prescriptions for sustainable development paths for different types of small island economies.

Hiroshi Kakazu is dean and professor at the International University of Japan.

Index

ADB. *See* Asian Development Bank
ADM. *See* Asian Dollar Market
Administrative services, 6, 57
AFTA. *See* Association of Southeast Asian
    Nations, Free Trade Area
Agriculture, 9, 37, 57, 66(table), 113–130,
    152–153, 176
    as agro-food industry, 117, 137(table 6.7)
    capital-intensive, 116, 126, 128, 129, 130
    cash crops, 11, 13, 119
    diversification in, 3, 37, 93(fig. 4.6), 117,
        122, 125, 126, 129, 137(tables), 161
    employment in, 116–117, 118–119, 125,
        126, 127, 129, 137(tables), 148(fig.)
    as growth sector, 123
    impacts on land/water resources, 128
    income in, 115, 118–119, 131(table 6.2),
        140(table), 177. *See also* Hawaii,
        income in
    irrigated, 126–128, 130, 149(fig.)
    product cycles, 119–121, 130, 141–
        142(figs.)
    products marketings, 143(table)
    traditional crops, 46, 119, 161
    See also under Commonwealth of North
        Mariana Islands
Aid. *See* Foreign aid; Official Development
    Assistance
American Samoa, 5, 6, 13, 35(table), 37, 47,
    57, 63, 87
ASEAN. *See* Association of Southeast Asian
    Nations
Asian Development Bank (ADB), 2, 44
Asian Dollar Market (ADM), 183
Association of Southeast Asian Nations
    (ASEAN), 183, 184, 185, 185, 215(n17)
    Free Trade Area (AFTA), 186
Australia, 63

Authoritarianism, 174–175

Balance of payments (BOP), 23(table), 44,
    48, 56, 59, 122–123, 155
    and possible growth paths, 40–42, 52(fig.)
    See also under Commonmwealth of North
        Mariana Islands; Singapore
Bananas, 39, 119
Banks, 42, 81, 88, 96(table), 162, 182, 183
Bartering, 119
Batam Industrial Park (BIP), 185–186
Batam Island, 180, 185–186, 187, 195(fig.)
Bellwood, P. S., 10
Bertram, G., 58, 61
Bhagwati, J., 55
BIP. *See* Batam Industrial Park
Bonuses, 115, 131(table 6.2)
Boomerang economies. *See* Economic
    boomerang
BOP. *See* Balance of payments
Britain, 63, 185, 188

Capital-accumulation spiral, 115
Capital goods, 5, 44, 46
Capitalism, 174
Census of Agriculture, 127
Chalmers, James, 11
China, 76, 80, 163, 175, 183, 186, 187
CINCPAC. *See* United States, Seventh
    Pacific Fleet
Ciriacy-Wantrup, S. V., 42
Classical/neoclassical economics, 8, 14, 40,
    55–56, 58, 125
CNMI. *See* Commonwealth of Northern
    Mariana Islands
Cocoa, 34(table)
Coconuts, 12, 38, 60. *See also* Copra
Coffee, 12, 32–33(table), 119